Robert Manning Strozier Library

AUG 3 1990

Tallahassee, Florida

Culture and Change
Along the Blue Nile

Culture and Change Along the Blue Nile

Courts, Markets, and Strategies for Development

Lina Fruzzetti and Ákos Östör

Westview Press
BOULDER, SAN FRANCISCO, & LONDON

Westview Special Studies in Applied Anthropology

This Westview softcover edition is printed on acid-free paper and bound in library-quality, coated covers that carry the highest rating of the National Association of State Textbook Administrators, in consultation with the Association of American Publishers and the Book Manufacturers' Institute.

All rights reserved. No part of this publication may be reproduced or transmitted in any form or by any means, electronic or mechanical, including photocopy, recording, or any information storage and retrieval system, without permission in writing from the publisher.

Copyright © 1990 by Westview Press, Inc.

Published in 1990 in the United States of America by Westview Press, Inc., 5500 Central Avenue, Boulder, Colorado 80301, and in the United Kingdom by Westview Press, Inc., 13 Brunswick Centre, London WC1N 1AF, England

Library of Congress Cataloging-in-Publication Data
Fruzzetti, Lina.
  Culture and change along the Blue Nile: courts, markets, and strategies for development/Lina Fruzzetti, Ákos Östör.
    p. cm.—(Westview special studies in applied anthropology)
  ISBN 0-8133-7788-9
  1. Applied anthropology—Sudan. 2. Rural development—Sudan.
3. Sudan—Economic conditions. 4. Social change. 5. Applied anthropology—Blue Nile River Valley (Ethiopia and Sudan). 6. Rural development—Blue Nile River Valley (Ethiopia and Sudan). 7. Blue Nile River Valley (Ethiopia and Sudan)—Economic conditions.
I. Östör, Ákos. II. Title. III. Series.
GN397.7.S73F78 1990
307.1'4'09624—dc20   89-14658
                                                                    CIP

Printed and bound in the United States of America

∞ The paper used in this publication meets the requirements of the American National Standard for Permanence of Paper for Printed Library Materials Z39.48-1984.

10   9   8   7   6   5   4   3   2   1

For Yousif El Mak
and the memory of
Dr. Adel Razak el Mubarak

Contents

List of Tables	xi
List of Figures	xiii
Currency Equivalents, Weights and Measures, and Abbreviations	xv
Preface	xvii
Acknowledgments	xxi

1 THE SUDAN, THE BLUE NILE, AND THE QUESTION OF DEVELOPMENT   1

Aims of the Study	3
Historical and Societal Contexts	10
Nomads and Agriculturalists	13
Anthropology and Development	15
Ideologies of Development	18
Notes	27

2 MERCHANTS, MARKETS, AND THE DAM   29

The Impact of the Roseiris Dam	29
The Suq in Damazin and Roseiris	33
Patterns of Trade in the Central Suq	41
The Suq, Mechanized Farms, and Development	52
Notes	55

3 FARM AND HEARTH: WOMEN IN A FARMING COMMUNITY 57

Women and Farms in Rural Sudan 59
Donor and Recipient Objectives 64
Women's Activities 66
General Implications 75
Notes 78

4 LAW, COURTS, AND REGIONAL DEVELOPMENT 79

Customary Law, Locality, and Society 80
Nomads and Agriculturists 87
Case Studies 88
Law, Courts, and Development 97
Notes 99

5 ADMINISTRATION, OFFICIALS, AND DEVELOPMENT 101
Mahgoub El-Tigani Mahmoud

History and Organization 104
The Political Framework 112
Muazzafeen Society 116

6 VILLAGE DEVELOPMENT PROJECTS: A CASE STUDY 125

Objectives of the Project 127
Results of the Research 131
Accomplishments and Failures 144
Notes 150

7 AGRICULTURAL SCHEMES: TENANTS AND INSTITUTIONS 153

The Role of the Gezira Scheme 154
Old and New Projects 160
Notes 168

Contents

8 CULTURE AND DEVELOPMENT 171

    Administration, Politics, and Development 173
    Subsistence Versus Modern Farmers 180
    Understanding Social Transformations in the Sudan 185
    Notes 191

Appendix 1: Ingessana Muazzafeen 193
Appendix 2: Methodology of the Survey 195
References and Research Bibliography 197
Index 227

Tables

3.1	Family and Contractual Labor: Changes in Farming Methods	60
3.2	Average Time Spent by Women Per Panel Family on the Following Agricultural Activities	62
3.3	Average Expenditure Per Panel Family of Women's Income in Sudanese Pounds	65
3.4	Average Women's Income Per Panel Family in Sudanese Pounds	70
3.5	Average Time Spent by Women for Selected Household Activities	72
5.1	Public and Private Investment	120
6.1	Number of Households and Average Family Size by Village	128
6.2	Tribal Affiliation of Heads of Households as Determined by Census	130
6.3	Professions Reported by Heads of Households by Village	132
6.4	Number of Heads of Household by Village by Age Category	133
6.5	Number of Heads of Household by Village by Level of Attainment for Both Religious and Secular Schools	134
6.6	Total Annual Earned Household Income in 1980	136

Figures

1.1	Development Schemes Along the Blue Nile	4-5
1.2	Map of El Roseiris	7
1.3	Map of El Damazin	8
2.1	Damazin Suq	34
2.2	Roseiris Suq	35
4.1	Native Court	84
4.2	*Gisim* Court	84
4.3	People's Court	85
4.4	Resident Magistrate's Courtroom	87
5.1	Administrative System	106
5.2	SSU Organization	114
6.1	Village Clusters	129
6.2	Rural Land Use	138

Currency Equivalents, Weights and Measures, and Abbreviations

CURRENCY EQUIVALENTS*

Currency Unit	=	Sudanese Pound (LS)
US$2.50	=	LS 1.00 (1978-79)
US$1.00	=	LS 0.40 (1978-79)

*Prior to 1978 the Sudanese pound (LS) was worth about US $2.8. Through subsequent devaluations in the late 1970s and early 1980s, it came to stand at US $1.00.

WEIGHTS AND MEASURES

1 hectare (ha)	=	10,000 m2 = 2.47 acre (ac)
1 feddan (fed)	=	1.04 ac = 0.420 hectares
1 kantar (large)	=	312 lb of seed cotton
1 kantar (small)	=	99.05 lb of cotton lint
1 kantar	=	100 pounds
1 kg/fed	=	2.38 kg/ha (2.123 lb/acre)
1 large kantar/fed (kpf)	=	337 kg/ha (300 lb/acre)
1 square kilometer (km2)	=	100 ha
1 kilometer	=	1,000 meters (m)
1 cubic kilometer	=	1 milliard cubic meters

ABBREVIATIONS

MOI	-	Ministry of Irrigation
SGB	-	Sudan Gezira Board
BNP	-	Blue Nile Province
GOS	-	Government of the Sudan
BNIADP	-	Blue Nile Integrated Agricultural Development Project
ESRC	-	Economic and Social Research Council of the Sudan
DSRC	-	Development Studies and Research Center (University of Khartoum)
MFC	-	Mechanized Farming Corporation
SSU	-	Sudan Socialist Union

Preface

We spent the summer of 1976 in Khartoum and Damazin/Roseiris discussing the possibility of long range research concerning the cultural aspects of development in a rapidly changing region of the Sudan. This venture was supported by grants from Harvard and Brown Universities. A cooperative, multi-pronged approach took shape and the details of teamwork were planned in 1976 and begun in 1977. We taught at the University of Khartoum from 1977 to 1979 and carried out research in Damazin/Roseiris in cooperation with the University of Khartoum and the Economic and Social Research Council of the Sudan. In November and December of 1977 we spent about five weeks in the field, accompanied by two graduate students from the University of Khartoum. Financial support came from a Ford Foundation grant through the Faculty of Economic and Social Studies. Lina Fruzzetti's part of the work was financed from a grant awarded by the Social Science Research Council (New York) and Ákos Östör's work was facilitated by awards from the Milton and Clark Funds of Harvard University. Field research continued in April 1978 when we returned to the South Funj region for over four months of continuous stay. Shorter visits totalling about eight weeks were made between November 1978 and January 1979. These phases of the work were financed from awards made by the Economic and Social Research Council (Khartoum). We carried out further research in the various libraries and institutions of Khartoum, while we were teaching undergraduates and training advanced students in research at the University of Khartoum.

We completed the basic library studies between 1976 and 1979, and we collected the available statistical evidence on the two towns and the region. We found much material in the Central Archives of Khartoum and in the Roseiris Archives now housed in the Rural Council Building in Roseiris.

Fruzzetti studied the People's Courts of Roseiris and Damazin and the Civil Court of Damazin. She observed court proceedings, interviewed court officials, and discussed legal issues with all participants. She studied the nomad-agriculturalist problem through court proceedings. She did research on customary law, law and development, and interviewed administration officials, merchants, nomads, and plaintiffs as well as citizens of the two towns. Later, Fruzzetti was able to carry out a study of the whole rural region as a director or co-director of several social impact studies for the Blue Nile Integrated Agricultural Development Project.

Östör worked in the markets of Damazin and Roseiris. He made a survey of the two *suqs*, interviewed about 230 merchants and traders, and collected basic sociological information about the background and origins, manner and pattern of trading, and conduct of business as well as patterns of credit, capital and stocks, and supply and distribution. He followed up the links between the market and administration, discussed government regulation of trade with officials, and worked on the development related aspects of market practices. He studied the mechanized farming system of the region and the trade in food grains. He cooperated with Mahgoub El-Tigani Mahmoud on a study of development administration and government corporations in rural development.

Dr. Mahmoud, then a graduate student at the University of Khartoum, carried out research on administration and bureaucracy in the two towns. His work included a study of provincial administration, local government, and the functioning of departments, agencies, and corporations. He interviewed over 200 officials and observed day-to-day governmental activities. He followed up the links between the officials and the town and rural councils and started research on officials as a society in the two towns. He collected basic sociological information about government employees and also worked on the administration of the current development effort.

In addition to these separate but related tasks we have made several joint trips to the villages along both sides of the river. We visited the Ingessana Hills, Keili, and Kurmuk several times. In 1978 Östör made a trip to Bikori and Geissan. We traveled to the Abu Gumai/Abu Sheneina and Jebel Agadi area on numerous occasions. Repeated journeys between Khartoum and Damazin/Roseiris by air, rail, and road throughout the 1960s, 70s, and 80s have helped us become aware of settlement and cultivation patterns, ethnic composition, ecology, economy, and communications in much of the Blue Nile Province.

Subsequently, Fruzzetti carried out a major survey of the Roseiris Dam area and of several major agricultural schemes during the winter of 1979-80 in association with the World Bank and the Economic and Social Research Council of the National Council for Research, Sudan. During the summer of 1980 Fruzzetti again cooperated with the ESRC in a survey of the Southern Blue Nile Region in preparation for a development project to be sponsored by the Agency for International Development and the Government of Sudan. During the 1980-81 academic year Fruzzetti was the project anthropologist on the Blue Nile Agricultural Development Project, which was implemented by Experience, Inc. (Minneapolis). During the winter of 1980-81 Östör was also in Damazin and Roseiris and visited

Preface   xix

the project area. Fruzzetti returned to the project during the winter of 1981-82 for further research. Several of these surveys resulted in publications by ESRC and Experience, Inc. (see Fruzzetti et al. 1979, 1982). These publications give full details of the work carried out and we have incorporated some of the data into the present volume.

The study was completed, more or less in its present form, in 1985, but research commitments in India and elsewhere prevented us from preparing the typescript for publication. Monographs published since then are not included in the discussion: This volume is a record of our fieldwork with the concomitant analysis and critical discussion. It is not meant to be a survey of the literature, hence our references to other studies, unless directly concerned with our argument, are illustrative and not comprehensive.

Many changes have taken place since our field study was concluded. Some of these are momentous, such as the introduction of the Shari'a law as the uniform system of justice, the extension of famine and drought conditions in the western regions, the eruption of civil war in the south, and the toppling of the May 1969 military regime in 1985. These events have caused untold loss of life, suffering, and destruction. In time, we may realize that changes in the legal system had the most far-reaching cultural impact and that political and administrative changes were less pervasive. In either case, the issues we discuss in this volume have a continuing significance. The problems of development and politics, administration, economy and ideology, regional imbalances and the decline of small scale societies, and the condition and status of women remain the same. Significant small scale changes that have, in time, a cumulative and lasting impact, are of course occurring and cannot be predicted. Hence, the major themes we consider here constitute a framework within which changes, with their still unforeseen consequences in culture and society, continue to take place.

L.F.
A.Ö.

Acknowledgments

We would like to thank our friends and all the people of Khartoum and of the Blue Nile Province, who extended their assistance and hospitality to us throughout our research. We acknowledge especially the people without whom we could not have completed this study. Lucia Tezba and Yousif el Mak were our family in Damazin. Hassan M. Salih, colleague and discussant, was our co-worker in the Abiyei Project. Ibrahim Hassan Abdel Galil (then Director of the Economic and Social Research Council) supported and in part funded our research; to him we extend our gratitude. Lidwien Kapteijns and Jay Spaulding, our "Sudanese" colleagues at Wellesley College and Kean College who discussed the manuscript at length: our deepest thanks for encouragement and support. Our daughters, Katya and Leila, put up with the inconveniences of cultural dislocation with patience and good humour. The experience of Sudanese life has made them citizens of the world; we treasure and thank them. For the patience of Shirley Gordon, who typed several versions of the manuscript, heartfelt thanks, and to Kerry Kohring, our journalist friend who edited the volume and still remains our friend, our deepest gratitude. Imogen Lim drew the maps and diagrams; Carol Walker set up the tables and layout; and Csilla Horváth designed the cover. The preparation of the manuscript was funded by the Dean of Faculty, Brown University. Earlier versions of several chapters appeared as articles or part of various reports: Fruzzetti 1979, 1985; Fruzzetti et al. 1982; Östör et al. 1978, 1981. We are grateful to Tavistock Publications, Economic and Social Research Council of the Sudan, and Experience Inc. for permission to use these materials and we express once more our heartfelt thanks to the funding agencies and universities that made our work possible.

L.F.
Á.Ö.

1

The Sudan, the Blue Nile, and the Question of Development

Positioned half way between the Arab and the African worlds, the Sudan is made up of numerous and diverse social groups and cultures. Long a home to indigenous chiefdoms, kingships, and sultanates, in the early 19th century the Sudan came under foreign domination: Turkish, Egyptian, and then British. After the defeat of the Mahdi, the great Islamic warrior-saint who attempted in the late 19th century to integrate diverse societies into a theocratic state, the entire country came under British rule. The British, in an effort to pay for the administration of the country, decided to develop agriculture. Several economic development projects were started by them, some of which have continued into the present. A model for future agricultural progress was established in 1905 when the colonial administration set up the Gezira Scheme. The British realized that the Sudan, though economically poor, was a country with great potential. Land was plentiful, the waters of the two Niles could be used for irrigation, but the country lacked sufficient capital for development. The Sudan achieved independence in 1956 and since then the expansion of the agricultural sector has accelerated. Most large projects designed or implemented in recent years have been funded and supervised by foreign agencies, such as the World Bank, the United States Agency for International Development and other development agencies from Europe and from Arab oil-producing countries.

The Sudan is the largest counry in Africa covering about 2.5 million square kilometers. It is sparsely populated except along the White and Blue Nile rivers and their tributaries. The majority of the 17 million inhabitants, subsistence cultivators and pastoralists, live in the rural area. Even though these two forms of livelihood exist side by side and often overlap, agriculture clearly dominates the economy. Beside providing a living for 80% of the population, since pastoralists also cultivate some farmland, agriculture contributes about 40% of the GNP and 95% of exports. Internally also the Sudan's economy depends on agriculture rather than pastoralism. But the renewed emphasis on agriculture has resulted in serious clashes between the two ways of life: as more land is brought under cultivation, the available pasture lands diminish. With even greater investment in agricultural development today, this sector will continue to dominate the economy.

What distinguishes Sudan's agriculture is the peculiar, local co-existence of a dual system: a modern mechanized and/or irrigated, and a traditional, subsistence sector of farming.[1] The former sector, based on the use of the Nile waters, is characterized by large scale, mostly state owned, partially or completely mechanized irrigation or rainland projects aiming at the production of cash crops such as cotton and sesame by modernizing the techniques of farming and expanding the area under cultivation. Irrigation costs are very high ranging from $2,000 to $5,000 and in some cases up to $10,000 per hectare not including government services which may add another $100 to $400 per hectare. (See Figure 1.1).

The traditional sector, mostly in private hands, receives little or no assistance from the state and very little technical aid to improve farming methods. It comprises rainfed subsistence agriculture. Rainland farms are usually small and poorly managed. As a result, production from these farms only suffices for the consumption needs of individual families. In the last few years the use of mechanized pumps along the White and Blue Niles has been increasing on private farms and gardens, whereas the larger pump schemes are government owned.

Though at present most large irrigated farms are state owned there is a tradition of irrigation in the private sector. At the turn of the century, modern gravity and pump irrigation replaced traditional flood irrigation, *shadouf* (irrigation by buckets) and *sagia* (water wheels), which were used up to that time extensively and successfully. The change in irrigation techniques necessitated the building of large and expensive dams and reservoirs to store the water. Over the last fifty years the Sudan has been able to irrigate 4 million *feddans* through reservoirs. Most of these irrigated farm lands are along the Blue and White Niles and use as their model the system of management and irrigation of the Gezira scheme. Away from the two Niles one finds a prevalence of small subsistence farms. This is also the case for the Western and Southern parts of the country where rainland farming and rainfed agriculture predominate. The kind of crops grown also differ in the modern and traditional agricultural sectors. The produce of irrigated farms is mainly for export while subsistence farms have taken care of domestic consumption. Irrigated farms grow cotton, groundnuts and wheat, while traditional farms cultivate sorghum, millet, sesame and wheat.

Post-independence regimes and states in the Sudan have committed themselves to certain kinds of modernization and directed change, and over the last few years the pace of development has increased dramatically. There is considerable concern on the part of government, universities, research institutes and the public at large with the rapidity and extent of change as well as the possible erosion of Sudanese values and ways of life. One shared expectation is that it should be possible to articulate economic development with the culture and values of Sudanese societies within the framework of a nation state. Following the resolution of a long and destructive civil war in the South in 1972, the government has embarked on an ambitious and expensive program of development. But by the mid 1980's the civil war resumed in the South, the development effort was near breaking down, and the military government collapsed. From its inception the new civilian regime has been confronted with major economic and social dislocations issuing from war, ethnic and religious conflicts, famine, and desertification, yet it remains committed to economic development and cultural change.

Aims of the Study

The argument of the book is that law, markets, and administration constitute, in part, the culture of development; ignoring these would lead to a lopsided view of social change. It is a commonplace that the societies which actually experience change themselves should be studied in order to understand the changes affecting them. But not only are villagers in project areas "societies," so are the people participating in markets, offices, and law courts. They also constitute a system of relationships with a parallel system of cultural categories, meanings and values. Our detailed narrative should reveal the complex interrelations of law, market, schemes and administration. We describe the social situation of large scale development schemes and smaller scale agricultural projects. All development efforts are doomed to fail unless local cultural and social contexts are fully integrated into the stages of planning and implementation. A cultural account can deal with aspects of development left untouched by the variety of economic approaches we criticize (modernization *and* dependency included). Even when these approaches do consider cultural phenomena they require the latter to be a separate and additional "input," secondary and inferior to economics and politics. Hence we discuss development in the context of market and exchange relations; civil and people's courts of law; administration and politics; projects, schemes and village social organization; and we attempt to find the links among these seemingly disparate parts that add up to, in our view, the totality we have to comprehend.

A more indirect aim of the book is to bring a concern with cultural values and meanings closer to the study of the economic, political, jural, and religious change and development in the Sudan. Having done extensive research in India, we came to study Sudanese societies utilizing the theoretical and methodological approaches we have developed in our previous work, with the eventual aim of arriving at a comparative understanding of continuity and change in South Asia and Africa. This wider perspective involves a dual attempt to generate anthropological theory from a comparison of societies analyzed and understood in terms of their own cultural categories and symbolic meanings, and to bring the

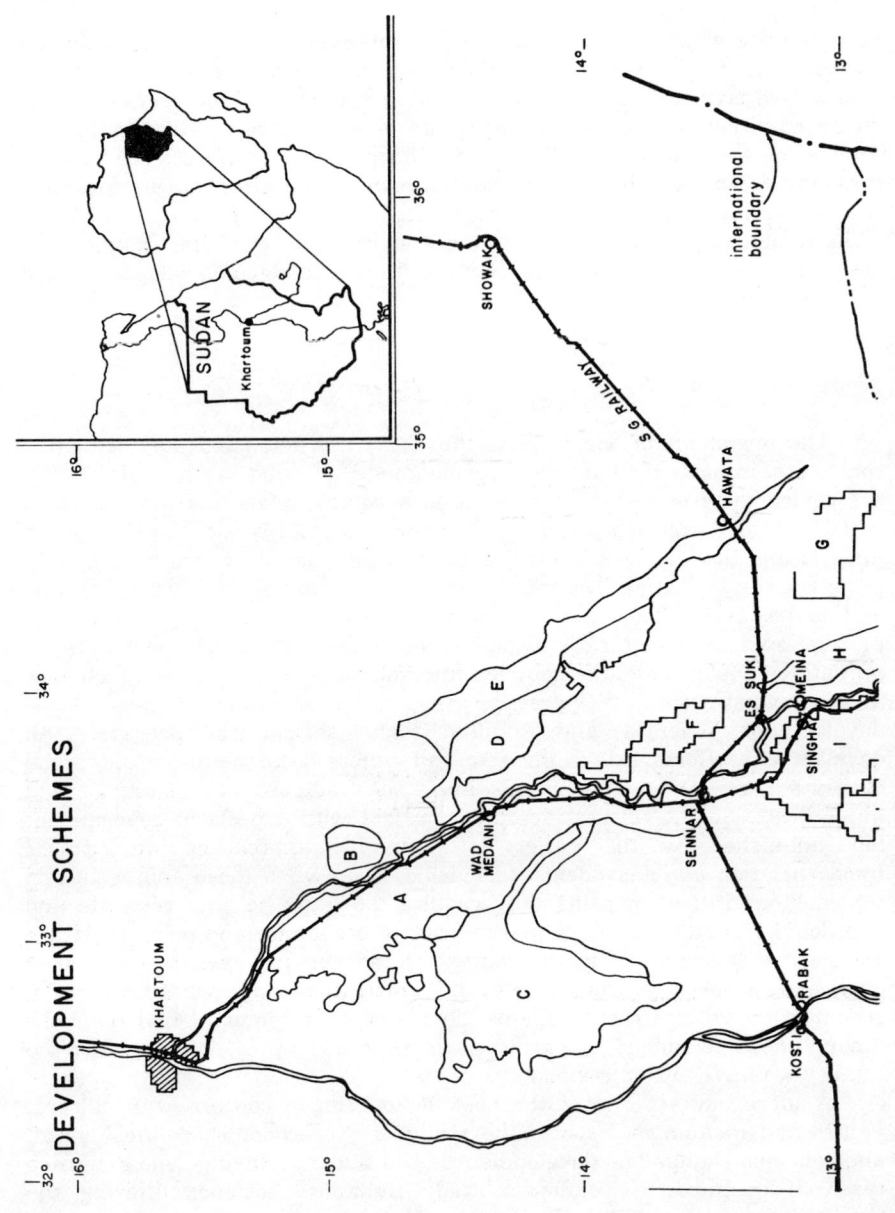

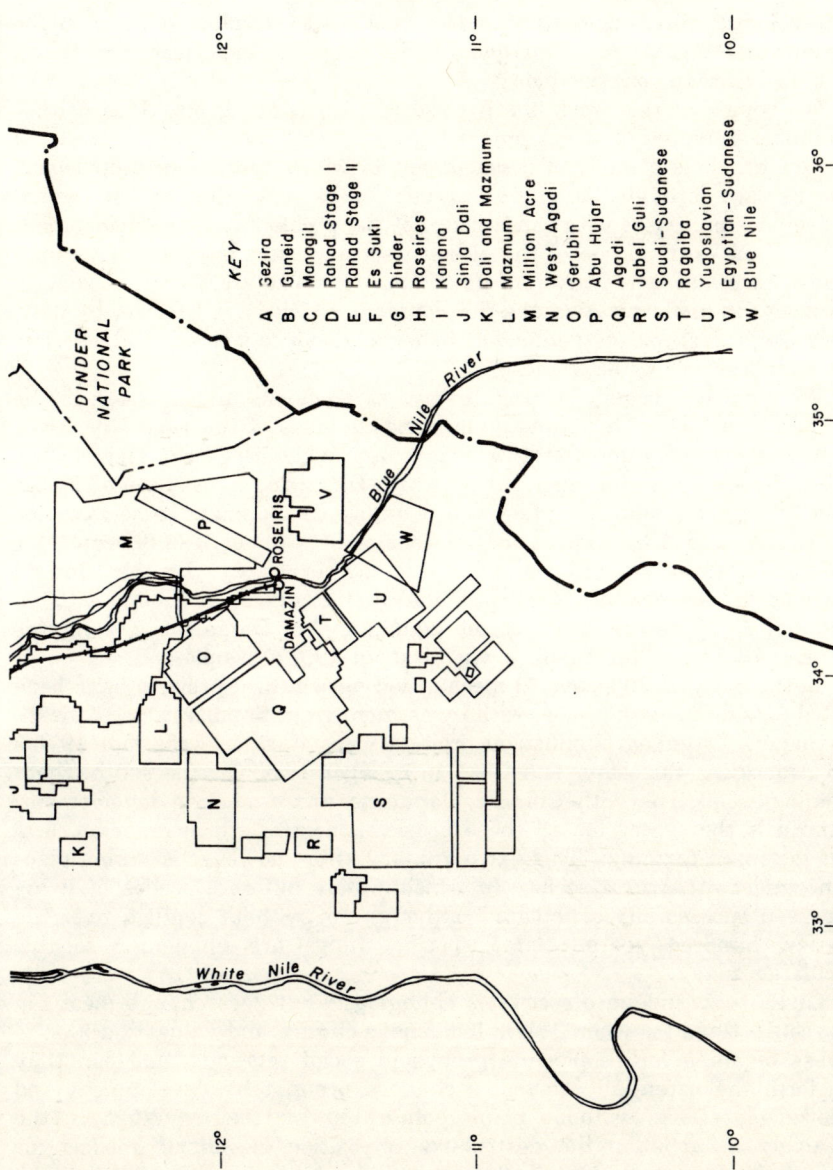

Figure 1.1 Development Schemes Along the Blue Nile

anthropologist's fine microstudy and cultural understanding to bear on the problems and dislocations of change and development experienced by South Asian and African societies today.

We hope that this work is a first step towards our goals. It is neither an ethnography nor a development report in the conventional senses of these terms. It is a study of development in which specific anthropological concerns are brought to the examination and evaluation of actual development processes. It is an account of the problems of the development effort and an examination of the affected social groups such as merchants, officials, farmers, women, and pastoralists. It is also a criticism of general approaches to modernization and development which have become, by now, the ideological staple of politicans, experts, donor agencies, and officials both Sudanese and non-Sudanese.

We studied aspects of change in two small towns and a region in the Blue Nile Province. The towns lie on opposite sides of the Blue Nile River which has been dammed at this point to provide irrigation and electric power. Roseiris, is the older town, while Damazin, a new town, is the center of regional administration and of many development projects. (See Figures 1.2 and 1.3). The 1955/56 census lists about 4,000 people for Roseiris, Damazin having been included in the rural area. By the 1964-66 household survey Roseiris stood at 7,300 and Damazin at 7,600, with an additional 1,400 as the "institutional population" of Damazin. The figures for the 1973 Census have both towns at about 12,000 people.

In the early 1970's several mechanized agricultural projects have been started outside the two towns, with investment from Saudi Arabia, Kuwait, and Sudan. Other agro-industrial projects were started in the late 1970's with American, Yugoslav, and German collaboration. To the south, there are mining concerns with Chinese, Japanese and American involvement. Damazin is the center for all these projects, most of which draw on local labor in tenant farming. This extraordinary effort however is taking place in the midst of a rural society in which widely different modes of living have been successfully articulated, although not without conflict, over the last few hundred years. Some specific things are happening to this articulation today.

Given that Sudanese society is changing, what does change mean, in what context and for whom? Will indigenous culture and values continue to express meaning for people and groups in social relations, and can they transform the potentially corrosive changes brought by development and modernizing efforts without being obliterated by them? What is the probability of avoiding the destructive imposition of outside models for change? Is there any chance of achieving national economic and political goals within the framework of Sudan's unique combination of African and Islamic civilizations and the indigenous cultural values of smaller scale societies? We do not believe that there are simple, overall answers to these questions. Ours will be given in a disaggregated form, in terms of the patterns and meanings we find in markets, law courts, villages, offices and development schemes.

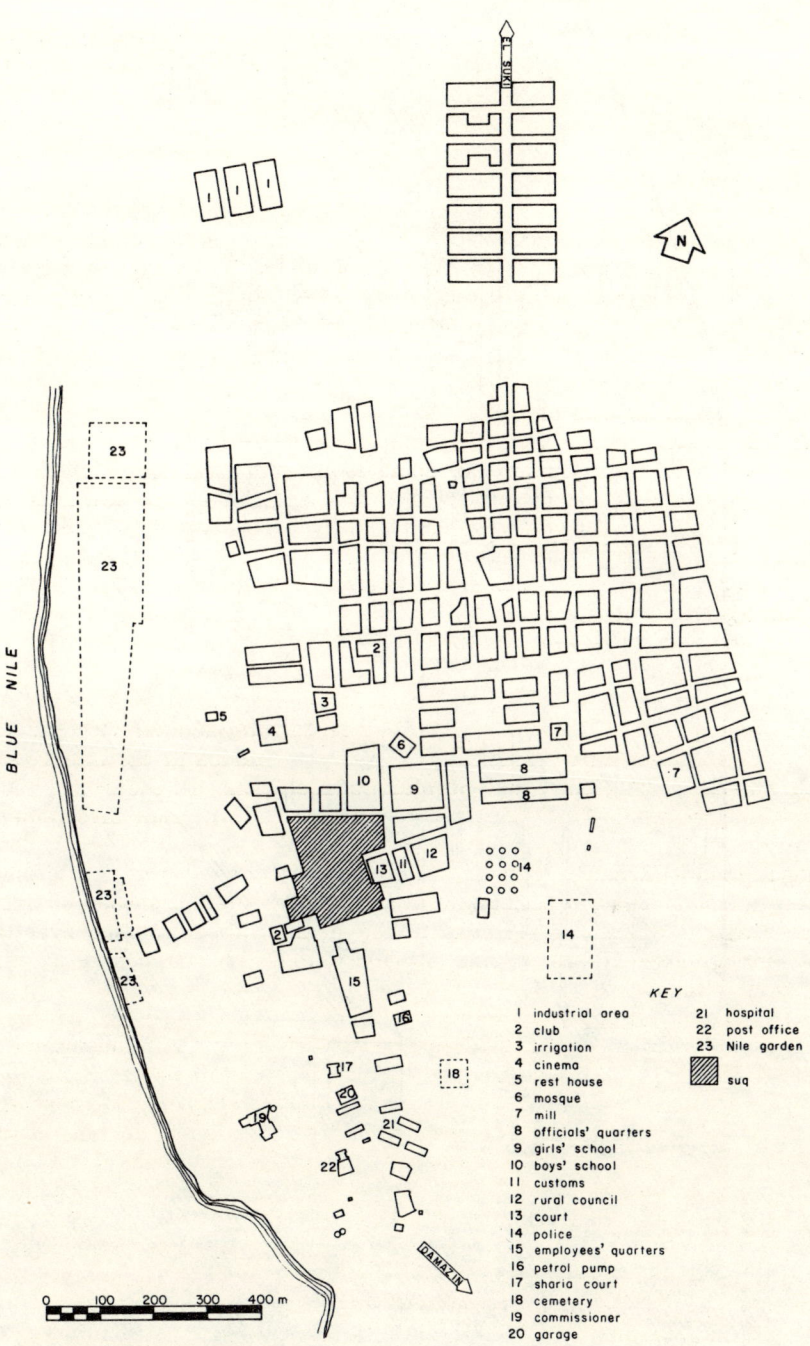

Figure 1.2 Map of El Roseiris

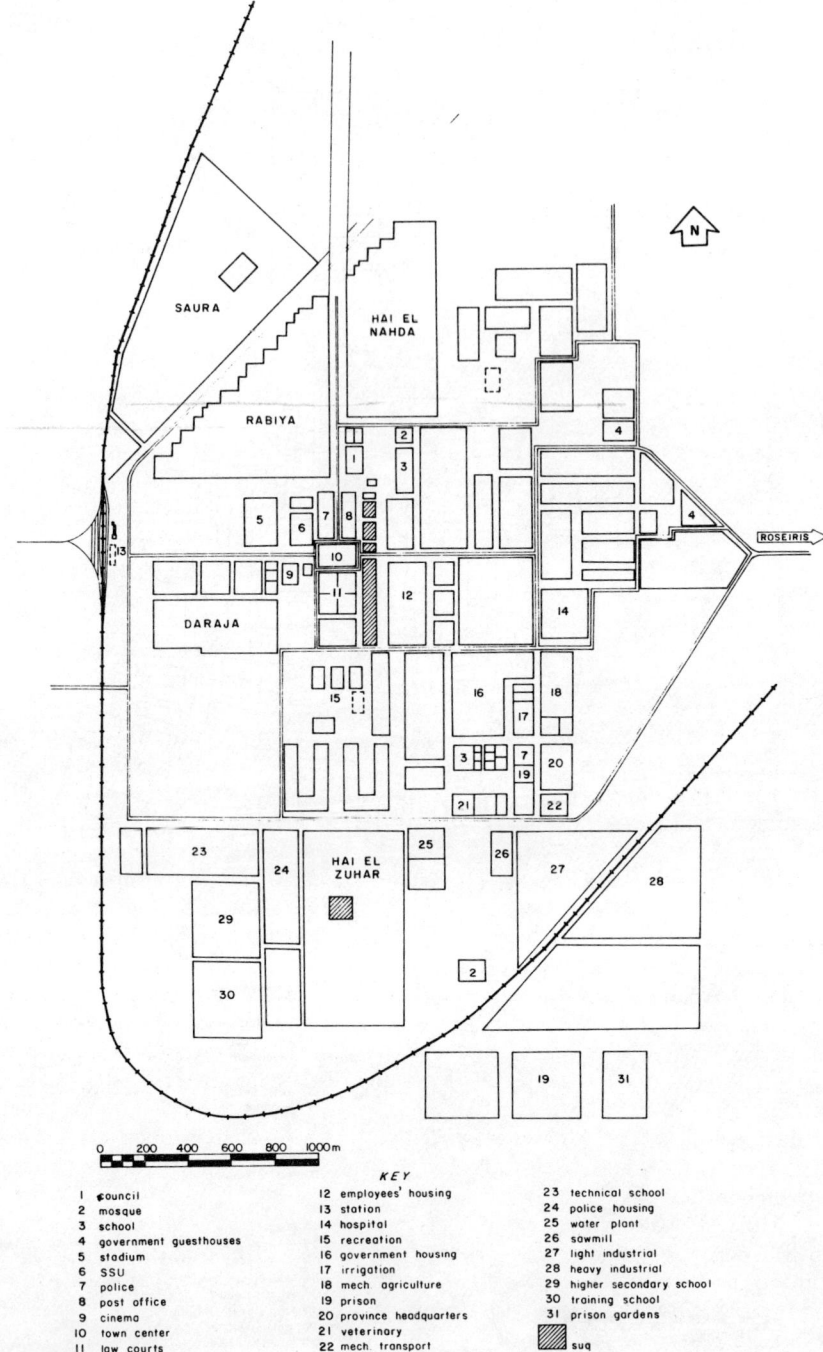

Figure 1.3 Map of El Damazin

Except for applied anthropologists most anthropologists have shied away from considering the problems of the societies they study. Applied anthropology on the other hand has been narrow in its approach to small scale problem solving, ignoring in the process the unique strength of anthropology: its holistic, totalizing, cultural perspective on society. It is this strength anthropology should contribute now in order to ease the disruption caused by rapid change and to participate in the search for indigenous values in approaches to development.

On a general theoretical level, we would argue for a more direct application of cultural approaches to the study of change. Too often the different aspects of social relations are left to the different methods and subfields of the social sciences in general and anthropology in particular. Economic, applied, political and cultural "anthropologies" proliferate and address different issues and audiences as if they were dealing with separate realities. Overarching approaches are not brought to bear on problems of economy and polity, while structure is thought of as underlying and not belonging to the domain of change, except to the extent traditional structures and values either hinder or ought to be rescued from change. Thus studies of culture, values, social structure, economic and political development remain divergent, each fitting into a neat typological niche. Yet an integrated study of all these aspects of society in the one locality is a precondition for understanding rapidly changing societies. One way out is to focus on change itself and posit some discontinuity between old and new, traditional and modern, past and present. Yet at precisely this point the endeavor can be questioned on the basis of a cultural approach: what are the categories chosen to reveal the contrast between these dichotomies? Do they really reveal change? Is change just posited on the basis of an extraneous universal framework or sociological theory? Another option is the study of values: the determination of new or modernizing values and the concomitent identification of traditional values. These approaches lead to filling out typologies rather than to an understanding of the actual changes that are taking place in particular societies or of the fundamental as against surface nature of these changes. Similarly, social structural studies alone are too static and synchronic to reveal the extent of change. On the other hand, diachronic approaches (inspired to a greater or lesser extent by rather self-absorbed Marxist methods) often cannot account for structural continuities and find difficulty in encompassing the cultural element as well as the moment of change from one kind or type of social formation to another. All these difficulties can be transcended to a degree by studying the relationship between culture, values, and social structure in a given context.

"Culture," in our view, is a system of symbols and meanings in society which may also provide the categories for the interpretation of social relations in indigenous terms. "Value" stands for indigenous construction of preferred, desirable and worthwhile ends in social action, relation, and being. "Structure" refers to the nature of the relationships among cultural categories and units in society, exhibiting properties of continuity, transformation, reciprocity, and replacement. The operations identifying the relationship between culture, values and structure within the context of an actually functioning society are crucial to successful development. The alternative is to intuit traditional and modern values independently of ideas and practices in given societies.

This book concentrates on sections of Sudanese society caught in the rapid changes of the 1970's. It gives case studies, each as complete as possible, of the cross-cutting factors and patterns present in the lives of local people. The rest of this chapter gives the historical background and the contemporary social situation of the Blue Nile region. Having taken a brief look at urban and rural groups, history, courts, markets, nomads and the problematic role of anthropology in development, we go on to criticize modernization and dependency theories which have become, by now, the twin bane of development studies. Neither approach is capable of giving a satisfactory account nor point a way out of the current impasse for countries like the Sudan. Chapter 2 is a study of Damazin/Roseiris townships, mainly through the marketplace *(suq)* and through the links between merchants, officials and development. We also discuss the impact of the Roseiris dam on the surrounding rural area. Chapter 3 is a study of women in agricultural schemes: the silent and neglected partners in development who nevertheless bear the brunt of change, both planned and unintended. Chapter 4 is a study of law courts, with special attention to the conflicts brought about by social change and migration. Chapter 5, written by Dr. Mahgoub El Tigani Mahmud, is a study of administration, politics and development on the national and local levels. It reveals a cultural system in the midst of a bureaucratic society. Various conflicts arise out of the difficult and contradictory demands placed on administrators. Chapter 6 is a case study of research in development: the ambiguous example of the Blue Nile Integrated Agricultural Development Project. Chapter 7 is a detailed survey of the major mechanized and irrigated agricultural schemes of the Sudan. The Gezira, Managil Extension, Rahad, Es Suki and the Guneid sugar schemes are examined in their structure and organization, as well as the position of their tenants. The last chapter presents the conclusions and implications of the study.

Historical and Societal Contexts

In the 17th and 18th centuries the region of our study was a part of the indigenous Funj Sultanate. Funj rule disintegrated in the wake of the Turkish invasion in 1820. During British colonial times the area to the West has been settled by West Africans, who came to the Sudan on their way to perform the *haj* (pilgrimage to Mecca). The indigenous inhabitants are still living around Roseiris and Damazin. Although little is known about them, recent work is beginning to document their societies. They have been a part of larger polities in the past. Coupled with relatively autonomous kinship - marriage, economic, and religious systems they are now being drawn into the changes affecting the country as a whole. The Hamaj, Berta, Gumuz, Koma, Ingessana, Uduk, and other peoples are collectively referred to as "pre-Nilotic," a linguistic rather than sociological grouping. It is not known precisely how many languages rather than dialects they speak although several may turn out to be dialects of the Berta language. In addition to the original inhabitants there are also the people referred to as Watawit, descendants of outsiders, Funj rulers and merchants, who made local political and marriage alliances. In addition, there are more recent immigrants to the area, merchants and bazaar people centered in the two towns who dominate the trade of the region. With these groups of northern Arab[2] immigrants are classed the government officials, administrators and development project personnel. Finally, there are the Arab nomads, such as the Rufa'a, whose lines of transience criss-cross the region. Sections of these groups alternate between nomadic and settled ways of living and the result of the interaction with the locals is a finely articulated cooperation and dependence between Berta, Watawit, Arab, Fellata (West African migrants),[3] nomads and merchants, but one that can also be the basis of conflict and stress from time to time. Over and above these local formations are placed the current attempts to build a nation state as directed from Khartoum and the regional centers. There is also the process of Islamization through merchants, Sufi orders and saints, and the resultant adjustments between idigenous culture of the Berta-speaking people and the Islam of the Watawit, the nomads, and the more recent immigrants, both from Khartoum and West Africa, who continue to come to the area and establish new settlements.

The southern Funj area combines the importance of Islam, the continued significance of customary law, and specific *tariga* (religious brotherhood) and *gabila* (tribe) structures in a meaningful historical and social whole. Islam spread into the Funj area at the end of the fifteenth century and the Funj rulers of local or immigrant ancestry associated themselves with and adopted a Middle Eastern Arab ancestry because this was considered to be prestigious. The controversy about the origin of the Funj kingdom will prove to be important if it reveals structural similarities between present political institutions and those of the past.

Historically, the Funj were probably nomadic cattle herdsmen, who migrated from the upper Blue Nile and gradually spread to the forest clearing at Sennar. The ruling families settled in Sennar, capital of the Sultanate from about 1616 A.D. They controlled much of the Blue Nile and even parts of the Northern Sudan also came under their control. They levied taxes on local and subordinate rulers. "The rulers in Sennar encouraged wandering Muslim teachers to settle and establish themselves in their area." (Voll 1972:88). It was through these men that Islamic society was established in the region. The Kings assumed the role of Muslim Sultans, established a state religion, appointed Qadis (Judges) and encouraged the *tariqas* (religious brotherhoods).

The military regime of 1969, led by General Nimeiry, tried to rationalize the customary law system by abolishing the privileges of the Funj rulers and establishing elected and appointed rural councils through which the immigrant and permanently settled populations could put political power to use against nomadic, Funj and indigenous priviledge. Yet the erstwhile Native Courts still exert influence and the People's Courts are in some ways a continuation of the previous system. Weekly courts are held in Roseiris amd Damazin to this day.

Roseiris is the older town with its courts, markets, and descendants of Funj rulers.[4] Here are also the older mosques and Sheikhs' tombs. The town is a loose collection of tribal *(gabila)* settlements and neighborhoods, many of which are Berta and Hamaj, while Damazin, an erstwhile village, is now the seat of government and administration. It also has a large *suq* which dominates the region. But like Roseiris it is surrounded by Berta, Hamaj and Gumuz settlements. The Ingessana hills are a short distance to the South where the Ingessana people surround new mining projects. The Ingessana have recently adopted a part nomadic, part settled way of life, and they trade with merchants and with the Arab nomads in and around Damazin. Further to the South, on the borders of the Blue Nile Province, the Nuer and Shilluk people are involved in similar cooperation and dependence with Arab nomads and Uduk, Koma and other "pre-Nilotic" peoples of the area.

Although the Sudan is made up of many social groups and religions, Islam being the dominant religion, the government's aim is for the people to transcend local loyalties. National identity and integration, not only in the South but in every region, are emphasized and the endeavor is to create a unified Sudanese society and ideology. Thus customary law will be abolished and civil law will apply to everyone, bringing about, in this way, a unified and singular judicial system. Similarly, the country's modernizing ideology claims that the benefits of development will accrue to the entire rural population since all the people of the country are considered to be equal.

Islam spread into the area from the North through merchants and religious specialists acting as missionaries. If the merchant was an agent of change, and still is in the remote areas, the man of Islam set the model for a new way of life to be emulated. Merchants and saints were the first to effect change in an area where Islam was unknown. Today Islam is becoming more and more dominant and while local tribes maintain their distinct cultures, they are increasingly affected by the culture of the North.

Fundamental aspects of Sudanese society have remained unaltered to this day: identity with a tribe *(gabila)*, loyalty to a religious movement *(tariga)*, commitment to the family. Within these continuities there have been changes, though the processes of change have not been fully documented (Sanderson 1963:61.)

In the history of modern Sudan, administrative and political institutions have changed hands many times. The offices of the Omda, Mek and Nazir have been replaced by a modern rationalized administrative system. Seeing that the position of traditional institutions was being undermined, Voll wondered, more than a decade ago (1972) what form Islam would take in the future in the light of basic economic and political changes. But the combination of old and new elements has been a conscious effort in Sudanese history since the 1930's. Alliances between political parties and religious groups have been a feature of the modern history of the Sudan as leaders of *tarigas* have joined hands with the "new men," of politics. (Voll 1972; Warburg 1973, 1978.)

In 1979 the old Blue Nile Province was divided into the Gezira and the new Blue Nile Provinces. Damazin was selected to be the new capital of the latter. The administrative changes and the implementation of mechanized farming in the province have changed the older pattern of alliance, trade and religion, and emphasized the significance of bureaucracy, politics, and religious movements. The role of the merchants became secondary. The new model for the local inhabitants to emulate is not the old-style merchant, but the *effendi* or *muazzaf* (government official) and the politician. Education and the possibility of acquiring an official position thus become the ideal.

Nomads and Agriculturalists

The Blue Nile Province is populated by many groups, (*gabilas*, tribes) indigenous as well as immigrant. Among the indigenous people are Hamaj, Berta, Gumuz, Ragreg, Watawit, and Jebelawin. There are a number of nomadic groups, Rufa'a Al Hoi, Ingessana, Um Bororo, and Fulani.[5] The Rufa'a Al Hoi are the largest and economically, historically and politically most important *gabila*. There existed, to some extent, a symbiotic relation between the Rufa'a and the settled subsistence farmers, but today competition for access to land and water has become a serious issue. Old, nomadic migratory routes are jeopardized by increasing mechanization and the growth of farming communities. The herder's way of life is threatened and migratory corridors, the ten mile wide "belts of fire," continue to decrease. All this is rought about by an economic and political push for development from the national and district levels. The nomads' choices are limited to following the migratory routes, accepting a sedentary way of life, or the drastic alternative of burning fields and trespassing on the farms. Cases involving nomads are a common feature in the People's as well as the Resident Magistrate's Courts.

In addition to the problems of nomadic and farming communities, there are increasing conflicts between the various nomadic groups in the Blue Nile Province. The non-indigenous (Fellata) nomads who have come into the province are the Um Bororo, Fulani, Nabaha, Nesah, Al-Kibashab and Sabhwho. The Fulani and the Um Bororo do not abide by the migratory timetable accepted by the other nomads, nor do they pay taxes to the provincial authorities. Their seemingly erratic movements across the landscape anger the sedentary farmers as well as the other nomadic groups.

The system of authority and social organization of the nomads differ from those of the sedentary groups. Among nomads, Omdas and Sheikhs are still important, but the national political role of these tribal leaders was dissolved recently, bringing all Sudanese under one rule and law. Nonetheless, the Omda system still operates on the local level, establishing peace and alleviating conflict and between nomad and non-nomad populations. Sheikhs and Omdas still maintain a high respect within nomad society. Whereas in the past they were responsible for the internal legal standing of the group, today their role is that of intermediary, attempting to solve cases by *suluh* (peace) before the problems reach the courts.[6]

Nearly 6 million *feddans* (1 *feddan* = 1.04 acres) have been allocated to government and private development schemes in the province. These exclude the farm areas which fall outside "government agricultural planning" but which have been mechanized and are used by well-to-do people at the expense of nomads and subsistence farmers. Villages in the province are scattered and sparsely populated. Cultivated plots move progressively away from the village. Each farmer can increase his plots by moving further out but not across the land, since other farmers are cultivating on his left and and right sides. Every 5 to 7 years, the cultivated fields are abandoned and new ones are prepared further away but still within the recognized village boundary. This process is common since fertilizers are not used and the productive capacity of the land diminishes. In time the fields move far from the villages and the process continues until the whole village or the individual families also shift. There is enough space for each farmer to expand his farm holding. The establishment of a new or a nearby sattelite village allows for further expansion. Villages can come into conflict over land, more so now when everyone feels pressed by the growth of the mechanized farms. In the past, these conflicts were settled by the local village heads (Sheikhs). At present, the courts have taken over this role and more subsistence farmers spend their time in courts arguing about land use and unwritten traditions which are no longer kept. Intervillage fights about land, trespass, burning of planted fields by nomads, and land displacement by large scale agricultural companies are only some of the cases handled by the local courts. Many conflicts go unreported to the authorities for a number of reasons; lack of transportation funds, fear of being involved in court cases, uncertainty of the local situation, misunderstanding of law, fear of litigation with large agricultural companies, or the possibility of nomadic revenge. The judicial changes are still unclear to the rural inhabitants, but most important, few can afford court fees, the travel and the stay in Damazin or Roseiris. Yet, it is in the rural areas that conflict is increasing and where the application of the law is most needed.

Anthropology and Development

Until recently few anthropologists worked in the development field. In the postwar period the only social scientists who took part in the design and implementation of development projects were economists.

When Third World countries began to concern themselves with the social aspects of their nationhood, they attempted to move from quantitative to qualitative development.[7] It was only then that economists and other planners welcomed anthropologists and even then the latter worked within an economic frame. Although now employed by some development agencies, the anthropologist is still a luxury and at times remains a "status symbol for the organization or department which possesses him, a sure sign of being up with the fashion of building in the social dimension." (Pitt 1976:2.)

Anthropological work in the Sudan ranges from help in the implementation and designing of new projects to evaluating old, existing projects. Anthropologists in the development field deal with practical matters that concern the lives of the rural poor. In the field, they are faced with the reality from which their theories about modernization dependency and underdevelopment are supposedly fashioned. Their information comes from living and working with the people rather than from impersonally collected and quantified questionnaires. But anthropologists have yet to make an impact in many areas of development. As Pitt noted, the anthropologist arrived, but has yet to reach the first floor.

Anthropologists differ in approach from economists and political scientists. They spend more time as participant observers in the field. They act as a liaison between the people and other project personnel. By including anthropologists, projects can foster a cooperative effort to help planners in addressing development issues from a cultural, as well as economic perspectives, without sacrificing one to the other.

The push for economic development in the Third World began during the struggle for independence and the subsequent decolonialization process. The paramount concern of the new leaders was achieving political stability and economic soundness for their countries. But the economic progress sought was often inhibited by political unrest. In terms of governance, these countries had to adjust to new administrative systems and, in many cases, had to contend with conflicts among ethnic groups which were opposed even during pre-colonial times but now became citizens of the same nation. In situations of this sort, national economic considerations have been sacrificed for political ones as leaders attempted to settle old disputes. Political issues took precedence in cases where primary loyalties were to primordial ties rather than to the state. It has been argued that individual loyalties that divide the nation along tribal, religious, regional, or other barriers must be removed before constructive changes can be introduced. Thus, economic development became a means to bridge or destroy existing barriers. The expectation was that in time the state will command the loyalty of the individual, since development within a national framework inevitably leads to the displacement of local by national dependence (Anthony et al. 1979:202).

Most development ideologies assume that "there is a continuous evolution that proceess from a traditional state towards a modernization goal and follows steps that are similar to those presumed to have been followed by Western industrialized nations." (Pitt 1976:10). Less developed nations expect to become more developed through economic progress, hence, economic arguments predominate in the quest for progress. Axinn compares the processes and theories of development to Durkheim's distinction between "pedagogy" and "actions," in that development today has become a matter of theoretical presentation. The major concern has been the "how to do it" aspect, ways of improving the world, not the relation of this pedagogy of development to past history, culture and social action. Nonetheless, there is a consensus among developing countries that the process of social and economic change is inevitable and necessary (Axinn 1977:10).

The capital needed for development comes from the West and is not generated from within the host country. The concept of development in the Western tradition carries with it the implicit notion of increased material consumption and higher standards of living. Furthermore, development is seen to follow a linear rather than cyclical progression. A technological analysis of economic development reveals success and failure in which high rates of success have not been achieved. In some instances, economic progress is apparent if we select for the indices of development the number of new buildings, the use of cars, the rise in the GNP and per capital income, and the wealth of the elite. Measuring the impact of economic growth in rural areas may however reveal the "poor," broadly defined, who, while designated as the target group for economic and social development, have not been the major recipients of benefits. "At times a broad classification of the poor...obscures the existence in the same country of a small affluent group that controls the means of production and the levers of economic and political power" (Parman 1975:13). Social justice and profit sharing will not automatically and in time reach the poor if these factors are not considered as a pre-condition of progress through growth. Development is not a concept which can be used to describe the lifestyle of individuals, small communities, regions or whole countries. There are no universal criteria for measuring development. "Neither economic indicators nor political ideals nor simple measures of life and death provide a universal development strategy" (Axinn 1977:10). In the 1950's and 1960's development, as a concept, referred to specific indices of wealth and the GNP. To understand such a concept in the Sudan, Barnett suggests that one must first try to place some of the features of Western "capitalist relations of production" in the concomitant widening of the wage labor base. Development is a relative term that has to be placed in a context rather than applied in a broad theoretical sense. In most cases, plans and implementation come from above. They are imposed from the outside by donor governments or funding agencies. Thus, as a result, "development reflects ethnocentric tendencies or similar structural features in the economic structure of the donor subculture" (Pitt 1976:4) Very rarely do such development plans begin at the grassroots level of the village.

Development generally refers to economic progress and fails to take account of social or cultural conditions and consequences. Although many leaders of underdeveloped countries are aware of the impact of development, few are able to separate the economic from social aspects, and by emphasizing the economic, incur a damaging cost to the people. One cannot impose economic development without affecting the ideology and values of the people to whom the benefits are supposed to accrue. "Since modern development implies deliberate choice -- development by design -- the social structure or the total system of rules operating in society at any given time is of crucial importance" (Anthony et al. 1979:199).

Despite the net contribution to society's wealth and progress, economic growth disturbs intergroup social networks and pre-existing intergroup relations. When a society initiates change, yet cannot channel it equitably, it may end with a situation in which the better-off will benefit more than those at whom development is directed. This has been the case in many projects, repeated in one rural area after another, where development has increased the disparity between wealth and poverty. Today it is widely believed, in the Sudan and elsewhere, that development really benefits the superior social groups rather than the targeted groups. "Increased income flows into the pockets of the merchants, who belong to a different subculture and the administration of development programs becomes yet an additional power in the already overpowerful central government" (Pitt 1976:16). Economic change is not directed towards an ethnic group or a local group, but at the nation as a whole. It is cast in a national context and provides individuals with opportunities and challenges. It is very difficult to predict the outcome and impact of any economic change introduced into a society, because the effect of an innovation in social relations may vary from simple adaptation to existing forms and no change in the social structure to the destruction of parts of the system and the emergence of entirely new social forms.

In recent years the outcry against the iniquities of development and the haphazard way plans are carried out have forced many developing countries to assess what development is about, who it should affect, and how it should be channeled; in short, to assess the pre-conditions for development before the inception of a project. Countries like the Sudan now ask that the society and culture not be sacrificed to economic progress. They insist that the rural poor have a direct say in designing, implementing and evaluating the projects which affect them.

The economies of many Third World countries depend on agriculture. Agriculture forms the basis of national income and is the major producer of foreign exchange. Ultimately, agricultural productivity determines a nation's balance of payments record and allows imports from advanced countries. Although the development of rural areas was neglected in the past, the recent world food crisis has been changing the existing, colonially inherited economic systems from a producer of raw materials for the industries of the colonizing power to producers of foodstuffs for direct consumption.

The modernization of agriculture in developing countries takes priority over all other concerns. The improvement of the rural areas and the efforts to bridge the difference between these and the more advanced urban sectors are on every leader's list of priorities. An increase in agricultural production was used in the past as the measurement for progress in the rural areas but, economic measurements, such as the those following the success of the Green Revolution, many instances did not reflect the social implications or the general welfare of the people (Nair 1979). Unbalanced social and economic development was disregarded and the questions of equity and social benefits were dismissed. Even positive economic effects were not enough to obliterate the social consequences. Today planners have to realize that the society of the farmer, the varied and interlocking institutions, values and beliefs of rural poeple must be considered in the process of agricultural planning. The view of the farmer as unchanging and unbending is a fiction because farmers are rational to the extent that they accept the challenges of innovations that improve their livelihood. There is a correlation between the decline in agricultural production, despite the introduction of advanced technological know-how and machinery, and the disruption of rural society. In order to succeed the modernization of the rural sector has to emphasize employment, equity, and contribution of the agricultural sector to economic growth (Sarah Voll 1980).

Ideologies of Development

The pervasive development ideologies referred to above derive from modernization and dependency theories, and can be found in most discussions of development projects, meetings of donor and host agencies, the exhortations of foreign experts and home grown officials. These sets of ideas can be found readily in the scholarly literature as well, not in every single publication, but in the manner ideas and assumptions make up a pattern, an ideological stance. Particular works may qualify a position one way or another but they still contribute to a general perception of modernization and development.

We discuss theories of modernization and dependency here because it is to these origins that we can trace back most of the rhetoric surrounding the issues of development today. A certain development ideology is shared by politicians, officials, project planners and academics in the Sudan and in the donor countries and agencies, whick rests on ideas that have been current for decades. Concepts may combine and recombine to yield any rhetoric of development. But those who so avidly use this language are the least concerned with a critical look at the implications of what they are saying. Theories of development and modernization have been with us, under various guises, but few have noted the many similarites between them. Not only do these theories converge but their effects in practice are not as different as we may expect. Hence a critical discussion is all the more important. The significance of our discussion is that the constructions of large scale systems are faulty and that even without regard to a particular locality, which is the burden of our study, the linking of different levels in a total system is inadequate, unnecessary and unconvincing. Later on we add the knowledge of a specific locality, the Blue Nile Province, to complete the critical argument we begin here.

The rapid decline of modernization theories, the equally rapid rise of dependency theories, and the self-proclaimed Marxist rhetoric in the Third World's confrontation with industrialized societies obscure the basic complementarity and even the similarity of these models for social transformation. The deeper roots of these circumstances are to be sought in the problematic relation between social science and society. Persistent calls on the social sciences to come to the rescue of revolutions on the one hand, and technology transfer and economic development on the other hand, present unseen dangers and focus our attention on modernization and underdevelopment as processes, theories, and strategies, as well as on values. In embarking on this discussion we will be general to a degree and programmatic to a fault in order to bring out the basic pattern of convergence between the seemingly contradictory approaches of modernization and dependency.

One significant problem is the relation between the social sciences and the concerned societies themselves. For our discipline, in Africa as elsewhere, this question has taken the form: what is, should or ought to be the role of anthropology and anthropologists in development? A whole host of fundamental problems and larger questions are hidden behind the innocent exhortation to become relevant activists. Current discussions of this subject confuse several distinct though related issues: the nature of social-scientific enquiry, the relation between science and society, the significance and relation of critique to ideology and practice, and the problems and contexts of development. At the same time, the question of "what is development all about" is left wide open. For anthropologists, the question of participation is often posed in terms of whether or not projects should have resident anthropologists, just as they have resident agronomists, engineers, and administrators. Note that while the latter are taken for granted, the former are prefaced by "should," and if the answer is yes then the question becomes "what are they to do"? In this way we are led to an underlying problematic in the study of society: the relation between the nature and the understanding of the structures and transformations within and across societies. However, a hasty application of received or intuited wisdom cannot replace, even in the name of one currently fashionable ideology or another, the investigation and analysis of this problematic. We have a good point of departure in theories of change that attempt not only to account for social transformations through time, but also offer models toward which societies may move.

In an endeavor to confront these questions there should not be even a trace of disciplinary chauvinism: in an immediate and restricted sense this means another look at the relation between anthropology and the other social sciences. Marx, Durkheim, and Weber, founders of modern social theory, studied societies in a comparative and unified manner. We can continue to learn from their example. Whatever we call it, our approach has to be holistic, systemic, historical, and comparative; we study societies as wholes, relating parts to each other and to the whole, and we make comparisons among societies. In anthropology, such an emphasis would go against the splitting up of a unified approach into economic, political, Marxist, symbolic or other "anthropologies."

The two ways of approaching change discussed below are symptomatic and indicative of a broad range of different and particular studies. We shall not be exhaustive in our narrative nor do we intend to give a survey of the literature. Our exercise is a means to an end, illustrating the problems involved in studying change and in trying to apply the results. First, we discuss the "modernization" approach. This includes economics, sociology, anthropology, and political science. More particularly it embraces development, neo-classical and liberal economics, theories of sustained growth, take-off, big-push, and human investment as well as theories of socio-political mobilization, differentiation, and development. These approaches are by no means uniform and there is considerable disagreement among them. Yet there is agreement on the broad outlines, processes, aims and desirability of modernization. Second, we discuss approaches to "underdevelopment" or "dependency." These also include a lot of economics and sociology but their main orientation is increasingly given by a self-professed Marxism. But this kind of "Marxism" goes beyond Marx himself to the century of theories and experiences after Marx.

Theorists such as McClelland (1961), Parsons (1951) Rostow (1956) and Gusfield (1971) need not acknowledge their similarities to be regarded as representing a trend and may include effective criticisms of each others' work in their own writings. Yet taken together and writing in the context of contemporary history, they converge more than they differ. More recently, events have brought yet another turn of the wheel with the rise of dependency theories which tend to lump all modernization theories together in critical condemnation. In their turn these also exhibit ideological and historical characteristics that allow *their* critics to speak of a "development of underdevelopment" theory and a "dependency" theory in the making. This discerning of trenss is in no measure restricted to critics: brethren of a trend, or in a more dignified way a "theory," read each other out of the orthodoxy with abandon.

The two major approaches we oppose to each other and yet find converging in important respects have long ago defined themselves and each other in these broad terms. Once this is perceived, the added insight of finding the same assumptions shared by both camps will not cause much surprise. It is no coincindence that the two approaches incorporate large portions of each other's territory presumed to be exclusive to their own camp. Through Weber, as well as modern economic ideology, Marx and Marxists have made a significant impact on modernization theory, and many of the assumptions of the latter are shared by dependency theorists. We note at the outset that we separate Marx and Weber from their followers, although we emphasize the former because of the nature of the theories involved (Giddens 1971). It should be said again that although social theories are to be understood in their social context and in their relation to practices, the latter of necessity cannot fully account for the former. Thus, facile arguments about economics directly reflecting capitalist society, about anthropology being merely an expression of colonialism, and about underdevelopment theory being explained by the exploitation of the Third World, cannot be accepted.

Theories of Modernization

Modernization usually refers to the multiple processes through which non-Western societies approximate the complex series of changes that took place and continue to take place since about the sixteenth century in Western Europe and North America. The characterization of the processes, the indices or at least the indications of measurement, the emphasis on the nature of the changes that occurred, the units of study (individuals, groups, institutions, countries, and states), the criteria for successful modernization and the practical implications of the studies vary a great deal; some are not mutually exclusive, others are opposed, even contradictory, but certainly critical of each other.

Modernization theories have been put forward in sociology, anthropology, psychology, political science, and economics, with significant variations within and across these disciplines. Nevertheless these approaches share certain central assumptions, criteria, and characteristics allowing us to refer to modernization in general, both as process and theory. The best-known theory of modernization comes from the sociological writings of Eisenstadt (1966, 1973), emphasizing social and political aspects, whereas political development is stressed by Deutsch (1961), Pye (1964), and Weiner (1968). In economics, widely different approaches to development have been taken by Rostow (1956), Myrdal (1968), Myint (1971), Hirschmann (1971, 1981), and Mellor (1976) among others, with little specific agreement beyond the fact, the desirability and even necessity of the modernizing process. Beyond the similar assumptions lie disagreement over the ways of achieving modernization. National and supranational issues have been emphasized by Shils (1975), Geertz (1974), Fallers (1974), and others in the early work of the Committee for the Study of New Nations at the University of Chicago (ed. Geertz 1963).

Although one or another of these approaches gives a central role to modernizing values in contrast to tradition, re-emergence of tradition, economic growth (take-off, big-push, investment in man, and integrated rural development), markets, planning, mobilization and/or relationships among different levels of a nation state, the critique offered below is not meant to refute specific studies. Rather we speak to general trends, realizing that many refinements and revisions have been made within this broad field of studies.

Evolutionary and diffusionistic assumptions are built into modernization arguments, "modern" is opposed to "traditional," but it is not clear what these polarities are about: types of society, kinds of social processes, description of facts, classificatory schemes, criteria for stages, traits, values or motives? For example, Shiner (1975) insists that "modernity" and "tradition" are none of these things, rather they are purely heuristic models. This may be a satisfactory academic way out but it does not face the problem of how to deal with categories that become part of the problem they mean to investigate.

Since theories of modernization refer to Western societies, they cannot account for the impact of the West on the rest of the world in other ways than the spread, extension, or triumph of rationality. As a set of theories, they have trouble explaining their own origin, development and shifts of emphasis during their long career (Dumont 1977).

Changes during the last two or three centuries are seen in social mobilization and differentiation through technology in the economic domains, the spread of power in the political, and the belief in progress in the cutural domains. "Modern" society is further characterized by non-ascriptive regulation through representation, markets, bureaucracies; dissociation between institutional forms and primary groups; the wider society being drawn into consensual mass society (Eisenstadt 1966, 1973).[8] These are all problematic and yet they require (in terms of the theories) indices and indicators, typologies, and measurements of progress toward goals. The issue is further complicated by doubts about the validity of these categories in the first place.

In erecting Western societies as a model for the rest of the world to follow, accounts of modernization tend to assume that we know all about the West. Yet this assumption cannot be justified since we do not fully understand the relations between social structure, history, and symbolic-cultural meanings and values even in Western societies. Such a comparative study of advanced industrial societies in relation to other societies is yet to be realized. Discussions of modernization are dominated by the primacy, even if not explicitly stated, of the "economic" and economics. There are peculiarities to the transformation of Western societies especially in the form of production and exchange and the centrality of certain categories of theory and action, all of which cannot be directly "applied" or even transplanted with fixed meanings, to other contexts. The task of carrying out a comparative study of economy and society in the West in relation to other hierarchies in other societies, has not been carried out by students of modernization.

More recently modernization theorists had to face the question: why doesn't modernization succeed? Studies of "interruptions" and "breakdowns" of and "latecomers" to modernization, and "recrystallization" of tradition try to account for post-World War II failures of the modernizing process (Eisenstadt 1973; Levy 1972; Rueschemeyer 1976). This time around "tradition" becomes the place to look for explanations: dynamics and modernity of tradition, primordialism and the like. Yet dichotomies remain and the novelty is merely in the chalking up of a few mere "pluses" on the side of tradition (e.g., Rudolph and Rudolph 1966). The more narrowly based economic theories are even more questionable: "stages of growth," "take-off," and "big-push" theories have been effectively criticized by Myint (1971) and Myrdal (1968). Yet when issues wider than the economy are considered, and valuations are taken to be basic to the discussion, as in Myrdal's study, after some temporizing we are quickly led back to the identification of "modernizing values" inimical to "traditional" backwardness, superstitution, inefficienty, and irrationality. In his general introduction Myrdal sums up and rightly castigates a generation of research and writing on development and change. He insists, emphatically, that indigenous culture and value premises have to become a part of our study and yet when he makes the attempt "modern" values are opposed to "traditional" ones with the latter condemned as a hindrance to change (Myrdal 1968 vol.1: chapters 1-3).[9]

Modernization is restricted to elite in opposition to class analysis. Thus modes and styles of living, political modernization and status groups become significant, implying a differentiation of economic and political domains, without, however, a discussion of dominance and/or hierarchy in the relations among domains. In the writings of Gusfield, Shils, and the Rudolphs, modernization often appears as a concern of elites, a set of motivations and inspirations, designating a datum rather than a social theory. The change it purports to describe is linear with functional requirements that demand continued extension. Hence the fear of obstacles, impediments. Tradition appears as a component unit and a feature rather than as a set of relationships. Hence elites are linked to tradition as well as to power (markets, production, administration). The modernizing disposition of elites is in turn linked to the extension of a particular mode of living. Beyond the above problems a quest for those features of modern (Western) society that seem to have contributed to the emergence of "modernity" can easily degenerate into trait hunting and a cataloguing of individualistic motivation (e.g., McClelland 1961).

The dichotomy of traditional and modern, and the inimical relations between them vitiate any attempt to understand what it being transformed and in what directions. The dichotomy is a part of Western ideology and the theory is itself a part of the actions it attempts to explain. Hence a critique of Western economic categories has to be carried out. The economic bias of modernization theories prevents the performance of this task. This is the measure of their embeddedness in Western (economic) ideology and an expression of their acceptance of specific (economic) categories as providing an objective framework for comparison across societies and times.

Theories of Dependency

Dependency or underdevelopment usually refers to the process by which European and North American countries have expanded, through mercantilist and capitalist production and trade, at the expense of the underdeveloped countries of Asia, Africa and South America. The underdevelopment of some areas is seen to be directly related to the development of others; as metropolis is linked to satellites, city to country, so "capitalist" is to "underdeveloped" countries in the world. (See Cockroft, Frank, and Johnson 1972; Jalee 1977; Rodney 1974) The unit is the world capitalist market in which exchange benefits the metropolitan countries. Among the satellites there are no "traditional" societies, only precapitalist societies deformed by their relation to the market, recreating the central form of dependency in the peripheries of the world market (Wallerstein 1976; Amin 1974a, 1974b).

Underdevelopment theory is best known from the writings of Frank and his colleagues on Latin America, but the bulk of contributions, not necessarily "Marxist," by Latin American students of society themselves has become known only recently due to the earlier paucity of translations (e.g., Furtado 1964; Cardoso 1972, 1973, and other "structural" approaches). There is also a substantial convergence between these studies and other approaches to Asia and Africa exemplified by the works of Amin 1974; Rodney 1974; Emmanuel 1972; Arrighi 1973; Gough and Sharma 1973. Although there are variations and differences of emphasis and theory among these studies to the point of contradiction and reciprocal reproachment, nevertheless they share a point of departure in a variety of seemingly Marxist theories of society and in more recent formulations of neocolonialism, peripheral capitalism, neo-imperialism, and unequal exchange. They all posit some sort of connection among these to produce a global picture of development and underdevelopment.

The critique we offer below is not applicable with equal measure to all these approaches, rather it speaks to a trend and its strictures apply to a wide range of self-proclaimed Marxist as well as non-Marxist approaches to the Third World, imperialism, and socialism. At the same time we recognize the fact that a significant critical contribution is emerging from both inside and outside these traditions.

There are some striking and immediate difficulties with these approaches: they tend to underemphasize the possibility of industrialization in the Third World; they do not analyze the phases of underdevelopment; they do not account for different forms of underdevelopment; they ignore possible bargaining positions in the Third World; and, most seriously, they fail to show a way out since, after all, domination is inevitable and peripheral capitalism is already rampant in the form of non-revolutionary class dependency.[10] They are also reluctant to examine their own genesis and development given their own social basis. They cannot explain underdevelopment except in terms of "as if" arguments: capitalist modes "are reproduced,"or peripheral capitalism "is established" in a curiously voluntaristic fashion (e.g. Andre Gundar Frank's numerous writings).

Attempts to resort to Marx in justification of these theories are faulty; as we shall see below there are major differences between Marx's practice and most theories of underdevelopment. The latter owe more to "Marxist" developments over the years than to an emulation of Marx.

The linking of capitalism and its phases to imperialism is oversimplified and without sufficient warrant from the evidence. The arguments suffer from inadequate assessments of both "capitalism" and "imperialism." Underdevelopment theorists tend to criticize and dismiss other theories on the grounss of their origins (e.g., Frank is at his shrillest in Cockroft, Frank, and Johnson 1972). Yet no theory can be refuted exclusively in this manner; the genesis of an approach does not fully account for its scope and meaning. Pointing to the "bourgeois" origins of something and dismissing it out of hand is no critique. Such argumentation, assuming direct links between theory and action, defeats all attempts at comparative social understanding and concomitant critique. Establishing direct links between production and exploitation is unacceptable practice because it ignores the problem of mediation and the mediating role of ideology, much emphasized by Marx himself. But forging yet another link and identifying exploitative persons with motives is a mere exercise in *reductio ad absurdum*, leaving the complex problem of levels in society and mediations among these levels quite untouched.

As a result, the possibility of a combined empirical, analytical, ideological and dialectical approach is vitiated. Due to an insufficient discussion of theory, practice, and rationality, the notion of development remains crude and almost completely economic. Particular studies take the form of applying the theory and illustrating the a priori nature of the theory from specific cases, rather than facing the more difficult task of investigating and understanding societies comparatively in general and in particular. (See O'Brien 1979 and Duffield 1981 in the case of the Sudan).

Accounts of dependency cannot account for development and change within advanced industrial societies. They tend to assume that these societies are static, monolithic, and that the differences among them are inconsequential (e.g., Kay 1975). This is due to insufficient understanding and differentiation of capitalism, capitalist society, industrialism, and industrial society. These are not at all the same thing. Industrialization need not lead to capitalism, which in turn is not equivalent to capitalist society, nor even to the capitalist mode of production.[11]

Class relations are also ignored or merely invoked and production relations are confused with several aspects of class relations. Abstract categories of classes differ from the structuring of class relations in given historical and social contexts. The articulation of production, social class, and/or status remains to be examined. The actual structuring of class relations varies according to the historical experience of societies, the nature of industrialization, and the extent of market forms of production. Note the differences between *capitalist* society and *capitalism* in societies of particular historical periods, the capitalist mode of production as an abstract model, and industrial societies.

The dichotomy of development and underdevelopment, like modernity and tradition, assumes a unilinear and uniform transition from one to the other -- an equation unacceptable in either case. The characterization of the U.S.A. as the ultimate capitalist society is also unacceptable since there are many historical reason why other advanced industrial societies will not follow the unique American pattern. (Frank 1972; Amin 1974).

The notion of imperialism which theories of dependency link to capitalist society without explicit discussion, is wanting both in its formulation and in its linking.[12] Here imperialism appears to be located outside "capitalist" society and is derived from an attempt to explain (away) the failure of revolution by the transference of class conflict to the underdeveloped world as a whole. This, however, ignores divisions and developments within the West and prevents the necessary comparisons between existing forms and variants of "socialist" and "capitalist" societies and leads to a rather naive and uncritical bias in favor of the former (see the writings of Amin). There are also major difficulties with the Hobson-Lenin theory of imperialism which remains widely accepted today. Wallerstein argues that imperialism cannot be made a phase of capitalism since in that case the former would become merely the voluntaristic foreign policy arm of the latter. The 1970's are not the watershed they are assumed to be, since the periods before and after 1870 exhibit similar features. The export of capital characterizes the whole market epoch beginning with the sixteenth century. Thus the export of financial capital may be another cyclical phase rather than a qualitatively different, final stage. Not all expansion is colonial; note the entry of the U.S.A. into Russian and Chinese markets, for example. Accounts of dependency also fail to explain decolonization, neocolonialism, Soviet imperialism, and the integration of socialist economies into the world market. The prognosis of capitalism is also wrong, since this form of production is in no imminent danger of demise. Wallerstein draws attention to several factors here: the commodification of factors of production is far from complete, anti-systemic organization is on the increase, and surplus values are being re-apportioned throughout the world.

Underdevelopment theorists assume that there are no "traditional" societies today, although the finite historical forms of the latter are known (cf Amin, Frank above). However, the differentiation of "traditional" and "modern" in terms of use-value versus exchange-value is too simplistic and does not allow a comparison of the many complex variants subsumed under these general categories. In addition, the concomitant conclusion that in peripheral capitalism "traditional" or pre-capitalist formations survive in a stunted, disfigured manner, is calmly asserted, but the nature and forms of these survivals, their articulation or lack thereof with other social formations are not discussed, much less demonstrated, in a convincing fashion. This is due to the complete lack of a comparative sociology, so that what is yet to be demonstrated is merely assumed: relations among societies have to be analyzed and understood through comparison, the dialectical relations betweeen ideas and actions, and the mediation of ideologies. Failing that, the construction of similarities and differences through sociological comparison falls by the wayside.[13]

The mode of production approach taken by some dependency theorists does not allow any serious consideration of differences among kinds of modern economies and the relations between economy and society in different social formations (see Amin, Rodney, Jalee). This is also the case with modernization theories where economy is taken to be a permanently fixed domain, making it impossible to notice the variously constructed hierarchies of domains in different societies. Most damaging, accounts of underdevelopment lack a theory of culture and fail to recognize the significance of symbolic meanings and value orientations in social processes. There is a consequent failure to comprehend genuine differences among societies. The so-called underdeveloped world has various historical pasts and these are different from the hierarchy of social relations in Western societies. By neglecting to make the *form* of difference a part of the investigation, accounts of dependency ignore Marx's fundamental problematic in the study of society.

Notes

[1] Concepts of tradition and modernity are criticized below -- here they appear in a specific, context dependent sense.

[2] Until recently, "Arab" in the rural areas referred exclusively to nomadic groups distinguished by their way of life.

[3] Fellata is the generic term used to refer to all West African migrants. Finer distinctions occur when the Fellata identify their own ethnic groups, such as Hausa, Fulani or Um Bororo.

[4] There is abundant written literature on the history, origin and social life of the Funj Sultanate, Holt 1963; James 1971; *Cambridge History of Africa* Vol. IV; Robinson 1929; Spaulding 1974; 1972a and b; Ahmed 1976a and b.

[5] The term Fellata is applied, in a somewhat derogatory way, to all people of West African origin. But Fellata nomads such as the Um Bororo are opposed to Arab nomads, such as the Rufa'a.

[6] Nomads are assumed by the rest of the population to have no respect for laws other than their own, and it is said that swearing on the Holy Book, the Koran, does not change their views about law, truth and justice.

[7] "Third World" refers to recently decolonized countries which are still economically dependent on advanced industrial countries.

[8] It should be noted that Eisenstadt is one of the few who keep revising their theories to account for social change in the 1970's. Most prophets of modernization remain silent in the face of the challenge issued to their theories by the comtemporary world.

[9] A central problem here is the systematic linking of values and cultural categories to the underlying structure of a society. Parsons has made a significant contribution to this problem, however his classificatory and compartmental appoarch did not establish necessary links and relationships. Values themselves are not structures except in relation to norms and rules which in turn are the expressed elements of an underlying structure (Piaget 1970: 103-4, Parsons et al. 1951).

[10] We are indebted to David Stark who drew our attention to these arguments.

[11] In the discussion of industrialism and class relations we are relying on Giddens 1975. See also the cultural critiques of Sahlins (1976) and Boudrillard (1975).

[12] For this argument we are indebted to Emmanuel Wallerstein who presented critique of the Hobson-Lenin theory in a lecture at Brown University 1977.

[13] See the critique of historical materialism in Sahlins 1976.

2

Merchants, Markets, and the Dam

The Impact of the Roseiris Dam

The building of the Roseiris dam marked the beginning of Damazin town. Laborers who came to work on the dam were given different tasks and responsibilities. A well-staffed hospital was built which made up for the lack of health services in the nearby villages. Several primary schools were built. Originally, these were co-educational, but now boys and girls go to separate schools. In contrast to Damazin, the villagers as well as nomads whose camps are near a village, send their children to village schools. The majority of the adult villagers only attended *khalwa* (Koranic) schools. Children are encouraged to attend government schools. The Fellata and Hausa do not send their children to the village schools.[1] Fellata children attend Koranic schools for two-three years, after which they participate in the family work. During the 1980's, post-elementary schools were constructed in Damazin town. Communication systems linking Damazin with other areas are fair. Besides being connected with the rest of the region by roads, Damazin is connected with Khartoum by rail. Sudanair has weekly flights between Damazin and Khartoum. In terms of telecommunications, telegraph and telephone services link Damazin with the capital, and the recently constructed satellite station has resulted in many people purchasing television sets. By making television viewing possible and radio reception better, the satellite station has helped disseminate national and international news and ideas.

Four or five contractors were responsible for the initial migration into the town. Each company had its own work to perform. Syed Abdel Syed Company and Hamid Humeida were responsible for constructing the buildings in the township. A Lebanese company, Mother Cat, built the airport; the Italian company, Impregilo, constructed the dam and Christian Noble built the bridge. Each of them attracted and recruited laborers from other provinces. Local inhabitants did assist in all of these activities, but they held the lowest paying positions. After the completion of the dam, some of the migrant laborers remained and took up odd jobs in the town. Others re-migrated to other towns and areas or decided to remain in BNP to become small subsistence farmers.²

The building of the dam has attracted people to Damazin for diverse reasons. Many *jallaba* (merchants) who came when construction began, lost their capital and left before being able to profit from the long term growth of the town. When the first *jallaba* left the town, they were replaced by later comers. The older merchants felt that after the completion of the dam the laborers would leave and, in turn, the town would die and its economic activity would level off. It was not until 1974, when the capital of the province was moved to Damazin, that the town again boomed. This time the government officials of the provincial administration arrived and with them came many entrepreneurs interested in the rapidly expanding mechanized farms of the province.

There are three residential areas in Damazin that house some of the early migrant workers who came to work on the dam: El Sanyo, El Nahda, and Hamid Humeida. All of these areas were characterized by inter-ethnic clashes. Some of the inhabitants now work as seasonal laborers on mechanized farms. Eighty percent of the laborers in the BNP are from other provinces, coming mostly from Gezira, Dar Fur, Kordofan and from the six southern provinces. As an example of a mechanized farm, the Takamal Egyptian-Sudanese scheme has 230 full-time permanent workers, but at peak harvest time, it employs 2,000-3,000 workers. Since other projects need labor at the same time, the competition increases every year. In 1968, a laborer made LS16 per month. In the early 1980's, he earned LS28 per month plus an additional allowance. Today, the laborers on some of the large projects feel they are being cheated and that the terms to their contracts are not clear. Therefore, they want to form a union to protect themselves. Many local merchants and officials own mechanized farms in the province. The presence of a large labor force helps support the markets of Damazin and Roseiris, with restaurants and cafes benefitting most. The buying power in the market is at its highest during harvest time and at its lowest from January to May. Clearly labor is still seasonal.

Construction of the Roseiris dam directly affected the lives of the nomads in BNP. First, the formation of a lake forced them to alter their traditional migratory patterns. Second, the grazing lands of the nomads are now being sought by entrepreneurs interested in starting agricultural projects on the nomads' grazing lands. Now that Damazin is a major town, it offers the entrepreneur all the urban conveniences and services. Being close to potential areas for mechanized projects, Damazin itself becomes an ideal place for the mechanized farm entrepreneur; owners can live in a major town in relative comfort and maintain close watch over their farm, at the same time.

Agricultural expansion has also affected the gum-Arabic industry for the nomad. Tapping the gum forests was previously a part of the nomads' livelihood. Now that the forests are being cleared to open up additional land for mechanized cultivation, gum collection is dying out. Merchants in

Roseiris feel that if the nation needs foreign exchange, gum-Arabic would be a good source.

Tribes and Migration

In the past, the town of Damazin and its surroundings were the pasture lands of the Rafa'a al Hoi and other nomadic groups. Today, as Damazin expands, newer residential areas are being created and what was once a homogeneous community is now divided into a number of residential class clusters, the *effendia* areas (for government bureaucrats), and the working class area (for mechanics and small shopkeepers). Some of the new neighborhoods are composed of people from different tribes. This results in daily clashes, which are generally resolved through the courts.

The local merchants in Damazin and Roseiris have built thatch roof houses to accomodate the influx of migrant laborers. The proposed heightening of the Roseiris dam has attracted even more workers. A typical residential area may accommodate Nuer and Dinka people from Dar Fur; Fellata, Hausa, and Fulani; Eritrean refugees, and Funj, Berta, and Ingessena groups (indigenous people of the area). Population mixture of this sort has been causing serious social problems for the townspeople and the local officials.

The first population increase in Damazin resulted directly from the construction of the dam. The newer, indirect influx is caused by the increasing number of mechanized farms (both planned state and private farms as well as farms outside the "planning area"). Owners and employees of the farms use Damazin as their base of operations, creating shortages and overcrowding the available resources. As a result, the standard of living in the town and its immediate surrounding area has deteriorated over the last eight years.

The subsistence farmer of the villages around the two towns earns from his farm and *juruf* lands, makes and sells coal, and at times works at odd jobs in the town. His options and opportunities are numerous. The existing situation has helped him avoid the indebtedness which is common in most rural areas. *Shail*, the traditional form of money lending, is almost non-existent in the areas around the reservoir.[3] *Shail* is prevalent in the rural areas of Sudan in both the modern and the traditional agricultural sectors. In the interior of the BNP the majority of subsistence farmers are indebted to local merchants. The entire sesame crop may be sold through *shail* in November-December, and a new debt cycle is begun in April, prior to the new planting. The subsistence farmers produce a surplus of vegetables which is sold at the Damazin market, where the demand is so great that the supply of locally-produced vegetables is usually supplemented by produce brought all the way from Khartoum. The vegetable gardens on the extremely fertile soil of *juruf* lands around the Roseiris reservoir have helped to cut farming costs and to stop indebtedness. Since the creation of the lake, fishing has also become an important economic activity that supplements local farmers' income.[4] Thus far, however, only the non-indigenous Fellata-Hausa groups engage in fishing as a profession. The non-Fellata groups supplement their farm incomes by making charcoal, burning forest wood. The provincial government gains from both these economic ventures in the form of taxes. As a result of these additional sources of income, there is a great difference in average yearly income between the subsistence farmers in the reservoir area and those in the interior part of the province. A farmer in the reservoir area has an average annual income of about LS625 (from field crops, fishing, vegetables, animals and the sale of charcoal), while a subsistence farmer in the interior has an average income of only LS195 a year. Before the completion of the dam, the income difference between these two groups of farmers was minor. The reservoir area farmers also have greater economic opportunities since they are not far from an urban center, Damazin. Many of these people are also employed in the villages or in the town. Their wealth is visually evident in the large number of bicycles, better houses and well fed and dressed residents in this area as compared with the surrounding countryside.

A local merchant explains changes in Damazin by pointing out that in the late 1960's, a shop in the market cost LS200, while in 1979 the same shop cost LS7,000. Similarly, he measures social change in the Southern Funj area by comparing the number of mosques and the spread of Islam between 1962 and 1979. In 1962, a mosque would be attended by five or six people, while today there are big crowds. The Southern Funj was a restricted area for Northerners from 1930 to 1953, when the British lifted the restriction. The first Northern pioneers who came into the areas were merchants, religious leaders, and a trickle of officials.

As grazing lands decrease, conflicts between nomads and agriculturalists increase. Nomads enter the cultivated fields and let their animals eat the crops and at times they burn the fields. Agriculturalists retaliate by killing nomads. In turn, nomads kill farmers. Damazin courts attempt to resolve these cases but offer no solutions to the underlying problem (see Chapter 4).

Historically, the relationship between the cultivator and the nomad was complementary. Now this traditional relationship is deteriorating. Finding themselves pressed on all sides, nomads not only encroach on existing farms but also compete with each other for available pasture lands. The nomad presents more of a danger to the subsistence farmer than to the mechanized farm owner. When a nomad grazes his animals on the four to six *feddan* field of the subsistence farmer, the farmer's major, and possibly only, source of income and family subsistence is lost.

Clashes are occasioned by nomads' animals, which graze on vegetables grown on *juruf* along the river banks. Agriculturalist-nomad conflicts over *juruf* lands are increasing at a faster rate today than conflicts over *dahari* farms.[5] During particular times of the season, nomads can make arrangements with *juruf* owners to graze their animals on non-cultivated land for a small fee. As the water in the lake recedes, farmers may sell to

Merchants, Markets, and the Dam 33

the nomads the grass that grows on *juruf* land.

The Roseiris dam has directly and indirectly caused a great many social and economic changes. The area has flourished since construction of the dam. A major administrative and market town was created, villages expanded, trade flourished, and production and rural incomes increased. New mechanized farms started and in turn generated additional labor opportunities. A new class of merchants emerged along with new middle-class elites. The dam has physically changed the area and has created new demands, wants, and needs for the local people. Opinions concerning the criteria used in determining change vary depending on whether one questions a local merchant, official, laborer, nomad, or villager. Some people have not evidenced any change, while others, in particular the elders, have very strong opinions regarding the emerging society and its conflicting needs and aims as economic concerns influence traditional cultural values.

The Suq in Damazin and Roseiris

The markets *(suq)* of Damazin and Roseiris look deceptively similar to the untutored eye. The former is new and rectangular having been laid out in parallel lines of long, low buildings. The latter is old and appears to be a jumble of differently shaped and sized buildings, dating from different periods of time, heaped together in one corner of the town. (See Figures 2.1-2.2). Nevertheless, there is order in both markets, and in terms of ordering categories, they are very similar. Both are situated near official-administrative complexes and are central to their respective townships. Roads lead into and out of them, reaching all residential areas. The functioning of the two markets is also similar. Despite their past, the differences are minimal in the patterning of business, but the volume and contents of trade are markedly different. Most people in Roseiris feel that the rise of Damazin hurt their market.

There are several sections in the *suqs* of both towns. The central part is occupied by major traders in big shops *(dokan)* and stores *(makhsan)*, built of bricks, with piles of goods and stocks.[6] This is the *suq* proper where *jumla* (large volume, wide ranging, long-term) traders, and *gattai* (smaller volume, shorter term, high turnover) traders hold court, where agents *(wakil)* and owners of mechanized farms, commodity distributors, lawyers, officials, smaller traders, buyers, customers, and acquaintances meet, drink tea, chew tobacco or smoke cigarettes, and discuss the market, trade, administration and related matters. The shops and stores of the biggest merchants *(tijar* pl *tajir)* are a focus in the *suq*: people can sit and talk and expect to find or hear about anyone they happen to look for. This part of the *suq* also houses the shops specializing in hardware and building materials, ready-made clothing, cotton and other materials by the yard, shoes, household utensils, and spare parts for cars and trucks. Further, there are general-goods stores (spices, oils, scent, and other manufactured

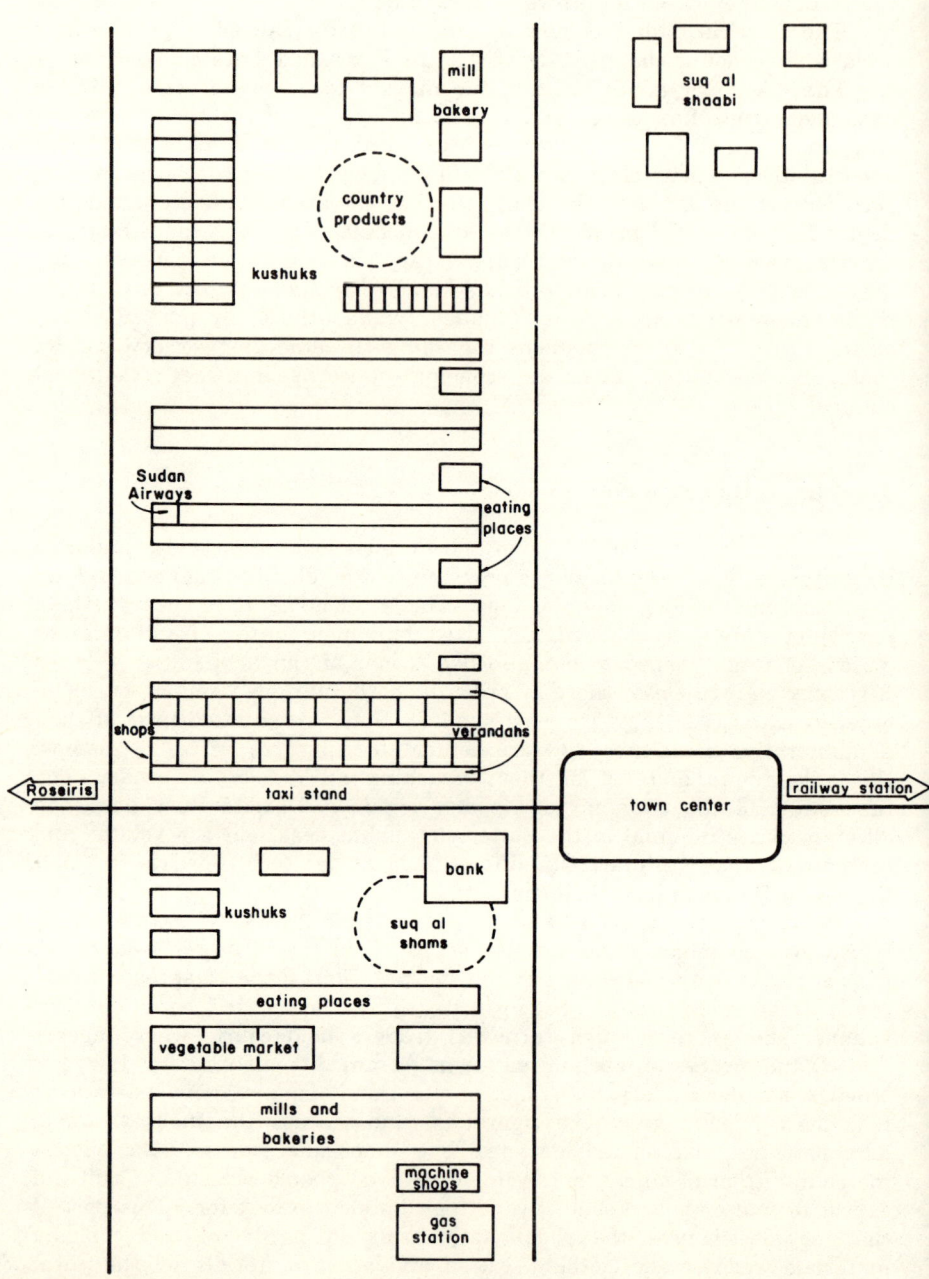

Figure 2.1 Damazin Suq

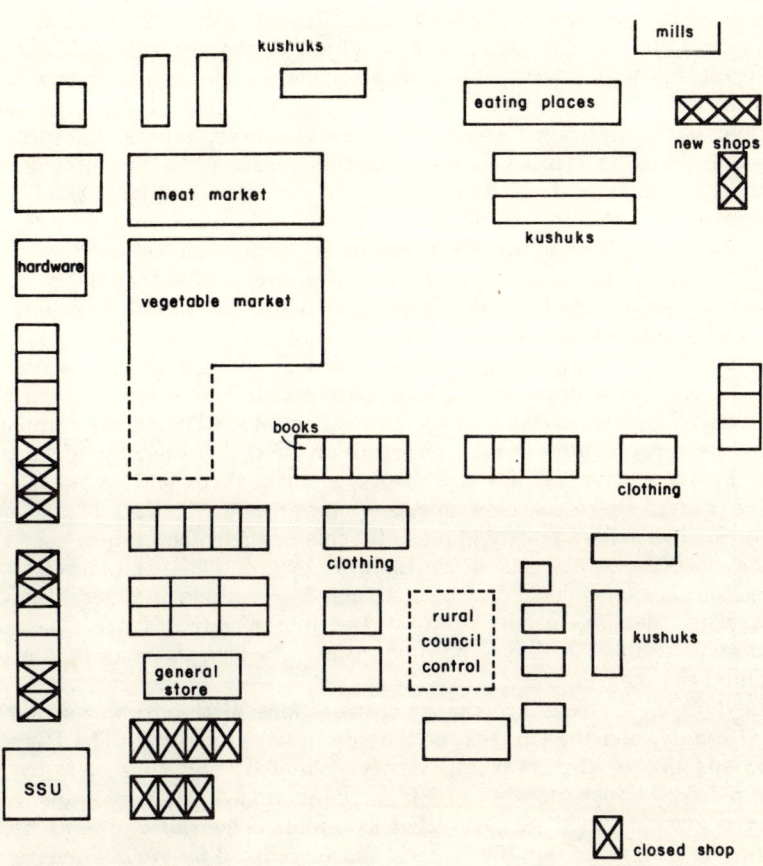

Figure 2.2 Roseiris Suq

items), dry-goods shops, restaurants, and bars. The spacious, covered verandahs also house minor traders *(farrashas)* and hawkers selling ribbons, pins, knives, mirrors, and hundreds of other small items. Tailors and barbers ply their trade here. Lawyers and a large trading company also rent or own shops and use them as offices in the central part of the market.

Beyond this area are the *kushuks* (sheds, kiosks), individually and together much smaller than the section just described. *Kushuks* are smaller shops of corrugated iron and tin sheets nailed on a wooden framework. In many ways this section is a smaller edition of the central *suq*, and with significant exceptions the same kind of goods, services, and specialization are to be found here as well. Some *kushuks* sell only cloth, or shoes, or pots and pans, or grain. There are general stores, tailors, barbers, and coffee/tea shops as well. But here we find most of the "country goods," stores selling local produce, handicrafts, spices and onions on a small scale, and products of the region (including *jebels,* hills, near and far) such as ropes, mats, baskets, gourds, clarified butter, honey, and coffee.

The vegetable, fish, and meat markets are also set apart, with the familiar division between the bigger, well-stocked stands exhibiting a variety of items, and the smaller, modest counters with one or two kinds of items to sell. The larger vegetable stands are terraced platforms made of brick and cement where a seller has space on all 3 or 4 levels, each block being shared by two traders, there being 8 blocks. The whole complex is covered by a corrugated iron roof resting on a steel frame, the sides being open. Fruits and vegetables are displayed in baskets and on mats. The smaller traders share space on long, low platforms at the back of the roofed structure. The sellers put up makeshift roofs of their own, improvised from wooden posts, sacking, and other light materials. They sit amidst their wares, potatoes, or onions, or fruits, and/or 3 or 4 kinds of vegetables. The meat sellers, dealing in beef, mutton, but mostly lamb, share a separate roofed structure. Fish sellers occupy stalls on a low platform in the open air behind the meat market.

Beyond these areas are the newest sections of the "people's market" *(suq al shaabi)* and the "market of the sun" *(suq al shams).* The former is an extension to the market, newly planned and licensed by the municipality. Consisting of small *kushuks* and open air stalls, it is clustered around the main lorry (truck) stand. The *suq al shams* has no specific location, referring to any open space occupied by small vendors who carry all their wares themselves and spread out their canvas sheets, displaying their wares in any available corner. The market expands periodically by the municipality moving the most perseverent of these traders, when their numbers and voices swell to a critical point, to a group of new *kushuks* or a *suq al shaabi*. The truck stand also houses the sheds of transportation and loading/insurance agents, official timekeepers, spare-parts dealers, light-repairmen, mechanics, and electricians who work on cars and trucks.

There is a large industrial area in Damazin, located at one end of the town. Major engine repairs, body works, and other activities take place here. Most of the skilled mechanics have set up shop in the industrial area recently. The municipality allocated the land and the craftsmen/artisans built the line of brick shops according to specification. In addition traders in spare parts, small manufacturers of tubular steel furniture, carpenters, building materials suppliers, steel door makers, and others have moved into the area.

The large volume trade in local wood for building, burning, and charcoal is conducted by merchants out of shops and offices in the *suq*, but the wood is stored, loaded, and unloaded on a large reserve just outside town. The livestock market is also located beyond the residential sections. Nomads bring animals culled from their herds and agents for the restaurants, and the meat market negotiate. The buyer for the *suq* does the slaughter, dresses and distributes the meat, holding onto the skins for his fee. Townspeople also come to this market to purchase *kharuf* (lambs) for feasts and sacrifices.

The *suq* area includes the taxi stand, bus station, and the stand for the ubiquitus *bokassis*. The latter, Toyota pickup trucks with elaborate roofing over the loading bed and benches along the sides for seating passengers, have started to ply the road between Roseiris and Damazin in increasing numbers, without cutting into the business of the taxis.

The Damazin *suq* is central to the town. All residential and administrative sectors are connected to the market by asphalt or graded roads. The railway station and provincial government buildings are equidistant from the market and police, courts, banks, and post-telephone-telegraph offices surround the central *suq*. The two mosques of the towns are on the same road at two ends of the market. The hospital, cinema, hotels, the cultural center, and the sports stadium are a short distance away. Damazin, new as it is, came into being fully planned with the market at the center of the town.

North of the market are the main residential areas situated beyond the benzine (gasoline) pumps, municipal offices, and schools at the edge of the *suq*. Recently these neighborhoods have been reclassified as a third-class residential area with a complement of new services, graded roads, and new taxes. Many *suq* people live here: a fast-growing section with brick buildings gradually replacing what used to be the exclusive domain of round, thatch roofed huts. Many offices of the provincial and central governments and government corporations are temporarily located here, until the construction of more permanent places. Building and renting have become a profitable business.

To the South is a large area temporarily occupied by the army, although the latter is scheduled to be moved outside the town. The light and heavy industrial areas are also located here, together with the water works and the sawmill. There are several fast-growing residential areas here, strictly speaking "illegal" (unplanned and not yet zoned), bordering on the planned section, laid out in a grid, and picturesquely named Hai El Zuhur (Neighborhood of Flowers). This neighborhood is home to dozens of different tribes and ethnic groups *(gabila)*, ranging from Dinka from the South, Ingessana and Berta from the hills and river's nearby, to Fulani and Bornu from West Africa.

To the east the *suq* borders on a large residential block built by Sudanese contractors for the dam building crews. These stone and brick structures are now occupied by lower and middle-level employees of the central government's Irrigation and Hydro-Electric Power Departments. Further east, beyond the road are the hospital, cemetery, and the first-class residential area housing the senior administrators (including the provincial commissioner), doctors, judges, and engineers. Much of the permanent housing was built in 1959-60 for the main contractors for the construction of the dam, and for the staff of various government departments.

To the west of the market are situated several other official buildings (police, post, telephone) and the town gardens, named after, as in many Sudanese towns, a young martyr of the 1964 Revolution. Beyond this are a fourth-class residential area (for the service classes), the railway station, benzine and fuel depots, and the airport.

The administrative and army areas have their own "market" sections with mechanized transportation supply and repair depots, commodity and ration stores, and officers' messes. Plans are in the making for new police, prisons, and Sudanese Socialist Union (SSU) headquarters, and a heavy industrial area. New junior-secondary and higher-secondary schools have been built recently some distance out of town. A vigorous town development program has been implemented following the re-organization of administrative provinces in the Sudan and the designation of Damazin as the new capital of the Blue Nile Province (1974). Much work was accomplished for the national Independence Day Celebrations held in Damazin in 1978.

A characteristic feature of Sudanese towns is the rapid growth of "unauthorized," and "unscheduled," or "overspill" areas. Although the main part of Damazin is constituted by the *suq* and *mudriya* (administration) center surrounded by merchants' and officials' residential areas, there are planned neighborhoods populated by lower-level government employees, laborers, and market-transportation workers, divided into 1st to 4th class sections. Many of these sections started as "unauthorized" settlements established by immigrants pouring into the town, attracted by the new dam, the new market, and more recently the developments surrounding the new provincial capital. Today, several of these new settlements on three sides of the town house people coming in from the countryside (especially Berta), and people from the West (including the generically designated Fellata). Some of these are multi-ethnic, others are exclusive to a group.

The colonial government exerted considerable control over Roseiris town and market: regulating the number, construction, and licenses of shops, the tribal composition of regional trade, attempting to keep West African settlers, "Arab," and Greek traders out of the region, allowing the latter only periodic visits, although a few traders from all these groups have settled in the region before colonial times. Like many colonial towns such as Wad Medani, Sennar, or Singa, Roseiris is laid out along the Nile with broad tree-lined, sandy avenues and substantially older buildings. Less regular in appearance than Damazin, primarily because of the hilly terrain and rows of big trees, nevertheless Roseiris, too, is resting on the ubiquitous grid. Nearest the Nile are the *suq*, local government offices, and the hospital. Adjoining these are blocks of residential neighborhoods occupied by the old trading families and the family of the local Meks, descendants of the Funj kings. Beyond these planned areas are smaller unauthorized settlements and villages that are engulfed by the extension of Roseiris or are directly tucked onto the edges of the town. These are mostly single tribal ethnic areas, especially Fellata (West African) and indigenous Berta, Hamaj, and Gumuz. Such settlements dot the 10 mile long road between Roseiris and Damazin in increasing numbers and one even had an elementary school built recently.

Most of the residential buildings are thatch-roof huts placed in compounds enclosed by fences. Officials and merchants live in brick buildings behind tall brick fences. Compounds have the same general layout and contain several buildings, even the brick ones include a group of thatch roof huts. Houses of officials are built in the bungalow style with verandahs and some local adaptations. New official residences are built in a standard style depending on the rank of the officer. These brick and mortar structures are hardly suitable for the Northern Sudanese life style, but the occupants make what adjustments they can, adding huts of thatch, fences separating the compound, trees and flower-beds, and quite often a section for domestic animals. Some merchants, and others of the well-to-do, live under no such constraints and their compounds are more clearly divided into public and domestic areas. Sometimes the kitchen, the women's quarters and family sleeping rooms, and the reception hall are in separate buildings. The latter *(maktab)* is a showpiece, containing armchairs, carpets, and mats. In many compounds of wood and thatch the *maktab* is a separate hut, and even in the poorest dwellings a semi-enclosed and roofed attachment to the main hut sets apart a place for sitting and talking.

Among the *kushuks* of Damazin there are about 20 general *khordawat* stores. About 15 are tailor shops; 13 are cloth stores; 8 are combined shoe, cloth, and ready-made clothing shops; and 5 are combined tailor and cloth-by-the-yard stores. Among the rest there are handicraft and country-goods stores (4); eating and drinking places (3); hollow-ware and glass shops (2); 1 car and lorry spare-parts store; 1 coffee *jumla* store-room; 1 bicycle repair shop; 1 blacksmith's workshop; 2 combined cloth and holloware shops; and 1 combined cloth and china store. The owners of these shops are mostly Ja'alyn or Rufa'a (about 14 each). The next most numerous *gabila* is the Fellata; mostly Bornu (12) and Hausa (5); followed by the northern Sudanese Saiquiya, Danagla and the Kawahla of the west (4 each). There are only 1 or 2 representatives of the following *gabilas:* Sukriya, Arakayin, Hamar, Kenana, Hawari, Baggara, and Mahari.

Among the Roseiris *kushuks* the pattern is somewhat different: again most are *khordawat* stores (9) but the rest are more evenly distributed (2 coffee drinking places, 3 eating places, 6 grain *gattai* shops, 1 iron-pot store, 1 baker, 1 welder, 1 shoe repair, 1 skin and hide shop, 1 traveling merchant, 1 general store). Among *gabilas* the Ja'alyn and Fellata are the most numerous (6 each), and there are also 3 Saiquiya, 1 Gumuz, 3 Arakayin, 1 Rakabi, 1 Magharba, 1 Abbadi, 1 Batahin, 1 Musallamiya.

Gabilas in the Suq

In the central part of the Damazin *suq* about a dozen merchant owners of mechanized farms maintain office cum store rooms. These men are the leading local traders in grains, and they also engage in other activities: *jumla* and *gattai* trade, supplies, transportation, and seasonal country produce trade. Several other owners of farms and traders in *dura* (sorghum) or *simsim* (sesame) do not own office-store space in the *suq*. Many of these men live in the Hai El Nahda quarter of the town and carry out their many-faceted work from their compounds. The latter are often spacious and cluttered with farm machinery, trucks, and implements. Among the shops of the main *suq* there are five large specialized cloth shops, some of which carry other general items on the side. There are also three large general stores (ready made clothing and cloth by the yard, shoes, bags, perfumes, and radios); six large building supplies shops; one flour mill; several bakeries; six large jumla stores (dealing in sugar, tea, soap, flour, oil, *tahnia*) and two large stores of country products *(dura,* ropes, oil, honey, butter).

The biggest single group of *dokan* owners are Ja'alyn, about 25 in all, of whom three are grain traders, three are *jumla* merchants, two are cloth merchants, two are building material suppliers, four are restauranteurs, and two are tailors. Among the rest of the shops, there are one each of pharmacy, barber, electrician, sweets, wood supplies, mill, book and stationery, and general country merchandize. The next biggest group are the generic "Fellata," men of West African origin (Bornu, Fulani, Hausa mainly). Of about 17 shop owners, three are barbers, who employ several other barbers; two are restauranteurs; three are tailors, one of whom employs six others; and there are one each of clothing, country goods, bicycle spare parts, radio repair, photo, watch repair, and mechanized farm *jumla* grain trade shops. One shop is the office run by the truck loading laborers' cooperative of the province.

Other groups in the *suq* are much smaller: There are three Shaigiya mechanized farm owners and grain traders (two of whom also run truck and car parts shops), and one tobacco merchant. Some *gabilas* have only one representative each: a Hamar wood merchant, a Tama, a Jawama engineer-TV repairman, a Bene Amer agricultural products trader, a Yagubab building materials merchant, a Rizigat photo-salon owner, a Zargawa carpenter, a Halabi carpenter, a Funj coffee shop owner, and there are several Kawahla eating-place owners. There is only one woman merchant in the *suq* who is of Eritrean origin and owns several shops, a bar and a restaurant.

The Roseiris *suq* is smaller and less diverse in every way. The central *suq* houses five large *khordawat* stores (including clothing); two large specialized cloth shops; two ready-made clothing stores; two *jumla* shops; five general merchandize shops (including ready-made goods); two wood supplies stores; and one each of photo, goldsmith, book stationery, carpenter, tobacco, mechanized farm-grain trade, restaurant, *gattai* grain trade, and leather shops. There are also four tailors and several stores of mechanized farm owners who do not keep their offices open throughout the year. The biggest group of *dokan* owners are again the Ja'alyn, about 13, while only one or two come from each of the Shaigiya, Fellata, Danagla, Abdallab, Ruwatab, Maghrabi, Yaubab, Arakayin, and Kenzi *gabilas*.

A more detailed discussion of *gabilas* will have to wait. Suffice it to say that these groups in the *suq* are neither the pristine "tribes" of the colonial administrator's imagination, nor the "ethnic groups" of currently fashionable parlance. *Gabila* identity is closely related to family (kin and marriage), *suq* and trade (especially in the links among credit, capital, circulation and time in the *suq)* and government and administration. There is also evidence that the Northern *gabilas* have by now established themselves in secondary centers (such as the Geizira). As a result, for many Damazin-Roseiris Ja'alyn, for example the Gezira has become the homeland and Ismailiya in the North was left behind. For those who would see this as "ethnicity," a word of caution. Obviously the Funj, Ingessana, Berta, and Ja'alyn present different aspects and problems of the *gabila* question. While these groups are neither autonomous nor self-sustaining, self-sufficient units, they do exhibit various gradations along these continua. Yet they are all far from the Euro-American phenomena of "ethnicity" within the context of advanced industrial societies with capital intensive economies. The relations and a possible directional transformation between tribe, ethnic, and class-like social formations in the Sudan is one of the central comparative sociological problems in Africa.

Patterns of Trade in the Central Suq

Most merchants in the *suq* try to practice all available methods of trade, mixing different lines of produce and manufacture, in localities near and far. But the oldest pattern is still pursued, and is being updated and transformed as a widespread way of doing business in Roseiris and to a lesser extent in Damazin. In this general pattern, merchants trade in all kinds of goods and perform many different kinds of services with a special view to the rhythms of production, locality, season and *suq* (including demand, prices, and distance). This way is still in vogue in the towns, and even more so in the *montega* (the region, referring to the hills and the non-riverine areas). The "wandering" or travelling merchants and some of the village-based merchants practice forms of it. There are many variations in the ways the trading is carried out, and the goods and information pass through many hands. The main virtue is timing: waiting for the right moment to buy, transport, stock, and sell. Each movement involves different people. Items may include leather, wood, food grains, spices and scents, honey, skins, local and "imported" produce of all kinds. Traders value a free market *(suq hurr,* independent, unbound market) where deals can be made unfettered by regulations. At some point independent brokers *(samasra* and *wasiq)* are used to "mediate" in the market and to scout out produce over a wider area. In earlier days all these men were *jallaba* (traders from the North). The *samasra* (also known as *jallaba)* used to work for a percentage of what the *tigar* purchased through their efforts. Today some agents range far across the land using telephones, telegraphs, trucks and airplanes as well as contracts, receipts and bills, items not deemed necessary by the old traders. There are still a few indigenous *(beledi,* son-of-the-soil) agents of this kind who became quite famous in their domain. Covering an area in the radius of about 25 km they know the people, the customs, the land and the produce, and what is being sold where, and in turn the people know them. These agents bring into the *suq* anything they can sell: honey, wood, snake skins, rope, butter, *simsim,* and *dura,* and take out items not available in the countryside: sugar, tea, cloth, onions, grains, and spices. They then receive commissions on what they sell, in both directions, all the while using the merchants' money, turning it over and over, through these many sided transactions. There are still several Northerners who trade this way among villages and towns, dealing directly with villagers or village merchants. But the pattern is changing: old merchants recall traversing the area between Roseiris and the Ethiopian borderlands on mules and donkeys, trading, in addition, in the more profitable gold, tobacco, salt, and coffee. Now there are trucks, but also more restrictions. Significantly, more indigenous people have taken up trading, and more brokers have taken to outright buying and selling rather than settling for commissions, and percentages. This way agents become traders and try to make their own prices in the field according to what is possible at a given time. Then they negotiate with the town merchants trying to gain the best possible terms. In this case they assume the risk of loss, since under the old percentage system the major risk was that of the *suq* merchant, not of the mediator.

More of these old traders reside in Roseiris than Damazin, but many merchants engage in this type of trade, at one time or another. The older men regret the eclipse of this trade but others adapt it to current conditions. The old way is exclusively pursued only by a handful of central *suq* traders and there are no more than a dozen or so "mediating agents" in the countryside. On the other hand, hundreds of other merchants and agents engage in similar trading, either periodically and/or in combination with other pursuits and other methods.

There is a significant reciprocity in this system: merchants realize that several intermediaries add to prices but they say that although they could go out and "mediate" themselves, and thus gain more, they do not because other *suq* people can earn their living from the market this way. Thus more people derive a benefit. There is another function: goods new to the area are introduced and others are imported, items wanted but not produced by the local people *(belediyin)*, and the produce of the area is taken to distant markets which the locals cannot reach. Traders freely admit that they make a profit on these exchanges but they are clear about their own contribution.

Some of the local production is consumed in the area but a supervising amount is taken to Damazin-Roseiris, Khartoum, and beyond. This is especially the case with grain from mechanized farms, and country produce such as wood, charcoal, skins, honey, butter, and handicrafts. Merchants who trade in skins, for example, sell their goods in Khartoum and then bring back ready made shoes.

Trading depends on good relations with everyone, a thorough knowledge of people, and contacts developed over the years. "Wandering" merchants and "mediating" agents may stay several weeks in a locality, and not having shops or offices, they work out of the verandahs and stores of their merchant friends. Traders with established shops exhibit a striking variation in the volume and range of their display of goods through the seasons of the trading year. They do not restrict their trade to a fixed line of goods but pursue what comes and goes best and is available at a given time.

The most widespread, small-scale, high turnover trade is *gattai*, conducted out of shops regularly supplied, and containing one or more lines of goods. This is conventionally, though inaccurately, translated as "retail" trade, a rather ethnocentric term which does not convey the range, nature, and interconnections of *gattai* trading. *Gattai* trade may involve specialized goods such as shoes or ready-made clothing, but also lengths or bolts of cloth *(tob)*, small manufacturers' items; buttons, thread, batteries, as well as soaps, scents, cigarettes, utensils, stationary, and even canned food items. Usually there is one major line of goods with several supporting lines. *Gattai* does not involve manufactured items alone; it extends to food grains, spices, and dry goods. The trader himself or a member of his family travels to the bigger towns, including Khartoum, for supplies. The use of agents *(wakil)* is not widespread in securing supplies. For the delivery of goods to Damazin and Roseiris transportation and consignment agencies are used. Owners like to make visits and choose goods themselves, partly because they know which goods move best in what season, and partly because they can renew contacts in the *suqs* of Khartoum, Omdurman or Medani, and can visit relatives at the same time. On these occasions the merchant calls on many different traders in making his selections. He would know most of the major traders but does not restrict himself to one steady supplier. He argues that *gattai* trade being small, he cannot rely on one man alone, but has to pick and choose from a wide variety of sources.

Some *gattai* shops combine a wider range of trading with supplying other shops and combine direct selling to customers with *jumla* (larger volume) trading, providing goods to smaller shops and to village merchants. They also trade in the usual *gattai* items of cloth and manufactured goods but add country produce, and whatever is available. The owner prefers to keep to himself as much of the shop's operation as possible: watching the shelves to see what is moving fastest, and making frequent trips, usually once a month, to the bigger *suqs* at Omdurman and Medani. Manufactured items from outside occupy the main part of the shop while the verandah houses the general line of country goods. The latter are usually displayed in baskets on a counter facing the street, physically separate from the rest of the shop. The goods here are supplied by village merchants, "wandering" traders, or agents *(wasiq)* in the countryside.

Gattai merchants believe that their trade cannot exist on an exclusive line of products; they have to carry more kinds of goods to sell enough. To "move" a single line is the preserve of the bigger shops with large stocks, or the smaller *gattai* traders in the *kushuks*. The smaller shops, carrying almost everything, cannot afford to be supplied from distant *suqs* so they take their goods from the bigger local traders and the travelling merchants. They also receive local produce from the countryside, and some of this they sell in the shop but give most of it to the travelling merchants to take to Sennar, Medani, Khartoum.

Gattai shops can and do specialize, most usually in cloth, combining bolts of cloth with ready-made clothing and tailoring. Smaller specialized shops buy from travelling merchants and local *jumla* traders, only the most popular kinds of cloth, and only a few bolts at a time. Prices are somewhat higher as a result but this is justified by savings on consignment agencies, transportation and insurance charges, *wakils*. These traders prefer not to travel for supplies and thus avoid costly journeys, entertainment and other expenses in town. Also the size of purchases counts; it is not worth travelling in order to spend under LS1000 on supplies. During the time the owner is away the shop is closed, unless a close relative is available to stay behind. LS1000 in purchases in Khartoum may mean LS25+ for the *jumla* trader, but the fees of agent and carriage are extra. The local *jumla* merchant puts 5% on top of the price and that is that, no more fees. Damazin or Roseiris *jumla* traders are also preferred by the mid-range *gattai* merchants since the former know the region and the market and have a larger selection of goods than the "wandering" merchants. The smallest shops and the *kushuks* rely on the "wandering" merchants since they can take small amounts frequently and choose from what is available thus benefiting from the advantages of the travelling merchant's restrictions. Specialization is thus oriented not only to goods and shops but the clientele and season of each section and trade in the *suq*.

In one direction *gattai* trade merges into *jumla* trade, in other directions into *kushuk*, general (old type), and *khordawat* kinds of trade. Prices are decided by the merchants in relation to the costs of supplies and transportation. The best months of trade are the late rains, August to November, when the market "rises." In late November the "decline" begins till the worst point is reached between March and July. At this time the *suq* "falls" and does not "move." At this point there is no work in the fields and people have no money to spend. But this is the time traders have to stock up for August sales.

Khordawat (general merchandize) traders stock small amounts of many different items: spices, incense, scents, small manufactured and ready-made items. Supplies tend to come in small amounts from a few trusted contacts in Omdurman, rather than Khartoum, who can be telephoned or sent a message without the owner having to travel. *Khordawat* merchants do not trade in the local produce of the countryside: their spices, onions, and scents come from other *suqs* or "wandering" traders. When owners travel to Omdurman they combine the journey with visits to relatives.

As we noted, some of the bigger shops may combine the four types of trade mentioned so far, with each operation taking a sizeable portion of store space. In several cases the various sections are actually separated. From time to time the owner himself travels to collect goods, and picking up small amounts from many different *suqs* and sources, and he entrusts his purchases to agents who book the parcels in trucks going to Damazin and Roseiris. In some cases the truck driver himself acts as an agent on the merchant's behalf and is given a percentage of the purchase price once the whole undertaking is completed.

"Wandering" merchants also supply *khordawat* shops since there are advantages to everyone involved. They travel up and down along the Nile, hiring trucks which they fill with goods and sell in small amounts in all the *suqs*. They then fill up with local produce and sell these on the way back. A *khordawat* trader buys from several of these travelling merchants, a number of whom can be found in the *suq* every day. This way the shop owner can respond to new demands (canned goods, for example) and taking from many different directions may also hold down his costs. Taking his contacts in other *suqs*, the travelling merchants, and the local *jumla* traders together, the *khordawat* shop can compare and choose. As a result, buying from the seemingly more expensive travelling merchants, who add transportation costs, does not work out to be more since the goods come from other directions as well. Thus the *khordawat* owner can derive small benefits on every turn.

Jumla trade is closely linked to the *gattai* pattern and often the same people engage in both. "Pure" *jumla* traders are few in both *suqs*. The biggest *jumla* merchants buy directly from factories or import directly from abroad through the appropriate licenses. This is the most lucrative way to trade and some Omdurman merchant-families can combine *jumla*, *gattai*, and import-export businesses. Government regulations forbid the pursuit of all three out of the same location, on the same license. However, the several phases of the combination can be separated. The combined total of these types of trade can mean 15% and more over and above all costs in the acquisition of goods. Pursuing one moment in the cycle means less percent "profit" for the trader.

Khartoum *jumla* merchants with a factory distribution license legitimately put 2.5% profit onto their costs, and pass the value added to other *jumla* traders who do not have factory or import/export access. The latter in turn pass goods to mixed *jumla-gattai* or *gattai* traders. There are a few of the former, called *shipi-jumla,* in Damazin-Roseiris. These men have licenses to trade both ways but they do not have direct access to factories and import licenses. Complete control is frowned upon both in government and in the *suq* because it interferes with the layers of "benefit" shared through many linkages in the market. Yet the combination of all types of trading in one family do occur. Nevertheless everyone who is involved in the cycle adds some "benefit" to the goods passing through his hands. The importer and the factory owner have fixed base prices, the *jumla* traders add a percentage, and so do the *shipi-jumla* and the *gattai* merchants, depending on the demand and on what the market will bear. The government often sets a ceiling to the allowable percentages, while some commodities (sugar, motor-fuel) are completely controlled by regulations.

Sugar, for example, is distributed in quotas by the government to the provinces. Within each province licensed traders in turn receive their quotas, the distribution being decided by the provincial administration and the local councils. The system is meant to prevent stock piling and black marketeering (thus driving up prices) by preventing traders from selling small amounts from their quotas and waiting for prices to rise before releasing more on the black market. But the system is cumbersome and higher prices are paid on the flourishing black market. The *mudriya* (provincial government) is aware of these practices and illegal stocks are seized from time to time. There are also periodic checks of the market and information flows to the administration through intelligence set up for this purpose. This too is cumbersome, however. The sesame-seed trade is semi-controlled (for export, not for domestic markets) and *dura* (sorghum) is sold at controlled prices in deficit areas during the rainy season. The Ingessana hills as well as some riverine and interior areas require such rationing every year.

Many traders say they feel that the black market is created by excessive regulation, and they argue that if there was a free flow of goods everybody would derive a share of the "benefit," more goods would pass through the market, and prices would eventually come down. Traders say they feel the burden of taxation and resent the increasing range and size of taxes. Earnings after costs of LS400-1000 are subject to 15% tax, higher amounts are 20% and more in taxes. There are other taxes, the above are on profit alone.

The smaller *jumla* trader takes goods from other *jumla* merchants in Khartoum. There are no fixed suppliers; the trader wants to choose, controlling the conditions as much as possible. Yet merchants know each other and expect and understand that any one of them may become party to a transaction one time or another. Nobody is locked into a formal position. The Damazin-Roseiris trader looks at the market, usually that of Omdurman, the biggest of this kind, with the most contacts, and studies

Merchants, Markets, and the Dam 47

how the *suq* appears, making frequent trips to renew contacts and witness movements in the market. He knows most of the merchants and the fact that the range of "benefit," the kind and quality of goods will be similar. The difference of + or - 1% increase in "benefit" (maximum 2%) will be due to volume, specialization. Traders may buy from friends, regardless of minimal price variations, but they will also mix the direction of their buying to reflect the relation with the *jumla* merchants, prices, quantities, and other market conditions. Damazin-Roseiris *jumla* traders are in the best position if they can use their own trucks (and several own trucks) to deliver their supplies. Others have relatives among the agents and truck drivers and try to avoid the maximum prices of the agencies.

Several of the bigger *jumla* traders work out of both Roseiris and Damazin markets. The older traders are in Roseiris but now more *jumla* merchants situate themselves in Damazin. The Damazin merchants handle more goods: *tahnia*, sugar, tea, soap, cigarettes, oils, cloth, batteries, and hollow-ware. Some rely on a close relative in the *jumla* trade in Omdurman, others look far and wide for supplies, but they all have two or three favorite contacts. Even the biggest traders deal in local produce: coffee, grains, butter, and wood. They have to estimate the *suqs* of different towns and the *suq* of particular goods since they do not work according to specific order, moving large volumes of goods. They build up relations with many different people in many markets and the nature of these relations sets the limit to the kind of trade that can be pursued: size, expansion, credit, and the availability of goods.

One of the biggest *jumla* merchants has several *gattai* shops in both *suqs*. At the same time the family holds *jumla* trade licenses with direct access to factories in Omdurman, Khartoum, and other towns. This kind of trade is very large scale with links in many directions, widespread credit arrangements and a lot of cash tied up at any time. Each trader is given a quota by the factory (hollow-ware in Khartoum) and has to take and distribute that amount. The quota applies to a specific area and the entire period of regional distribution and arrangements with *gattai* shops have to be covered by the *jumla* merchant. *Jumla* trade ranges from food-grains to manufactured items. Smaller traders cannot meet the range, volume, cash-credit, and especially, the rhythm of time involved. In this way Damazin merchants eventually reach Port Sudan and export produce to the Gulf and other states.

Trade in local wood is also lucrative and is controlled by a few merchants in the Damazin *suq*. The wood comes from the forests on the west side of the river around Bikori village. Several merchants form patnerships and either hire trucks to move the wood or use their own trucks. Labor is hired locally. Permission is secured from the Forestry Department to cut the trees and a number of licenses and tax fees have to be met. The season lasts from November to May. Local wood is of excellent quality and can be used for furniture as well as construction. Merchants estimate that only 10% of Sudanese demand is met locally, so the trade will expand upon payment of the fees, the Forestry Department gives a written permission which the trader takes to the department officer in Geissan. The area, kind and number of trees to be cut are specified. The forest guard and guards at the road check points see that the specifications are complied with. The great boom in trade is depleting the forests, so now the Department has begun to plant and manage the forests. Merchants approve of this management and they also want to learn from the officers, especially the use of high speed mechanized tools, which if proven useful, they would purchase themselves. They expect that managed forests will yield better and more produce.

Restrictions of space preclude us from detailing other kinds of trade in the *suq*. These latter include the work of artisans and craftsmen, *angareb* (string-bed) makers, tailors, barbers, carpenters, mattress makers, goldsmiths, and photographers; merchants and repairmen, electricians, engine mechanics; watch, bike, TV and radio-repairmen; the shops of pharmacists, bar and liquor supply owners, eating and drinking places (*mata'an* and *mashrubat*) book and newspaper dealers, building material suppliers, electrical appliance dealers, hollow-ware, and chewing tobacco sellers.

Trade in Grain and Mechanization of Production

We already noted some peculiarities in the trading of food-grains. Small volume *gattai* merchants in *dura* (sorghum) and *simsim* (sesame) take produce from the *jumla* traders at the rate of about 5-10 sacks and sell small amounts in high turnover trading. They store as much grain as they can but they cannot hang onto their stocks throughout the non-growing period. Hence they are dependent on the bigger merchants. Small traders also tend to deal in other local products and in addition to food items they sell carved sticks and handicrafts. Wood is taken from the forests with the permission of the Forestry Department, and craftsmen and artisans are retained in the villages to turn all their production over to the merchant.

Before it reaches the small shops, the grain trade is a big volume, large sum affair, dominated by *jumla* merchants, trading companies and agencies. Truck loads of grain are moved from Damazin to the North, South, and West, reaching Khartoum, the Northern Provinces, and international markets through Port Sudan.

Big merchants of Damazin and Roseiris run their trade out of "shops" and storerooms in the *suq*. These offices are unlike the usual *suq* shops. The big double gates open onto a desk with a telephone where the merchant sits with sacks of *dura*, drums of oil and diesel fuel, spare tires, and goods that he happens to be moving at the time. Often the big room is completely empty. Most of these merchants own mechanized farms in the surrounding countryside.

Mechanized farming of the rainlands started in the mid-1950's with the introduction of tractors, but without any other improvements. However, it did not begin in earnest until the early 1970's when hundreds of thousands of *feddans* were put under mechanized cultivation. Each farm is 1500 *feddans*, 1000 being under cultivation and 500 left fallow at any given time. Merchants may have several farms and put the cultivation under the supervision of an agent. The owner visits the farm several times a year and camps out during the harvesting season. The rest of the time he pursues trade in the *suq*, secures supplies for the farm, and arranges seasonal labour, always experiencing bottlenecks at the crucial time.

Grain merchants have other activities as well, dealing in various local products, and often running transportation and other businesses. Some traders handle only the produce of their own farms, others take the produce of fellow owners, many of whom are not merchants, and yet others buy from village cultivators in the region as far away as the Ethiopian border to the East and Southeast. Traders would take grain to the bigger *suqs* and bring back oil, sugar and other items in the *jumla* pattern, distributing these to *gattai* shops; others just purchase more grain in order to store more for the lean periods ahead. The main factors here are season and time: waiting for produce, holding, storing, and moving stocks at the right time and in the right place.

Some traders use agents *(samasra)*, others try to avoid commission, interest, and loan payments, these being against, in the strictest interpretation, of the way: *din*, Islam. Trading is integrally linked to the respect *(ihtiram)* due to "free" merchants, which in turn is linked to work kept within the family, and not extended to hired strangers.

Big merchants sit in their offices and wait for cultivators to bring the produce to them. Commanding information from the town they encompass the trade of the region. Some merchants who do not maintain shops go out into the countryside at harvest time with trucks and collect produce from the villagers and the mechanized farms. Grain traders prefer a "free" market in which many people are active, buying and selling in high volume, with a high turnover trade where no one person has total control, dictating terms to all. Through the many transactions, prices are set to the obvious detriment of no one section in the *suq*. This also allows regional variations in prices and works to the advantage of merchants with wide contacts. Transportation is always a problem, but on hearing from their contacts in the *suqs* of the south, north and west, some traders can dispatch large amounts of produce. Trains would be suitable if they were not so problematic: delays, and long waiting lists require extra payments to ensure speedy delivery. In the south especially, officials today tend to enforce price ceilings on a range of goods, with the result that traders divert produce to higher price *suqs*. Merchants say they believe that officials will eventually appreciate this and they regard the Damazin market as still, by and large, "free." But prices do not, initially at least, dip below certain minimum levels agreed to by the bigger traders in the *suq* before the harvest is in.

Sesame trade differs in that the government retains a monopoly on exports through the Oil Seeds Corporation. Internal trade is "free" and there are price fluctuations as a result. Government buying prices are fixed but they are raised several times after the harvest to keep pace with internal prices. Buying prices for the export market are set by region, with the highest being paid at dock-side in Port Sudan. However, in the fields merchants often pay higher prices than those set by the government since they have to compete with the internal market. Still they benefit because the corporation allows transport, loan interest, collection and cleaning charges to be added on top of the fixed price ceilings. Merchants with their own transport and cash arrangements reap the benefit. Some merchants are not disturbed by government monopoly. They point to the freer flow of sesame in contrast to *dura* as the beneficial side of controlled competition. There is less opportunity to hoard and prices move despite government intervention, but are not inflated artificially to a great extent. Some such control is necessary, they say, so that even under current conditions more people become a part of the trading cycle. Some would prefer all export trade to come under similar terms. But they insist that internal trade be "free" and that there be a link between internal and export prices.

Mechanized farm owners in the *suq* stress their difficulties: problems concerning soil, water, and weather, but most of all they worry about the availability of supplies, labor, machines, spare parts, and fuel. Most of these men do not regard their agricultural pursuits as the center of their interest in the *suq*. Their shops, trade in grain, and other things make them persevere with agriculture. They regard the latter as a risky, uncertain, and unpredictable business, something out of which one ought to get as much as possible in the shortest possible time, and proceed to put the profit into a trade. Merchants think of agriculture as a good business in the short run but one on which one can only lose in the long run. Trading is more prestigous, stable, safe, and rewarding. In trading merchants get to know each other, develop many contacts, and deal in many kinds of goods. In cultivating, they point out, everything rides on a single season of one crop, and this is repeated every year.

Fuel supplies are effected through the allocation system of the *mudriya*. But even if the right amounts are authorized, the farm owner cannot expect delivery before the planting and weeding seasons. Black market prices rise as deliveries are delayed and the cultivating season approaches. Owners travel to Khartoum to secure sufficient fuel. The costs of land-clearing are rising even faster. Harvesting by laborers is becoming more expensive. Yet most traders set these against the rising prices of food grains and claim that they are not losing on the grain-trade. However, since much of their available cash goes into the setting up and operation of the farms, many owners have little left over to market the produce, let alone to effect improvements. Thus the field is left open for the big merchant-owners, trading companies, and agencies. Merchants in the farming business prefer to keep in the family the different moments of their trade. The merchant himself looks after the overall trade and close relatives tend to the farms (on agency or direct salary) and to the other ends of the business in other *suqs*. The large majority of farm-proprietors are absentee owners, only 10-15% reside in the Damazin-Roseiris area.

Merchants, Markets, and the Dam 51

Many merchants from the Blue Nile towns, especially Sennar, Singa, Suki, and Karkoj, own farms and make regular visits to Damazin. But increasingly ownership is concentrated in Khartoum-Omdurman, from where companies and cooperatives cultivate thousands of *feddans* through agents and professional staffs. Some of these companies and "cooperatives" represent wealthy professional people. Large tracts of land (recently a cooperative of lawyers was given 75,000 *feddans)* are approved and ceded by various ministries in Khartoum. The local, Damazin selection system is often by-passed, since it was set up primarily for the 1500 *feddan* farms. Vast amounts of money are required for the clearing and planting of the bigger farms. Loans are a necessity and while the smaller owners go to the *suq* for money, the better placed ones can go to the Agricultural Bank. The latter enquires into past performance, the extent of other property, and the amounts already invested and still available, as a requirement for backing the loan. Repayment is also negotiated in volumes of harvested crops fixed in advance. In the *suq*, giving and taking loans depends on the relationship between the parties, trust, and prior arrangements. Repayment also differs. A farm-owner may give his produce to the loan giver on a first-chance-price basis: the amount paid for grain on the arrival of the first crops in the *suq*. This price tends to follow what the biggest merchants and buyers will pay for newly harvested grain, the largest volume buyers of course exerting the most influence. But prices are not "fixed" in advance, since buying is pursued from many directions in many *suqs* and the initial prices cannot hold over vast areas. If prices rise as the crops are brought in, the big merchants and loan givers gain but there is a risk involved if prices are steady or less than expected. Smaller farm owners (traders as well as others) cannot afford the chance and pass the risk on to the big merchants and companies by selling their entire stock.

Labor is also viewed as causing increasing problems. There are seasonal bottlenecks of availability. There are now several large, permanent villages in the area of the mechanized farms and many inhabitants of Mazmum, Dali, and Gerebin work on them. They form groups and select a representative to lead negotiations with owners and agents. The latter in turn entrust their drivers (if they have trucks) to secure such groups from near and far and to transport the workers to the farms. Food and temporary accommodations are paid by the owner, excepting tea, coffee, and *marisa* (local beer). Many laborers are brought in from the villages of the *jebels*, the interior as well as distant riverine areas. Agents specializ,e in recruiting people from the Berta, Gumuz, and Ingessana villages for 3-4 months of seasonal work and then take a commission from the scheme operators. The practice is giving an impetus to organization among the villagers. Recently groups of indigenous people held out for better wages and conditions, especially in harvesting the sesame crop which has to be done quickly to prevent the bursting of pods. This pattern of organizing is being extended to the smaller operators and to tribal-ethnic groups *(gabilas)*.

In a marked departure from *suq* patterns described above, a few years ago one of the big Khartoum trading companies set up an office in Damazin and started to trade. It hired a shop in the *suq*, employed 11 men (2 accountants and 9 salesmen, 4 of whom work in the countryside). The company is a family business and two brothers look after the Damazin operation. The company trades in all "Sudanese products" *(masurat Sudaniya)*. It owns no land but uses its salesmen to gather information about produce and arrange deals with the cultivators. It runs about 17 Fiat gondola-trucks, which makes it the single biggest transportation entity in the province. The busiest season starts in October when the company begins to gather produce. Since transportation is at a premium, the company gains most "benefit" when it takes produce directly from the fields. But it also buys from merchants in the *suq*, from mechanized farm owners, and from small cultivators in the villages. The company prefers to estimate the crop while it is still standing and then negotiate for the whole lot. At harvest time, the produce is loaded in the field and transported to Khartoum and Port Sudan to be sold in other *suqs* or to be exported. By June the work is done and during the wet season the company does its accounts and other office business. Given the size and facilities of the company, no one can compete with it in the volume of grain moved.

The Suq, Mechanized Farms, and Development

One central component of development policy is the mechanizing and projectizing of agriculture for increased production. Mechanized farming is administered through the Mechanized Farms Corporation (MFC) headquartered for the province in Damazin. Records of the mechanized farms are kept here, including lists of owner-tenents, annual yields of crops and sizes of plots under cultivation. Applications for new farms are processed through this office once new areas are authorized from Khartoum. Administrative and technical staff of the Damazin office participate in carrying out the various tasks of the Corporation. There are four sections covering the activities of state and private farms, agricultural production companies, and cultivating cooperatives. The Agadi State Farm is headed by a manager who coordinates the three divisions of the farm: agricultural, mechanical, and administrative. Companies and large cooperatives cultivate vast tracts of land and are not directly supervised by the Corporation. In effect, only the 1500 *feddan* private farms come directly under the umbrella of the Corporation's Damazin office since the State Farm is run autonomously by its own management. When an area is opened up for mechanized cultivation, applications are taken from prospective owners who have to fill out long, complicated forms about their past experience of cultivation, current activities and financial and property background. Applications are scrutinized by a local board consisting of officials from the corporation, provincial administration and the rural council. Decisions about large cooperative and company cultivation are made in Khartoum, by the presidential palace and/or the Ministry of

Agriculture through the MFC. The soil and land-survey departments, as well as high officials of the provincial government and the SSU may be involved in these decisions. Several other corporations of the Ministry, such as rural water, agricultural research and development and forestry, may be consulted. From the moment of decision the farm owners, as well as the companies, are left largely to their own devices. Nor are there any links between the various units. Most numerous are the 1500 *feddan* farms, 900 farms with 700 owners, but these figures do not include multiple ownership by the same family or other kin-related people.

The State Farm, other corporations, and the various farm-specific corporations throughout the country such as Rahad, Nuba, and Khashm El Girba, do not provide any access to each others' accumulated experience nor is there any link between these units and the private farm owners in regard to research and development. The Agadi State Farm does supply improved seeds and mechanized equipment to interested local scheme owners on a fee and rental basis.

The MFC is frankly production and investment oriented. The past experience of cultivators is relevant only in the "business" sense of an ability to run a sizeable enterprise, not necessarily agricultural. The only other decisive factor is financial: how much money is the prospective farmer able to put into the farm. Officials stress that mechanized farming is expensive and success is directly related to the size of initial investment, commercial experience, and the likelihood of attracting loans. Cultivation is risky, a lot of equipment is needed, so the MFC is not interested in the seemingly less tangible socio-cultural factors and contexts that may make a difference in the long-term outcome of private cultivation. Beyond the initial decision, the Corporation does not participate in the cultivation process: there is no agricultural extension service, no soil conservation, no improvement (suggested or required), no application of research results from the State Farms and other corporations. Owners are allowed to plow the land in a circular pattern without regard to contours, there is substantial run-off in the rainy season and topsoils are washed off, and there is no provision for keeping moisture in the soil. One improvement in recent years has been to increase the size of plots from 1000 to 1500 *feddans* with the suggestion that 500 *feddans* be kept fallow. There is no crop rotation nor can the MFC insure that its recommendations are followed. Even the yield figures are estimates of standing crop before harvest, and although experienced field-staff can make reasonable estimates, many officers say that per-acre yields are consistently under-assessed. They would err on the lower side for good reasons, but the low figures also mean lower government revenues and more earnings diverted from production to trade. Furthermore, despite best intentions and good technical ability, not all plots can be surveyed, hence estimates are applied to vast tracts on the basis of a few surveyed plots. Thus, limited by their technical and administrative composition, structure, and isolation from each other, the various government units cannot provide reliable measurements of yields, prices, incomes, social constitution of agriculture, produce distribution, and local market exchange linkages.

These circumstances are not produced by government and administration alone. The farm owners as well as the companies and cooperatives, but not necessarily the State Farms, are absolutely committed to holding costs down. Since initial clearing costs are very high and harvesting and other seasonal labor costs are increasing rapidly, other aspects of cultivation are neglected, especially long-term conservation and productivity measures. Cultivation is also very risky: under certain conditions whole crops can be lost easily. Sesame is a profitable crop but it carries the most risk and heaviest labor costs because of the nature of the crop, which has a 10-day maturation period after which the pod shatters, so many farms revert to the safer *dura* cultivation. Even the State Farm relies on manual harvesting ever since the Russian supplied combines broke down. No new methods are applied and yields quickly fall from the initially high figures achieved in the first two years of cultivation. The tendency to get as much as possible for as little as possible, even to the extent of weeding only once per season, results in low yields ranging from 5-15 sacks per feddan, with an average of 7 sacks. These yields brings mechanized cultivation close to the range of production achieved by subsistence agriculture in the nearby Berta and Ingessana villages. A mechanized farm produces an average of 7,000-10,000 sacks with about 20-25 sacks needed for seeding. We may note that averages are much higher on the mechanized farms of the Kassala province.

Private mechanized farms suffer most from the erratic supply of diesel fuel. The allocation is government controlled yet local agents of fuel companies play a central role, holding one of the most profitable market positions in the two towns. Farm owners normally receive only 1/2 - 2/3 of their fuel allocation and have to scramble for the rest in the "open" or black markets of the towns between Roseiris and Khartoum. As a result some owners cannot cultivate all their land while others divert their allotment to the more profitable black market. Nor can farm owners plan ahead since fuel supplies are government controlled and the provincial administration cannot assure or forecast a steady movement of fuel to the farms.

Risks of cultivation, variations of rainfall, unpredictable fuel supplies, difficulties of credit on the one hand, and the rapid exhaustion of soils under existing methods of cultivation and decreasing yields on the other hand make mechanized farm-owners regard agriculture only as a short-term interest. Since the rapid expansion of mechanized cultivation in the early 1970's at least one major area was closed because of soil exhaustion. Estimates of yields continue to rise in the region as a whole but this is entirely due to the addition of new farms and not to improved productivity. Many farm owners, among the first to take up mechanized cultivation, chastened by the experience, are giving up cultivation and moving into market trading, garden horticulture and other schemes along the Nile. At the same time more companies and cooperatives are being formed by outsiders, mainly from Sennar, Medani, and Khartoum, for commercial agriculture, managed by personnel hired on contracts. Vast development schemes based on shared partnership between the Sudanese government and international companies, financiers, and projects funded by European and American aid programs also continue to multiply.

The *suq*, as we see it, is a cultural whole with particular values and meanings. The new economic, political, and administrative changes are beginning to affect this system. Especially noteworthy in this regard are the concepts of respect, trust, fate, reputation, and the ways of thinking and acting associated with trading, free markets, benefit, capital/credit, supplies/wants, as well as family, *gabila*, and regligious brotherhoods. Any regional development effort involving, as it has to, people in social groups, and a hoped for increase in production, will have to come to and contend with the complex cultural system of the *suq* in Damazin and Roseiris.

Notes

[1] *Gabilas* not indigenous to the area, having originated from Nigeria.

[2] The Fellata especially tended to cultivate along the river banks.

[3] Of 1,477.5 *kantars* of sesame, 42% were sold through the *shail* system.

[4] A refrigerated truckload of fish costing LS800 in Damazin is sold in Khartoum for LS3,000.

[5] *Dahari* are farm lands where *dura* (sorghum) and sesame are grown.

[6] The discussion of trade and merchants is based on field work in the central *suq* areas of the two town. All in all 79 *dokans* in Damazin and 24 *dokans* in Roseiris were surveyed. Similar data were collected for 90 Damazin and 27 Roseiris *kushuks*.

3

Farm and Hearth:
Women in a Farming Community

Just as men dominate the markets and offices of Damazin and Roseiris, so women are the invisible partners in rural development. What is the productive potential of women farmers in the rural areas? For all the research on the impact of mechanized agriculture on rural society and economy, there is hardly anything about the changes affecting women in subsistence farming communities.

This chapter deals with the unrecognized contribution of women to subsistence agriculture. We document the women's role in the production cycle and income from agricultural and non-agricultural activities. We are concerned here with women's labor input into the various activities on the farm and in the household. We emphasize the productive role which women can play in the development process to counteract the destructive politics of food and the spread of hunger in rural areas.

Using the family as their unit of investigation, development planners impose their own cultural biases when dealing with sex role divisions and hierarchial structural models rather than utilize the cultural constructs of the societies they set out to examine. Thus, the push for economic growth and progress and the plans for agricultural development or modernization, have focussed on male participation in the production process. Here we are alluding to classical models of division of labor in private and public spheres where male and female roles are assigned exclusively to the one or the other, and where the home is clearly separated from the work place, in this case the farm. Over the last two decades, development projects have reinforced a mothering role for women, as well as a welfare orientation in the designing and implementation of programs for women (Germain 1976-77). This treatment has resulted in the exclusion of women from any meaningful consideration in development goals. Generally, the separately designated projects for women, and the systematic effort to exclude women from more significant projects, result in a merely symbolic representation of women in whatever plans ultimately materialize. Women are neither required nor encouraged by local government or planners to participate in any substantive sense in the development process as the latter relates to resource allocation (Papanek 1979).

The persistence of this discriminatory representation of women in the planning process serves only to intensify and reinforce inequality which may already exist in the rural areas. In fact, the work performed in farming communities is shared by both sexes, adults as well as children. However, the work carried out in the house is performed by women alone, so that current designs for rural development employ a model which in many areas is contrary to the existing social organization and structure. Thus modern technology continues to restrict the participation of women in the development process while simultaneously perpetuating their role as producers of food for household consumption on their traditional plots of land.

Many reasons are offered to explain why women are ascribed such low priority in economic status, some of which can be attributed to two prevailing biases in modern economic ideology. One is the continuing perception of a division of labor in which women are viewed as belonging to the traditional sector while men are seen as the natural participants in modern economic activities; the other is the irrational association of occupation with sex role stereotyping (Tinker 1979). Economic growth and progress -- in a word, change -- are seen as male-oriented phenomena whereas women continue to be viewed as the standard bearers and bulwarks of tradition, even to the extent of being consciously perceived as obstacles to economic progress. Women's role in agriculture is further modelled alongside two contemporary trends: 1) no longer are the social relations revolving around agricultural production determined by family labor, but rather by contract, which introduces a non-kinship element into the farm sphere; 2) women's, unlike men's, role in agriculture can be significantly altered by overall changes in the structure of production such as capital intensive operations, the scale of farms, and the separation of land ownership from farm operation and the traditional notion of work by the family unit. Thus, efforts to modernize agriculture through technological inputs, high-yielding crops, marketing innovations, and other infrastructural interventions such as loan extensions and other forms of financial assistance can result in undermining the role of women in farming communities. Big farms tend to increase the number of the landless in proportion to large landlords or corporations, and the agricultural productivity of the subsistence farms, which is affected by all of these factors, continues to decline. There follows a veritable exodus of farmers to better-paying occupations.

Given the accepted prejudices about women in development, it is not surprising that women have not been included in the modernization of agriculture. Women, who provide the bulk of labor for subsistence production should be included in rural development projects, and the policies and institutions should facilitate their participation in mechanized forms of farm production. Unfortunately, this potential remains unrecognized by the planners (Lele 1975). What is the root of this prejudice, since the rural male farmer must recognize the impact of female members of the family?

Women and Farms in Rural Sudan

The primary objectives of rapid agricultural development are to increase the productivity and income of the farmers, as well as to reduce the post-harvest food loss. These three goals are expected to be effective in alleviating world hunger. Yet in no instance have any strategies attempted to enhance the role of women and make use of their economic contribution, a surprising fact given that more than half of the actual agricultural labor in developing countries is supplied by women. On the other hand, the responsibility for post-harvest food processing and preservation is relegated almost exclusively to women (Tinker 1979:147-79). The results of our study illustrate how women farmers are an integral part of a family based community, despite the recent and disastrous consequences of some agricultural planning. There is a two-part argument to be made here: first, agricultural development is presented as the precondition for change and the ensuing sex role stereotyping; the second is the study of women farmers in the Blue Nile Province of Sudan, which serves to show the inconsistencies between an ideology of agricultural improvement and the resulting demise of women farming.

The model through which agricultural development is conceptualized tends to separate the renumerated from traditional activities, the latter being considered non-monetarily oriented. Thus, in seeking to modernize agriculture, planners stress crop specialization, surplus production, and improved marketing facilities. This effectively excludes the involvement of women in the process and relegates them exclusively to the stereotypically appropriate activity of post-harvest food processing and preservation. A dichotomy comes into play regarding the type of crop being cultivated: cash crops are handled by men, while consumable crops become solely the concern of women. Marketable crops such as cotton, groundnuts, coffee and cocoa are income-producing on a national scale. Sorghum and sesame are produced for immediate or local consumption and, in the past, these crops were rarely marketed (See Staudt 1978; Boserup 1970).

It becomes increasingly clear that the division of crops into marketable and consumable kinds does not result in greater scrutiny of the role of women's labor. In fact, this issue has yet to be included in major agricultural surveys.

The primary discrepancy between earners and laborers in the field results from the separation of the control over production from the actual work invested on the farm. In many countries, such as Sudan, Kenya, and Uganda, women contribute as much as 80 percent of the labor on subsistance farms.[1] In many cases, these women are not paid for their labor since it is considered part of their family obligation. Table 3.1 illustrates the contrast between traditional and contractual labor and farming methods as elaborated in Boserup's recent paper.[2]

Family labor is based on kinship relationships where the norm dictates a form of communal labor.[3] Paid labor is based on a contractual understanding drawn between the farmer and another party.

TABLE 3.1

FAMILY AND CONTRACTUAL LABOR: CHANGES IN FARMING METHODS

FAMILY LABOR (unstructured)	PAID LABOR (structured)	
HOUSEHOLD LABOR	WAGE LABOR	
	SUBSISTENCE CROPS	CASH CROPS
CULTURALLY EXPECTED	MARKET BASED AND DETERMINED	
	HOUSEHOLD CROPS	COMMERCIAL CROPS
FEMALES CHILDREN	MALE CONTRACTUAL ROLES	
	CHANNELLED BY WOMEN	MARKET
	HOE	PLOUGH
LABOR UNPAID	PAID LABOR	MALE CONTROLLED

Modernization in agriculture introduces the concept of paid wage labor within organized and planned rural development without attempting to understand the relationship of work and family in the rural setting.

A sample of eight villages were included in our survey of rural communities in the Blue Nile Province, located in the southeastern part of the country, each village consisting of about 50 to 300 households. Although a study of the role of women in developing countries was not intended to be the major concern nor the ultimate objective of the Blue Nile Integrated Agriculture Development Project (BNIADP), the results of the various surveys and research undertaken illustrate the significance of the participation of women in farming communities.[4] Recording the social organization of women farmers, we are pointing to the disappearance of a world as a result of progress. The dissolution of subsistence farming is clearly marked by the demise of the rural family.

From the sample of the eight villages, and from the experience of many developing contries it is clear that the continuing decline of smallholder agriculture adversely affects the daily food intake and nutritional requirements of the family as well as the general well-being of the community. In the Blue Nile Province, male emigration from the villages continues, because being employed as daily wage laborers is a more lucrative occupation for men. Women and children are left behind to manage the farms, at times completely alone. Yet frequently, due to increasing household chores, women's workload becomes overwhelming and they, too, abandon cultivating small plots. Table 3.2 assesses, from a cultural perspective, the time spent by women in the field, assisting men in farming the land.

We are not suggesting that women are incapable of managing small subsistence plots on their own. Throughout the agricultural season, women work alongside their husbands or brothers as a part of a household or family unit. While in theory the workload is shared equally, in fact, more of the burden falls upon the women. Nonetheless, women give up some of their other income generating activities in order to attend more fully to the farms. The crucial issue is the necessity of obtaining credit, which is needed to manage a farm. In the Sudan, credit *(shail)* is extended to men by shopkeepers and merchants who are also male. Men are deemed "farmers" and women "farm workers" even though both men and women work on the farms. In addition, rising costs and the limited land now available for cultivation prevents women, who are small farm producers, from competing with large farms. In time, women also leave the village and migrate to other areas where they hire themselves out as laborers. This shift has had some devasting consequences for women and the family.

As providers for the household, women farmers depend on the subsistence farms, and the occasional remittances from male members of the family who left the village. Additional income earned by men is not necessarily spent or invested in the family, nor does it always go towards improving the small farms. Instead, consumer goods and alcohol are purchased, and in many cases, an additional wife is brought into the house.

TABLE 3.2

AVERAGE TIME SPENT BY WOMEN PER PANEL FAMILY
ON THE FOLLOWING AGRICULTURAL ACTIVITIES

	Type of Work			
	Land Clearing Days/Year	Planting Days/Year	Weeding Mur Days/Year	Weeding Kabeb Days/Year
Dan Dan Azaza	8.25	3.92	12.30	8.00
Illyas	13.76	4.32	16.95	9.65
Shaera	14.00	7.15	17.69	10.35
Abu Shenina	9.37	5.28	9.95	8.44
Dan Dan	13.00	5.38	21.52	14.08
Abu Gumai	13.60	29.75	16.00	31.38
Karan Karan	19.23	7.48	20.06	11.75
Esseil	18.50	5.54	15.66	9.77
	Other Weeding Days/Year	Sesame Harvest Days/Year	Sorghum Harvest Days/Year	Other Days/Year
Dan Dan Azaza	-	10.09	8.33	17.09
Illyas	-	8.73	6.68	14.09
Shaera	-	16.28	17.50	22.43
Abu Shenina	-	8.66	5.20	15.22
Dan Dan	-	10.52	12.66	24.38
Abu Gumai	9.3	28.91	7.86	31.83
Karan Karan	-	8.88	5.10	12.62
Esseil	-	19.16	20.00	-

By contrast, women generally spend their income on social occasions, household, health and schooling (See Table 3.3).

The literature on the decline of subsistence agriculture points to land ownership as the central issue. Some development projects would have been more successful had they recognized the centrality of labor, especially in areas where land is neither owned nor sold or disposed of by individual users. Concentrating on the importance of labor and not land might have led the way to establishing sexual equality in the community for work and benefits. It is clear this is not a goal for economic planners.

In the Sudan, land is owned by the government; the people have a right to use the land and are entitled to transmit that right to others but not to sell it. In a village, land is shared according to an individual's capacity to farm it. Though the majority of people in the country are of the Islamic faith, culturally the women in rural areas have enjoyed a freer status in the public domain than in the more urbanized areas. Rural women are very active in the fields and naturally can often be seen outside their houses during the day.[5] Though in many parts of the world, land is associated with male control and ownership, that did not use to be the case in the Sudan. The labor invested on the land is important especially since land is still plentiful in some parts of the country but labor is not. Because planners are often lacking in cultural awareness, they are insensitive to this issue in their development projects, which consequently have shown no great intent to improve the lot of women farmers. Rather, agricultural projects continue to concentrate on the ownership of land. The issue of labor and, specifically, who performs what task, rarely seem to concern project designers. Planners work with models which assume that men own and control land, a perception which is almost universally assumed. Development follows the thrust of such universal assumptions.

The explanation for this inequality is complex, including the assumptions built into programs, staff structures, and, most important, the lack of demands by women for agricultural services (See Staudt 1979:7). Men are viewed as breadwinners so to enhance, expand, and modernize agriculture, development staffs naturally work with men. Secondly, the all-male staff structure of donor development agencies is unsuccessful at working with women in villages thus the existing structural inequalities are further exacerbated. Uma Lele (1975) argues that the attention accorded women by extension services resulted *not* in an increase of their farm productivity, but in the reduction of their participation in farm land activities.[6]

Though women have national representation on the political level, elite women are not concerned with rural farming communities and urban women's aim is to be distanced from such activites. The ideal of urban women is to engage in the new non-agricultural occupations available to them. Thus, between the cultural biases of the development planner and the difference of urban and rural women's goals, vital issues and concerns of rural women are misunderstood and ignored.

Donor and Recipient Objectives

In 1973, the United States Congress passed the Foreign Assistance Act. This law, sponsored by Senator Charles Percy, allowed the Agency for International Development (AID) to shift its direction and focus attention on meeting the basic needs of the rural poor by moving from capital intensive to labor intensive projects. This made it necessary for the beneficiaries to actively participate in the projects so as to assist the poor in expanding and increasing their capability to step up production and food distribution. Also as part of the act, a new office was established within AID, Women in Development (WID), to monitor projects and assess the impact on women. This office, while still in operation, has yet to offer substantive proof of its efficacy.

Since most of AID's recent projects deal with agricultural improvement, we can understand from the preceeding argument what kind of sex role models donor agencies introduce to developing countries. Women are designated as producers and earners of non-marketable goods and so they are viewed as invisible agents in the productive force, remaining unaccounted for and receiving few, if any, program benefits. Because the family is the unit of investigation, we are not alerted to sexual imbalances within the household in terms of labor invested and income earned. Women remain in a peripheral position vis-a-vis development goals and results. At the project level, their inclusion in implementation is justified as ..".a service rather than productivity issue."

The problems of development are due to the concerns in the way in which economic growth is structured. Capital intensive projects are not the only solution to the alleviation and eventual elimination of poverty (Traore 1975:11). Many Third World Countries have experienced difficulties as they endeavor to obtain a larger share of the gains from their own production and trade. Trade barriers, restrictive business practices and political pressure to adhere to Western models of development all suggest that nations do not necessarily make predictable and steady progress through the various stages of economic growth, but rather find themselves encountering economic barriers along the way. Heilbroner referred to this as "aggression in the normal direction," which in practice means simply aggression by the powerful producer against the poor (Erb 1975:43).

Far from improving the lot of poor people, many development efforts have strengthened the grip of an already privileged minority. Applying the Gross National Product (GNP) measurement as a test of development in countries broadly classified as poor does not necessarily lead to an observation of "the existence in the same country of a small affluent group that controls the means of production and the levels of economic and political power" (Parmor 1975:13). Development is not a process in which growth will differentiate between the resource quantities available and distribution and utilization, nor will it tell who used these resources and to what end. The quantitative and resource-dominated approaches to

TABLE 3.3

AVERAGE EXPENDITURE PER PANEL FAMILY OF WOMEN'S INCOME IN SUDANESE POUNDS

Village	Household Expenses Daily				School Expenses Monthly				Health Expenses Monthly			
	Mean	Med	Min	Max	Mean	Med	Min	Max	Mean	Med	Min	Max
Dan Dan Azaza	.60	.50	.02	1.50	.50	.22	.05	1.50	.45	.25	.10	1.00
Illyas	1.23	1.25	.50	2.00	.70	.25	.05	3.00	.25	.25	.25	.25
Shaera	.91	.75	.26	2.00	.33	.25	.25	.50	.27	.27	.03	.50
Abu Shenina	1.09	1.00	.40	3.00	.11	.10	.10	.15	3.65	.70	.05	33.00
Dan Dan	.64	.50	.10	2.00	.07	.07	.05	.10	.65	.70	.05	1.00
Abu Gumai	.90	.75	.10	3.10	.39	.10	.06	3.00	.73	.25	.25	4.80
Karan Karan	1.46	1.00	.10	9.60	12.06	.10	.10	36.00	10.00	10.00	10.00	10.00
Esseil	1.00	1.00	.50	1.50	.05	.05	.05	.10	.31	.25	.25	.50

Village	Social Occasions Monthly				Agricultural Expenses Per Annum				Debt Repayment Per Annum			
	Mean	Med	Min	Max	Mean	Med	Min	Max	Mean	Med	Min	Max
Dan Dan Azaza	1.02	.50	.10	5.00	.55	.55	.10	1.00	.22	.22	.20	.25
Illyas	2.15	.75	.25	12.00	-	-	-	-	3.48	1.00	.20	8.00
Shaera	.32	.25	.25	.50	-	-	-	-	4.66	2.00	2.00	10.00
Abu Shenina	6.56	1.00	.25	36.00	6.06	3.50	1.00	20.00	3.62	3.75	1.00	6.00
Dan Dan	.40	.25	.25	1.50	3.41	2.60	1.00	8.50	11.25	5.50	4.00	30.00
Abu Gumai	.98	.25	.05	10.00	5.78	3.20	.50	20.00	2.48	.50	.10	12.00
Karan Karan	5.30	.25	.20	52.00	7.12	7.12	.25	14.00	-	-	-	-
Esseil	.43	.50	.25	.50	1.00	1.00	1.00	1.00	.50	.30	.20	1.00

A. Data for Tables 3.3-3.6 was collected for the Blue Nile Integrated Agricultural Project in the Sudan.

B. There were no values for "Other" categories of income.

development have drawn criticism from many sides.

Development planners and investors tend to equate the order and logic of a given society with the existing pattern of its power structure. Investments in a country require security and stability, thus they contribute to maintaining some of the components that serve to perpetuate the problems of distributional inequality.

Briefly then, Sudanese rural women, like women in neighbouring East African countries, are not the beneficiaries of the numerous agricultural projects. Most, including AID, projects make orthodox assumptions about agricultural improvement, and see women as earners of non-marketable goods and therefore invisible agents in the productive force. Women then remain unaccounted for and receive few if any program benefits. Furthermore, the criteria for measuring the projects' impact on women are flawed. Project evaluation is not broken down by the sex of labor as the unit of investigation, but rather it is the group, the family, the village, or the region's overall improvement which are assessed. Information based on sex is not available, but the least percentage increases in income or production are greatly emphasized. Thus it is impossible to infer from such data whatever improvements may have resulted for women.

Women's Activities

Although a study of the role of women in developing countries was not intended as the major concern nor the ultimate objective of the BNIADP, the results of the various surveys and research undertaken illustrate the significance of the participation of women in farming communities. Here we concentrate exclusively on the women's survey (See Chapter 6 and Appendix 2 for further detail) which was a part of the research on the rural community. We recorded the number of women residing in one compound and also their relation to the wife of the household head. Very distant kin occasionally turned up, but more common were husband's mother and sister, husband's sisters' children, a woman's own mother and sisters, paternal or maternal female cousin, husband's grandmother, or even husband's father's sisters and mother's sisters. The pattern which emerged here showed the women in a household to be either a man's wife or his unmarried sister or mother. These women would be related through a man in the patrilineal descent system. It is not common for a man's maternal relations (relatives on his mother's side) or relatives by marriage (unless from his own father's side) to reside in the same compound. Protracted visits from the maternal side are allowed from relatives who live in a different village.

In the villages, the number of women in residence per compound varies from four to ten. One kind of rural family consists of one wife and her children. An equally important family model for the area is that of three to four wives plus children, and the mother of the male head of household. In large households, a lax kind of social hierarchy exists among the women, based on the lines of age and seniority (first wife, second wife and so on). The eldest woman, mother of the head of household, controls the other women of the house. The household chores and different activities are divided daily according to the number of women available. In a large household, one will cook, while another prepares the local bread *(kisra)* and a third is responsible for chores such as preparing tea and coffee (the latter being very time consuming) and tending the children. In smaller households, it is necessary for both male and female children from the age of six years on to become involved in these activities.

The larger the number of women per household, the easier is the work and the more complicated and tension-ridden are the family replationships, especially if more than one wife lives in the compound. The first wife, no matter how old, runs the household, the joint unit of consumption. Every day two main meals are prepared. Men are fed first, then the women may eat. Traditionally wives are expected to eat from their husband's leftovers. Foodstuffs are brought to the house by men, while women are in charge of organizing the preparation of the food itself. The shared kitchen becomes a source of conflict among the women in the household. Each wife eats separately with her children in her own compound.

Household expenditures extraneous to those generated by household activities are the men's responsibility. Delegating household chores remains the women's domain. Although their relationship is theoretically one of respect and humility, tension between wives exists and affects the internal management of the household. Younger and newer wives are not allowed to appear in public or to work in the fields. The eldest woman remains in the house whereas older women, especially those past childbearing age, are expected to work in the fields. This scheme of things results in the daily pestering of the younger women by the older women. Managing the household means delegating chores and supervising the performance of the work, and keeping an eye on the behavior of women.

Social and Cultural Obligations

Symbolically the house represents the cultural constitution of woman in terms of male lineality. Both the positive and negative actions of a woman affect the deeds, actions, and honor of the husband, husband's brothers, and children, both in public and private. Women are a reflection and custodian of values. It is said that a woman's actions can result in either the downfall of her man or cause an elevation in his social standing. A woman, even within the confines of the compound, can harm her own man by manner of speech and dress, tone of voice, and gossip with male kin.

One gains prestige and high status by conforming to the cultural ideal of the good woman and by associating with such women. Status and position in the society have to do with men, but women are a major instrument of status dynamics.

It is incumbent upon women to honor social and cultural obligations. It is also they who are responsible for the performance of rites and prestations concerning birth, marriage, circumcision, or death. Men merely supply the capital for such obligations. Table 3.3 illustrates how much of a woman's personal income is spent on various household activities. Expenses for social occasions are supplemented from women's spending.

Numerous social obligations are required of women. These may be met by visiting, gift giving, taking part in life cycle rituals, or sharing in religious and sectarian festivals. The social occasions held and observed by the wives of the heads of households include major life cycle events (marriage, birth, death, circumcision), various religious festivals, and other local celebrations observed in the eight villages. Women make offerings of either money or food at social occasions. Money is offered in the amount of one Sudanese pound or less. Many women reported offering food, or *dura* (flour, raw or in cooked form, *kisra*, the local bread). For many it is easier to offer *dura* since cash is not always available. It should be noted that women do not offer jewelry or clothing as gifts since these are very expensive items. Rarely is new clothing worn by village women and children. Most own only one change of clothes. Jewelry worn in the villages consisted of glass, beads, and only rarely gold and/or silver. Most women participate at least once a year in a life cycle ritual. The estimated cost per year of participation per family averaged LS5. However, up to LS20 or more are sometimes spent annually on these obligations. Such spending represents a kind of savings, for the nature of the gift is recorded and then repaid by the recipient to the giver at the a life cycle ritual or other celebration held by the latter. Families which have no occasion to perform a ritual will declare a household feast and invite those families to whom they presented gifts on past occasions. Thus one's credit, prestige, reputation and position in society depends on and is influenced by the number of families one gave to, the nature of the gift, and the extent of pleasure experienced by the recipients.

It was surprising to note the number of life cycle rituals attended by women outside their village at which the usual offering was made. It is not rare for a family to travel two or three times a year in order to attend festivities outside the village. Women are acompanied by men especially on long journeys. Buses and cowcarts are used for travelling between villages. Men need not accompany their women, if the distance is short. The high rate of intervillage participation observed is reflective of the strength of family and friendship ties, and also of the importance of these social occasions to the village and the family unit, especially women.

If relatives or members of a village are invited to attend and to participate in a marriage ritual, the occasion definitely disrupts the women's daily chores in their household. The invited women are expected to literally close their houses and move into the place where the rituals or festivities are held and at times remain there for two or three days. Partaking in ritual action means assisting before, during, and after the performance, helping to cook and feed the invited guests and provide entertainment in the form of singing and dancing. Women in these social occasions remain secluded from the men. Women then entertain invited women guests from the neighbourhood. Men are housed in the male section of the compound or in nearby compounds appropriated for a few days' use. Food is cooked in the women's section and younger men carry the large trays of cooked food over to the male side. Though in the farms men and women work side by side, it is in the performances of social or cultural occasions that the separation of the sexes is clearly demonstrated.

Marriage or death rituals are attended by friends, relatives and acquaintances. Circumcision rites are attended by members of the extended family in the male line, but the feast following the ritual includes a wider circle of invited guests. Basically these rites serve to cement ties and return obligations and social services rendered in the past. In a village marriages, circumcision, and other social festivities are usually held after the harvest of the crops.

The range of activities engaged in by women throughout the year clearly indicates that it is not only the household chores, the farms and the vegetable plots that need attending. The social obligations of women are not confined to their own villages, but extend far beyond these boundaries. They vary according to the time and season of the year. Life cycle rites such as marriage, birth, death, and circumcision are celebrated by inviting friends and relatives to a feast. All those invited present a token gift of money or food to the people holding the festival. Refusing to attend such occasions reflects negatively on the family. Participating in the festivals without a gift is also frowned upon. Festivals of any sort are common ground for sharing in communal sentiments and ties. The annual observance of the Islamic religious festivals such as Ramadan, Id, or the Prophet Mohammed's birthday, constitute yet another occasion during which relationships are strengthened and renewed. So significant are these events that women maintain reminder calendars listing who attended which festival and what kinds of gifts were exchanged. One gives in order to receive, to be fully accepted as a relative or a friend, and to reinforce one's standing in society. The responsibilities for performing these social obligations rests with women, while the reward for the act is vested in the men. Men are publically praised by other men for the success of well-planned, lavish feasts which their women have presented. Such praise is never given directly to the women, it is the men who are rewarded by a society of men.

Social obligations cut across kinship and tribal lines as well as village boundaries. The stress and enactment of social obligations are indicative of the intricate social organization of women, mobility within and outside the village, and the value of social expenditure. Not only are these obligations time consuming, but they also constitute a drain on already meager incomes. Some families even mortgage their crops before maturity to the local merchant in order to fulfill their family and village communal obligations. Thus it is not uncommon for farmers to obligate themselves beyond their means, and for women to spend large portions of their

TABLE 3.4

AVERAGE WOMEN'S INCOME PER PANEL FAMILY IN SUDANESE POUNDS

Villages	Type of Activities				
	Poultry Pounds/Year	Sale of Vegetables Pounds/Year	Handicraft Pounds/Year	Making and Sale-Kisra Pounds/Year	
Dan Dan Azaza	2.25	3.50	2.25	53.12	
Illyas	2.00	-	3.65	10.66	
Shaera	4.00	4.30	5.66	-	
Abu Shenina	7.22	3.74	7.50	11.72	
Dan Dan	1.82	3.15	13.65	4.00	
Abu Gumai	31.62	53.03	173.64	104.97	
Karan Karan	8.00	-	2.15	-	
Esseil	7.50	1.33	7.76	20.00	

Villages	Hired Wage Labor Pounds/Year	Rope Making Pounds/Year	Traditional Hairdresser Pounds/Year	Sale of Dried Okra Pounds/Year	Other Pounds/Year
Dan Dan Azaza	1.69	-	-	-	2.12
Illyas	4.32	-	-	10.00	15.37
Shaera	4.66	-	-	-	6.18
Abu Shenina	8.54	3.50	-	2.00	19.00
Dan Dan	1.50	6.00	-	2.00	-
Abu Gumai	32.58	336.49	6.10	10.83	336.00
Karan Karan	2.51	68.58	-	1.00	402.00
Esseil	2.70	-	-	4.43	2.40

Farm and Hearth

personal income earned from non-agricultural activities (See Table 3.4).

Rural women, in fact, can hardly be said to have free time. After the daily farm labor and the household chores, women engage in a variety of work around their compound, weaving, drying vegetables, tending vegetable plots or working as daily paid laborers. Women have more opportunity to earn after harvest; during the cultivation season, a total of two to three hours is the maximum a woman can devote to generating personal income. Tables 3.2-3.5 illustrate some of the activities available to women which are within the accepted cultural norms of what women may do.

Farm Work and Hearth: Public and Private Roles

Women are not expected to work or to have a profession like their husbands and brothers. Rather they are considered simply to be wives, mothers and/or sisters. Nevertheless many have an independent source of income from a variety of activities.

The community allows its women, whether married or unmarried, to work at home and in the fields with the understanding that they are *assisting* the household financially but not holding a profession. In this way, women are able to take an active role in the work force and gain an income. This income, as we shall see, is dispensed primarily in areas involving household activities. Women are publicly relegated to a position inferior to that of the men and there is an assumption that division of work along sex lines should prevail. Indeed, private and public are seen as clearly delineated domains of action. Women are expected to work at only household related activities; rope-making for example, is regarded strictly as a man's occupation even though women can be found performing the same task at home.

There is an ambiguity concerning what women can actually do and what is culturally accepted. Farming is considered a male role, yet women are active on the farm. There is no conflict in the lives of these women, whether in their public and private activities or in their status and role at home. Perhaps because women underplay its importance, the ambiguity remains dormant. As a result they are able to work in the field whenever possible and then stop as necessary to attend newborn or sick children and adults at home. It is this ability both to do the farm work and leave the farm responsibility to the household males which affords them the leeway to acknowledge a less active participation in public work. The temporary nature of this work permits the cultural assumption that they are not holding a public occupation, but rather providing a strong support base for the male work force.

Women maintain a social distance from men, remaining in the background while performing public roles, even though they are clearly a visible component of the work force. They play an integral role in the local male economy, without appearing to contribute to it.

TABLE 3.5

AVERAGE TIME SPENT BY WOMEN FOR SELECTED
HOUSEHOLD ACTIVITIES
(hours/day)

Villages	Child Care Hrs Min		Food Preparation Hrs Min		Collecting Wood Hrs Min		Fetching Water Hrs Min	
Dan Dan Azaza	2	28	2	35	1	42	1	25
Illyas	1	50	2	32	1	42	-	17
Shaera	1	06	2	26	1	34	1	28
Abu Shenina	2	11	2	28	2	00	1	20
Dan Dan	1	47	1	46	1	37	3	20
Abu Gumai	2	11	2	35	2	15	1	46
Karan Karan	1	55	1	25	1	43	1	51
Esseil	2	34	2	06	1	54	1	55

	Work on Veg Garden Hrs Min		Handicraft Hrs Min		Poultry Hrs Min		Animal Husbandry Hrs Min		Other Hrs Min	
Dan Dan Azaza	3	42	3	13	1	13	-	-	-	-
Illyas	3	10	1	58	-	04	-	13	-	-
Shaera	4	45	2	01	-	11	-	20	-	-
Abu Shenina	3	15	2	08	-	07	-	14	-	-
Dan Dan	2	20	-	08	-	10	-	-	-	-
Abu Gumai	4	15	2	47	-	13	1	50	1	00
Karan Karan	-	-	2	01	-	05	3	06	-	-
Esseil	-	30	2	26	-	04	-	24	-	-

Table 3.2 indicates the number of days spent on various agricultural activities in which the women of the household are involved. Table 3.5 assesses the total time spent by women in non-earning household chores. It is clear that some women work harder than others, but all in all women form a valuable part of the agricultural cycle, except in the cases of wealthier families which forbid women to work. The wealthier classes consider women's work to lower their standing in society.

Children are also active participants in agricultural endeavors. There are specific ages at which they work on the different types of lands. Girls betweem the ages 5 and 12 are assigned duties to perform on the land. Between the years of 13 and 15, upon coming of age, young girls are kept in the house till they are given away in marriage. During this period, the girls learn about household maintenance and cooking. Shortly after marriage they are not allowed to work in the fields, resuming work after the birth of their first child. This norm varies depending upon the family's economic standing. Newly married women might be required to work sooner if scarcity or the need so dictate.

Male children on the other hand, are sent to school and many opt for a non-agricultural occupation after completing their education. If families are able to make a choice regarding their children's education, boys are sent to school before the girls are even considered, regardless of the child's ability.

Expenditure of Women's Income

The average and the maximum expenditures for various household expenses are shown in Table 3.3. These payments or debt settlements are made strictly from the separate income of women which they are free to dispense as they please. Some of the more common areas of this spending involve the daily household expenses, health, and school costs. Social obligations, purchasing and repairing agricultural implements, and the settlement of debts are secondary considerations in the allocation of income. Table 3.3 shows household expenses to be the most common and frequent area of expenditure with a range of LS9.60 at most to a low of 2 piasters, the lowest average for the families in the eight villages being 39 piasters, less than half a Sudanese pound. In each of these households, all purchases were made in the local shop. Since many of the farmers do not produce enough for their own annual consumption and do not accurately calculate their annual needs, some have to buy back grain sold in December-January to the local merchant. Grain is re-purchased, however, at a higher than the original cost. Throughout the year, household needs on a daily basis consist of salt, oil, red pepper, coffee, sugar, and other occasional needs. It is during the April to November period that most families lack the cash to purchase the above commodities.

Thus women's income serves to cover the costs of essential needs for the house. Beyond this, school expenses can amount to as much as 30 piasters or as low as 5 piasters per family per month, including purchasing pencils, paper and other essential items. Every village has an elementary school and in the larger villages one finds the upper-level schools. Schools are government run and no fees are required to attend, though some expenses are incurred by the families. All children, male and female are encouraged to enroll in the village school, though one finds a higher enrollment of boys.

Some families send their children to upper-level schools outside their village. In cases where families have children in boarding schools (about three or four families in some villages) the expenses are naturally higher. For example, in the village of Karan one family spent LS36 for schooling, having sent their children to study in a town. Expenditure on health is, however, less than that for social obligations. Though medicine is supposed to be freely administered by the government to the village clinics, in 9 out of 10 cases medicine is simply not available. The nearest place to purchase whatever medicine is needed may be 20 to 30 miles away. Among the eight villages, one spent LS10 per year on health, while in another, LS33 was spent for the same purpose. However, such high expenditures are not common. Normally, an average of 2-3 pounds per month may be spent on visits to the village nurse for medication. Expenditures for health covered by women's income are usually made for children and female relatives and women feel that it is essential to save some cash for this purpose. In caring for both the children and women relatives of the household, women feel that their husbands, brothers or fathers can concentrate better on other issues outside the house.

Health is a major concern in the rural areas, especially in predominantly farming communities. The occurence of high rates of malaria, children's fever, miscarriage and more recently, the emergence of schistosomaiasis, make it difficult for families to save for health purposes. Though medicine is subsidized, compared to their income, the villagers find it very expensive.

In case of an illness, women will try folk remedies first. For these remedies, women seek the advice of the village Faki or Sheikh. The former recites specific passages from the Koran and dispenses roots and herbs. The latter depends on writings from the Koran; pieces of paper with appropriate passages of the Holy Book are given to the sick person to wear close to his or her body. If the above cures fail, the women seek the assistance of the village nurse. In some cases, older women with curing knowledge can also be found in villages, if available they are approached before the Faki or the nurse. We found that the wealthier people tend to ignore folk remedies and depend entirely on the Western system of medicine.'

Our study shows that depending on one's income, the expenses for social occasions and agricultural purposes are higher for some families than others. Some women contribute money toward payments for agricultural implements and debts, though these two areas fall theoretically within the male jurisdiction. In the village of Karan Karan, women contributed a maximum of LS14 and an average of LS7.2 for agricultural expenses, but did not cover expenditures for debt. As previously discussed, social obligations play a pivotol role in the lives of rural village women and large sums are spent annually on these occasions. Since these occasions are important, the participation of women in them is essential for their own social organization, as well as that of their household members, and their tribe and village. Women's social organization is a loose, informal network of women in any one village. The gathering of women takes place whenever a household has to celebrate a marriage, birth or death ritual. In contrast to the major Islamic festivals, life cycle ceremonies are not fixed events, so women are called by other women for such rituals. In fact, it is only during the performance of a life cycle ritual that large numbers of women gather together. Men do not take part in these celebrations. Thus an organization of women is to be found in almost all villages. To participate in village festivals where women are both the organizers and the audience is a source of enjoyment for women, especially since it offers a change from their rather mundane daily chores. It is expected that they cooperate in such ventures.

Women carry such cultural obligations and they contribute a relatively high portion of their income to this sphere of activity. In fact, without the use of the independent income of women, the household would not meet its obligations or adequately support its members. Clearly women's income is not spent on luxurious or frivolous items, and social obligations are not considered to be an optional spending which a family might consider eliminating. To do so would result in ostracism from the sole source of well-being in the life of the community and village.

General Implications

Sudan does not fall under the category referred to by Boserup (1970) as "female farming systems," in which women perform a large share of the agricultural activities, and are involved in controlling and dispensing the crop. Rural women in the Sudan control neither the subsistence nor the cash crops. While Islamic culture continues to play a role in delineating some of the sex roles and the positioning of the sexes in a hierarchical fashion, it does not serve to constrain development.[8]

Writers on Muslim women has stressed that economic growth has tended to contribute to the paradoxical tradition of veiling of women. Yet, in rural Sudan, Islam has not affected lower class women by relegating them to the household domain in an orthodox fashion. Rather it is the upper-class women, those with a high and stable family incomes, who have opted for a more conservative social position, consciously adhering to the sex roles prescribed in an Islamic community. Veiling, or the modern *shari* dress, are fast becoming an urban middle-class phenomenon. This trend can be viewed as an attempt to right what is being perceived as a wrong turn in the history of the country. Recently some urban Sudanese women have begun to wear a stricter form of veil, more in line with the Saudi

Arabian garb.

Islam is considered by many Westerners to be incompatible with economic progress. Yet far from ruling out economic growth, Islam in fact endorses several tenets of the latter, such as private property, recognition of the profit incentive, tradition of hard work, and the link between economic success and external reward.[9]

Since World War II, elite or working women have moved out of food production, and their movitation has not been religious, but but social, aiming to emancipate women. The "Free Women Movement" *tahrir al mara*, was launched in Cairo around 1952 and quickly spread throughout Egypt. By 1967, urban upper-class women began appearing in the public arena and holding public positions. Lower-class, rural women are unaffected by these developments and remain in their traditional roles, though they fear *inhilal* (social disintegration), and seek to protect the family, society, and moral values. (See Esposito 1980, 1982.) Rural Muslim women in the Sudan continue to work on their family plots, and try to maintain at the same time an acceptable public image.

It is not enough to blame Western-style economic policies as the sole cause of the breakdown of traditional society and the resistance to progress. In times of crisis, rural Muslim farmers have resorted to religion to solve an immediate economic problem. For many these farmers this escape from the existing tensions of socio-political changes or imbalances was of a temporary nature. Men may join various *tarigas* (religious brotherhood). Though the *tarigas* are not meant to alleviate socio-economic problems resulting from loss of income, decline in productivity and threat of famine, still the followers find spiritual peace and solace in religious movements. Men attend the weekly *tarigas* meetings without their women. At times of economic crisis, the stress of the family most severely affects the male members who are the traditional earners and the providers of food for the household.

Although women are partners in work, male earners sustain the family and female private income supplements the household expenditures. The inequality resulting from the ever-increasing gap between the owners of the means of production and the laborers, has resulted in the dispersal of farms, families, villages, and other social organizational mechanisms. It has also begun to affect the workings and stability of the rural family.

The incursion of secular ideas upon Islamic community ideals have been emphasized recently, the literature asserting that Islam and modernization or economic progress are incompatible (Esposito 1980; also Smith 1980, Strobel 1979). Moreover, the results of recent economic growth and progress have tended to contribute to the gradual establishment of a less egalitarian society. Women are forced into less profitable positions and sexual asymmetry is reinforced in the name of economic progress and efficient production.

The issue to consider here concerns the relationships between Islamic ideologies and social structures in a Muslim world in which population growth, urbanization, media exposure, education, industrialization, mechanized agriculture and the highly uneven distribution of income and new wealth are simultaneously reinforcing gender inequality and upsetting whatever balance there is in the existing political system. What is to become of male and female roles? What direction will male and female roles take in the creation of a new state?

At the present time, there are few occupations in the farming communities where kin groups control both the means of production and consumption. Men in search of better jobs and higher income, migrate to cities and desert the farms, while women remain behind where they continue to be ignored by the planners and the local governments. The processing and storage of food stuffs are not deemed a high priority in the final tabulations of the GNP. This is one more example of the way in which women's activity is ignored by development agencies (Tinker 1979:25). Yet theoretically, technology could improve this picture by preventing post-harvest food loss and fostering improved agricultural practice.

Women are largely confined to the farms, where agricultural activities naturally consume most of their time and effort. As previously described, it is not surprising that urban-based women's organizations totally ignore agricultural interests of women or alert the overall political process to the demise of rural women. Unless women become visibly integrated into development projects at the design stage, there will be little chance that they can be incorporated in any future progress, especially in a setting where the resources are limited (Staudt 1979:15).

Women are given only marginal consideration in terms of the projects and larger economic objectives in planning. Their participation is not accounted for since the measurement unit of performance is the farmer, and farmers are males. Thus the total labor invested on the farms is assumed to be male labor since the results of work are not disaggregated on a sex-role basis.

Although women play a crucial role in the agricultural cycle, their condition has not improved as a result of agricultural modernization. As farming turns to the production of cash crops, women are not encouraged to participate. Thus rural farming women continue to concentrate on providing food for the household and the major bulk of financial support for the family. Yet they are finding it difficult to continue providing food in the midst of agricultural modernization. Women who are left to tend the subsistence farms are restricted in their ability to engage in other forms of income generating endeavours and farm labor becomes their full-time occupation.

Insofar as technology remains the basis of development and development is the means of change, we have emphasized changes in rural values and ideology. Development and change comes at a high cost, in this case, the transformation of traditional male-female relationships, with attendant consequences for the position of women inside and outside the household. Economic change does not affect production alone, it has major implications for gender. One meaning of development can be seen in the inimical consequences for women, men and the family.

Notes

[1] In evaluating a nation's economic status, the GNP does not incorporate the value of non-marketable crops or any other household-related activities which in fact do generate income. In this way, women's contributions remains financially unquantifiable and so are invisible in terms of government and economic development efforts. This feature persists as capital intensive agriculture becomes central to the economy: antiquated farming methods are left to women (non-cash producers) while progressive strategies emphasizing capital inputs concentrate on technological improvements beyond all other social concerns.

[2] The question of land ownership (separate from labor) introduces a new dimension towards generating and furthering sexual assymmetry (Boserup 1970).

[3] "Small holder agriculture is the production system evolved by rural families living on the land to provide their basic human needs of food, clothing, shelter, security for the young and old and other family supports" (Chaney 1980:1).

[4] The BNIADP will be described in Chapter 6.

[5] Religion has not constrained rural women from working but poses an obstacle for the progress of urban middle and upper-class families. Despite image held by elite women, the rural women abide by the cultural norms for Muslim women.

[6] Furthermore, "It must be emphasized that in a subsistence economy, the establishment of a public office along Western lines serves only to widen the gap that has always existed between government workers and peasants." Development projects introduce a hierarchical structure which is not accepted in a subsistence economy because it serves no role for the society and the people. Rural society in the Sudan has a more egalitarian view of itself in the village. (See Traore 1975:114).

[7] See Staudt,1979:32, for an excellent criticism of AID projects vis-a-vis women.

[8] Women we talked to in the course of the survey all claimed that they did not have an occupation because they were either wives or daughters. So out of a number of identified male occupations, women had none which could be publicly claimed though they did engage in a number of these occupations. See also Fruzzetti 1985.

[9] Esposito 1980:45; see also Smith (ed.) 1980; Fernea, Warnock and Bezirgan (eds.) 1977; Strobel 1979; Rodinson 1979.

4

Law, Courts, and Regional Development

The meaning of change can be profitably approached through an account of law and courts of law. In the 1970's, the government of the Sudan decided to expand the agricultural economy, hence the emphasis on mechanized farming in areas where rainland agriculture was possible. At the same time the government began to stress agro-industry. The move to establish mechanized farms was based on the availability of large tracts of uncultivated land and on the encouragement given by rich oil producing countries, which were ready to fund programs that would aid subsistence farmers and benefit all of Sudan.

In order to understand what is actually happening in the Sudan we have to take into account the problems of land ownership, the way development is affecting those who are supposed to benefit from it, displacement from the land, and labor migration. Should some agricultural projects be implemented as fast as they are drawn up, even before a social understanding of the region is attained? We would presume that the people, the types of social organization, and the differences and similarities of culture ought to be known first. The pace of development has to slow down and changes already brought about have to be explained to the people who are affected. Also, the government's notion of development differs substantially from what the farmers expect or what they are ready to accept. There are diverse economic arguments for long-term benefits but people are affected in the short term and not only economically. What may be beneficial to the country as a whole, in the long term, may drastically disrupt people's lives in different regions now and later as well. No time and effort is spent by those who draw up development plans in considering the people who will have to evacuate their traditional lands and houses, and are left with no alternatives. For an ideology of development to succeed the message should be consistent with the aims: the improvement of the farmers' lives and livelihood.

Customary Law, Locality, and Society

Numerous large and small scale agricultural industrial development projects are taking shape in the Blue Nile Province. The relationship between economic and political changes on the one hand and social and religious development on the other is also accessible through descriptions of civil laws, customary law, and native courts. While we are concerned with the social and political problems which reflect and apply Islamic and non-Islamic principles, we will emphasize customary law and the native court systems more than the manuals of Islamic faith and practice.

The social and political problems of the Sudan cannot be understood, without a specific consideration of the relationship between customary laws, Islamic Shari'a law and Civil Law. To do this, a number of questions have to be asked. Historically how did the two legal institutions, the Shari'a and customary law, establish a working relation? Did the introduction of a third legal system, British Civil Law, cause any discrepancies in the other legal systems of the Sudan? Considering customary law in the Sudan, does the law of each tribe (*gabila*) form a corpus which parallels other aspects, such as the land tenure system of the group? Islamic Shari'a law deals with the personal and private matters of the individual. Customary laws are the legal system of particular tribes, so one ought to find a direct relationship between family, tribal structure, and the legal system.

In traditional Sudanese society, a man's strongest loyalty is to his family and to the tribe (*gabila*). The *gabila* offers its members an identity and a base for loyalty, over and above a religious loyalty to Islam. Sudanese people differentiate themselves, within the shared Islamic beliefs, in terms of tribal membership and religious orders *(tarigas)*. Abdel Ghaffar (1976) argues that there is a process of "detribalization" and that "classes" are replacing "tribes". Such claims, however, are difficult to substantiate and need further consideration. "Tribe" and "tribalism" are knotty issues. Fallers distinguishes the classical use of the word "tribe" from its present day use. The classical meaning may have applied only to some precolonial African societies. Today "tribalism" means "ethnic divisiveness," which cannot be denied. "African states do contain diverse primordial solidarities...and these solidarities, in Africa as elsewhere, sometimes rise insistently to self-consciousness and become divisive, occasionally threatening the integrity of the states." (Fallers 1971:36-37.) The same argument can be applied to the use of the *gabila* concept.

Sanderson commented that during the modern period of Sudan's history, political and administrative institutions have changed hands and transformed the ruling machinery. What remained seemingly unchanged and maintained a level of consistency were the three "traditional" institutions, family, *tarigas*, and *gabilas* (Sanderson 1983). Numerous traditional roles and services have either been replaced or continue under a different guise. To some extent the traditional role of the Mek, the secular tribal chief who used to preside over customary law courts, continues. On the other hand, the Faki, a religious or spiritual leader, has had many of

his traditional services replaced. His importance is now limited to local village and tribal activities, whereas before he held national religious significance.
Voll argued, as recently as 1972, that the structure of Sudanese Islam is undergoing dramatic change and that traditional institutions are being transformed. The question he raises is: "...if the traditional institutions are declining and society is rapidly changing what is left for Islam and what form may Islam take in the future of the Sudan?" (Voll 1972:74) Such worries are meaningless today in the light of Islamic resurgence in the Sudan, while the ethnic and political implications of the resurgence remain worrisome indeed. There have been attempts by political leaders to ally their parties with religious *tarigas*. Such were the efforts to form alliances between the Khatmiya brotherhood and *walis* of other religious groups with "new men", political leaders (Voll 1972; Warburg 1973). Combining new and traditional groupings has been a part of Sudanese history since the 1930's. Many such alliances have been and will be created and destroyed in the efforts to build a modern nation-state.
The legal structure of Sudan, a form of legal pluralism, took its contemporary form during the time of Anglo-Egyptian rule. One of the many functions of indirect rule was the "preservation" of indigenous forms of political institution. By indirect rule the British administration aimed to constitute and develop a native authority, single and autocratic, but still a part of government machinery, with defined judicial, fiscal, and executive powers. The system aimed to preserve the rule and uphold the authority of local, tribal chiefs (Bakheit 1976:258). Indirect rule favors autocratic chiefly power whereas native administration was aimed at a different problem. It sought not the preservation of the chieftainships but the evolution of representative local governments. Sir Donald Cameroon described the Indirect Administration system as "...the recognition of native authorities as self-governing local executives with clearly defined responsibilities, judicial, legislative and executive..." (Bakheit 1976:229). Indirect administration in effect spells out the importance of tribal divisions and the revival of tribalism. The Mahdist attempt to detribalize society had only a brief success at the end of the 19th century. During 1931, the Chief's Court Ordinance was instituted, followed by the enactment of the Native Court Ordinance a year later. These Ordinances reveal that the colonial powers recognized customary law as a viable judiciary system in which each tribe had its own law and courts. Furthermore, this system served to fix the tribes permanently in their original homeland. Since local disputes were settled by local laws, even though different tribes shared the same Shari'a law, it was to the advantage of people not to move unless they were a part of a mass tribal migration. Shari'a or divine law was derived from four sources: Koran, Sunna or practice of the Prophet Mohammed, *ijma* or consensus of the doctors of law, and *qyias* or analytical deductions of the jurists from given primary sources.
Today, unwritten customary laws are under scrutiny. Some question whether these laws are compatible with the interest of a modernizing and

developing state. According to planners, there is no potential for the resolution of future problems if the numerous Sudanese tribes, representing various languages, and social and economic patterns, continue to function under their own customary laws. Labor migration is noted as one potentially central problem. During the colonial era, the institution and mechanisms of customary law suited a less mobile population than is the requisite of a modern state embarking on economic development. In a modern setting, the migration of peoples from rural to urban areas necessitates the knowledge of various systems of customary laws. This creates a situation in which courts call for the standardizing of customary laws, a codified legal system.

But are customary laws necessarily incompatible with or counteractive to economic development and modernization? By definition, customary law is a living organism which endures through time due to its inherent ability to adapt to changes in a society. These laws reflect the value system of a society, the cultural and societal patterns of the population to which they apply at any given point in time (Verholst 1968). Today, many African nations are re-evaluating their legal structure. The literature on law and development offers some suggestions; first, an African nation can continue with the legal system as inherited from its colonial predecessors; second, all the customary laws can be codified into one written and documented body. Seidman (1966) suggests that due to the "stagnatory" nature and present day "irrelevance" of such laws, they should be completely replaced. Verholst (1968) and Fallers (1968) take issue with this. They argue that the so-called modern approaches to economic and social change must take into account the past traditions and cultural values of the people. To replace or abolish customary laws during the process of modernization would create a vacuum and would disrupt the lives of the people.

New nations attempting to build an enduring sense of nationhood and citizenship can develop by synthesizing the "...cultural unities of traditional Africa" with the modern aspect (Fallers 1963:72). In independent Sudan, out of 1,000 local court cases heard in 1966, 55 - 75% were under the jurisdiction of the native courts. Here is a strong case for the continuation of the court system, without ruling out modifications. On the one hand new African elites proclaim the uniqueness of the African personality and heritage. It is well to recall that "...tribal traditions, law and customs are clearly among the most authentic and fundamental expression of this heritage" (Kuper 1965:25). On the other hand Baade argues that traditional studies of law are misleading because the institutions are on the periphery and melting away, and that divine and traditional laws are ideologically based, which poses obstacles to reform and modernity (Baade 1963:2). Instead of dismissing customary law and replacing it with some alien model, we believe that the Sudan should opt for new approaches to the uses, organization, and working of the older "traditional" systems.

Local Courts and National Policy

Sudanese policies of national unification are also felt in the rural areas. Today many Sudanese doubt that customary laws are compatible with the interests and the growing economic and social demands of a modernizing state. National efforts de-emphasizing local particularism ("detribalization") and stressing unity and cohesiveness, a national culture, have forced many newly independent states across Africa to unify and integrate their customary laws into a single body of law.[1] Native customary law courts have been dissolved in the early 1970's in the Sudan, and there was a push for the establishment of a single code of civil law. There are only two courts left where customary law is applied. One of these is in the Kurmuk area of the Blue Nile Province. Abolishing the practice of customary law is still a slow process, and the actual ruling is not as yet clear to many rural inhabitants. The rationalization of so-called customary law is a policy of the current regime. Since 1969 the regime aimed at a structural reformulation of left-over colonial administration and organization. Thus the native administration as well as the native courts and the residing officials in the above institutions were abolished and new officials were elected. The Funj rulers were replaced by elected and appointed people from the area, mostly local merchants, traders, and older migrants in the Blue Nile Province, to head the People's Courts and the Rural Councils. New appointees to the People's Courts find themselves in a situation where, in principle, the erstwhile Native Courts still exert influence and guidance. Even in practice, the People's Courts are a continuation of the previous system. The new appointees belong to the one approved party, the Sudan Socialist Union, with a specific term of office. Under the previous system, formal English law was applied to supplement the "native law or custom", when the latter was found to be "repugnant to justice, equity, and good conscience."[2] Before Independence, all Native Courts followed the same pattern (Figure 4.1).

The *gisim* (section) Court (Roseiris Native Court) was located in Roseiris, the traditional seat of the ruling Mek family of the Southern Funj area. Power and authority were divided in a hierarchical system, with the Mek ruling over 10 *omodias* with one or two Omdas in each. Persons in charge of each *omodia*, an area under one Omda, were the Sheikhs who controlled one or more *mashiakhs*, a number of villages which fall under the jurisdiction of a Sheikh (Figure 4.2).

The Mek's jurisdiction over the Native Courts *(El Mahakim el Ahliia)* corresponded to 10 Roseiris Rural Councils. Each *omodia* had a Rural Council as well as its own judicial structure. Having set a timetable with the Omdas, the president and his clerk would travel once a month to each *omodia* to hear cases. Each case was recorded and settled right away. In case of an appeal, the court case would be referred to the District Magistrate. The procedure of the new People's Courts is in fact less complicated

FIGURE 4.1

NATIVE COURT

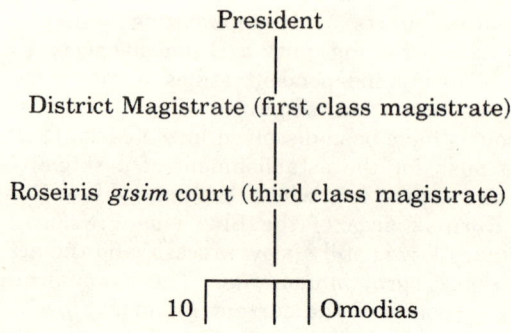

FIGURE 4.2

GISIM COURT

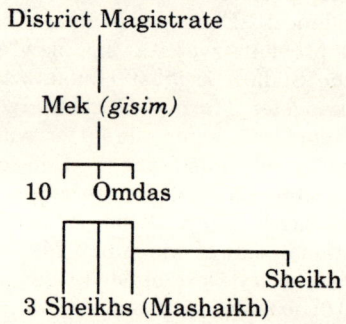

but not as effective (Figure 4.3). There are police posts at the village where civil and criminal cases are reported and recorded. The police collect a number of cases before they present them to the Resident Magistrate. The more complex structure of shared authority and responsibility of the old system is limited to a dual relationship between the Resident Magistrate and the People's Court.

The power and authority of the Omdas were dissolved. Presently the Sheikhs function in a subsidiary role on the village level; whenever a court

FIGURE 4.3

PEOPLE'S COURT

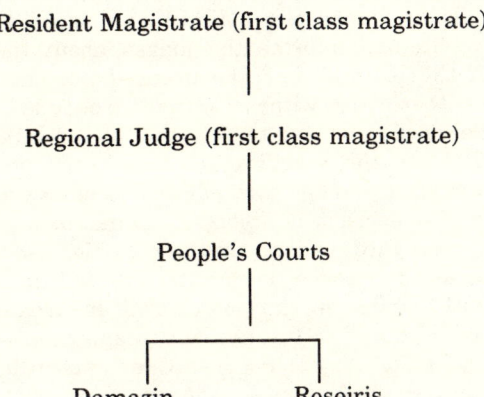

summons is given to a person in the village, the Sheikh reminds him and sees to it that the person attends the court at the appropriate date either in Damazin or Rosieris.

People's Courts

The People's Courts in Damazin and Roseiris are responsible for civil cases in the two towns. There are two Judges, a President, a Clerk, and a Messenger in each court. The President of the court is appointed by the Resident Magistrate who, in the past, did not interfere in the three-tier court hierarchy.

Presently, the plaintiff *(shakhi,* the person who is complaining) does not present his problem to the village Sheikh, or to the Omda. He/she has two options, first to report the incident to the police and open a *balakh* (information). The police *balakh* is soon followed by the collection of information *(tahrir)*. Once enough evidence is collected, the case is presented to the Resident Magistrate. Secondly, to present a *shakwa* (complaint) in a written *arrida* (petition) directly to the Resident Magistrate. The features of the case are presented to the Judge in the *arrida* and recorded in the *arrida* book. Every morning the Resident Magistrate reads the *arridas* and looks over the *balakh,* both having been recorded separately. He then decides whether to refer the specific cases to the People's Courts, the District Judge, or himself. Deciding where to allocate the cases depends on the magnitude of the crime and the damages incurred.[3] Some cases are cancelled for lack of evidence and some are sent to the District Judge for a magisterial enquiry.

The People's Courts consist of a one-room building in which the two judges, clerk, policeman, plaintiff, and accused come together. Sometimes one feels that the whole town is outside the courtroom arguing and even interfering with the case. The judges at the People's Court first hear the criminal cases *(gimaii)* which are reported to the police station. One by one the policeman calls in the people: plaintiff and accused along with their witnesses. The policeman informs the judges about the specifics of the case. Then both the plaintiff and the accused present their side of the story. Whenever there are witnesses they are called upon to answer questions. All the people involved tend to talk at the same time and argue with each other. Once the specifics are heard, the people involved are asked to leave the room and the two judges discuss what they heard. In most cases the judges' decision is accepted. Sometimes, however, the case continues in the courtyard, where the two parties debate, quarrel, and fight. The judges and the police try to interfere and in extreme situations the police book both parties on charges of civil disturbance. At times the disputed verdict is petitioned to the Resident Magistrate who may hear the case again if he sees fit. At the People's Court, the policeman leaves the courtroom once the criminal cases are heard, taking with him those who received a prison term, and those whose cases did not reach a solution for lack of evidence. Civil cases *(madaniia)* are heard soon after.

The procedure at the Resident Magistrate's courtroom allows the participation of a lawyer as the intermediary between the law and the people. The judge is separated from the rest of the courtroom. The lawyer, the accused, and the defendant are in the middle, but they are also separated from the people and the judge. Here we do not concentrate on the Resident Magistrate's court, but highlight the differences between the People's Court and the more complex Civil Courts.

Resident Magistrate's Court

At the Resident Magistrate's court, the Judge works on his own, occasionally calling on the aid of the two People's Court judges for specific cases. The two types of courts are very different, the latter allowing a lot of arguing, discussing and explaining, much in line with the older system, whereas the Resident Magistrate's court is structured through its own system of questions and answers. Once a person enters the courthouse and faces the judge, he or she usually looks lost. The court language is high-class Arabic which tends to be unintelligible to both plaintiff and accused. In the Resident Magistrate's court, a rural inhabitant or a nomad will try to talk to the judge in the way he/she would discuss a case with the local Omda or Sheikh: telling a story. Thus he/she would begin by saying "when we were going, we met...," or,"in the past we...," or "we were friends and then...," or "once I was in the fields and then...," or "and then we sat...." But the judges want answers to questions and the formal procedure is very difficult for the participants to comprehend.

The style of modern interrogation is most alien to the tribal people and the nomads. Wherever possible they attempt to manipulate the law, the judge, and their own lawyer. In most of the traditional disputes, the people involved in the case are divided into two groups, "us" and "them". The groups argue for the individuals involved, acting as speakers for them, and solving problems in a group effort. As many as fifty to a hundred persons stand outside courtrooms, having come to take part in the hearing but the court structure allows them no role unless they are specifically involved.

If it takes three days for a case to be decided, the supporters will wait before returning to their villages. Court cases do not always close with the passing of a sentence, arguments are continued outside the courtyard, in the markets, neighborhoods, and villages. One decision can trigger a number of other cases, and one will find the same groups again outside the courtrooms. Taking justice and the law in one's own hand and revenge are a common feature of local level judicial manipulation.

The Resident Magistrate's courtroom is shown in Figure 4.4.

FIGURE 4.4

RESIDENT MAGISTRATE'S COURTROOM

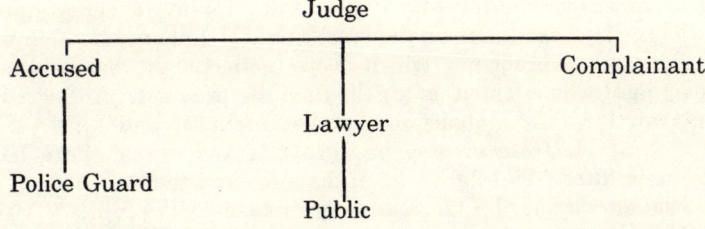

Both accused and complainant are responsible to the judge, and the lawyer intercedes for either of them. Sometimes the lawyer has to ask his defendant to answer the questions of the judge. The court procedure is often incomprehensible to the rural people who are alienated and frightened by the judge and the court structure. The shift from the local, traditional court to the more advanced one was too abrupt for most people.

Nomads and Agriculturists

Given the layout of the mechanized farms, it is clear that very little consideration was given to nomadic pasture lands and passage routes. The ten mile wide passage known as the "belt of fire" allocated to the nomads for their movement to the southern part of the province, becomes narrower every year.[4] Thousands of nomads are expected to cross the province using the same route, but when we consider that more than five nomadic groups have to use the same passage, sometimes only a day or two apart, not much grass is left for the cattle. Though the cattle are expected to keep within the ten-mile belt, many of them wander into the cultivated fields on either side, creating damage that triggers major conflicts between farmers and nomads. The farmers then turn to the law and the courts. The nomads are forced to pay steep fines to the farmers for the damages the cattle have incurred. The nomads do not have a central body of responsible people to whom they can present their increasingly difficult plight. The 1975 conference at El Dali and Mazmum on nomadic and agricultural issues set down certain written guidelines. These were supposed to be applied in the case of nomads clashing with farmers. The farmers set up local committees to assess damages incurred by the cattle. Today this committee is responsible to the judge during the hearing of a case. The committee usually includes a member of the nomadic group in question.

Conflicts between the agriculturists and the nomads, or among nomads, farmers and migrant laborers are but a few of the daily cases heard at the different courts. Small thefts, disturbances in residential areas, drunkenness, problems with *juruf* (river) lands, *talef* (trespass) on private fields, the farms or house gardens, are other cases heard daily in the courts. Cases of land dispute include *harig* (setting fire to fields), *taadi* (vegetable garden and field trespass with intent to cause damage), and *juruf* (disputes over lands on the river banks). Labor migration has brought about types of problems which were non-existent before the push for development was adopted as a policy for the province. An increase in labor means an increase in housing, market produce, and services. With the influx of people from diverse backgrounds and areas, there has been an increase in inter-tribal fights, labor disputes and thefts.

Though we heard a large number of cases between 1977-1979, we will be selective in the actual cases reported here, limiting the account to cases directly resulting from the impact of the massive development program. The cases considered here were heard in the two People's Courts as well as in the Resident Magistrate's court. We will conclude by noting the problems of the judicial system as these demonstrate conflicts inherent in development.

Case Studies

We spent equal time in the three courts. At the Damazin and Roseiris People's Courts, the judges were local merchants, and often they had to judge their friends, relatives or co-workers. The courtroom people strive for the same friendly and amiable relations as in the market not the rational and impersonal behaviour of the higher courts. Because of the familiar and less hostile atmosphere found in the People's Courts, most of the cases there are settled by the *suluh* method (peaceful negotiation) instead of the strict application of a law. The People's Court takes the form of a close-knit society, where kinship tie, tribal loyality, and professional solidarity play a dominant role in the decisions. In this situation, the concept of law has not completely replaced custom, and the change from custom to law is still in process. *Adat* (custom) is the old system and people want to live by its principles. But there are times when complainants will not agree to *suluh* and the plaintiff's only reference is the older system. In this situation, the judges have to apply the law as stated in the books, even though it might not make sense in the particular instance. The idea of *suluh* is to stop or avoid fights among the townspeople or villagers. The judges try to convince the people concerned to settle the case outside the courtroom and to give consideration to the older, sacred, and respected values. They also try to avoid sending people to prison, since that leaves a "bad mark" on the individual and the family concerned, a mark which remains with a person for a long time. It may mean a loss of prestige, status, and respect in society.[5] If the judges foresee that someone is about to end up in jail, they attempt *suluh* to avoid sentencing. *Suluh* also has a purpose in small towns where people are not strangers and where revenge is still active. Settling a case by peaceful means involves more than just a decision. It is a way of maintaining equilibrium in a society which is undergoing changes at every level. It may also prevent revenge, especially when someone is to be sent to prison, and he or others on his behalf will take the law into their own hand. But once the specifics of a case are heard and registered in the Magistrate's court, then *suluh* cannot be applied. The judges cannot interfere in their capacity of mediators and settle the case outside the court. That would mean making a mockery of the law. In a dispute between nomads and farmers, three nomad children were killed, and the case was heard in the higher courts. Because the nomads insisted that two particular farmers shot at the children (the oldest boy was sixteen years old), and the case was heard a year after the incident, the only way to find out whether the bullets were fired from one or two guns, was to dig up and re-examine the bodies. The nomads, due to their beliefs about the sacredness of the dead, did not allow the the corpses to be exhumed, and as a result the case had to be settled outside of the courts. The nomads withdrew their case and *dia* (blood money) was paid to them.[6] Often an incident is repeated in different areas and with different nomads, but the solution is often similar. In the People's Court's we still find such old Sudanese values at work, a claim we cannot make for the higher courts. Because of this, the absence of lawyers does not affect cases at the People's Court. Values act as the buffer between people and the law. In the higher courts, lawyers replace the tribal advisors in feuds, or village Sheikhs in the attempt to settle fights. Lawyers are beginning to play an important and constructive role. They are the intermediary, for those who can afford it, not only in defence but in explaining the structure of the courts, and in advising what to say, how and when. A lawyer is highly regarded. The lawyer is not merely the middle man in court negotiations, he is also the only hope in a judicial system which is still not trusted. The modification of all Sudanese law into a single system is misunderstood by many rural people and as a result the law of the country is surrounded with suspicion and fear. People find the judicial system to be harsh and devoid of social understanding. It is feared rather than respected at all levels.

The courts hear daily a number of minor cases from newly settled residential areas of the two towns. These cases invariably involve intertribal fights (Dinka versus Nuer, Nuer versus Shilluk), fights over debts, personal property, family feuds, drunkenness, or small theft. There are also cases which involve different tribes in conflict with each other, such as Fellata versus a Hausa, or a Fulani against a Rufa'a al Hoi, or a Kenana in cases of insult and other disturbances. A typical residential area that has grown over the last 10 years is Hai El Zuhur, on the outskirts of Damazin. It includes new arivals from every tribe, a phenomenan not common to rural settlements. Normally one finds separate Berta, Hamaj, Funj, or Fellata villages. The mixture in the new "fourth-class residential" areas is extraordinary; an almost city-like neighborhood where hired labor and a technical service "know how" are all that is shared by the working people. Most of them have come seeking work in the new, expanding town. The crime rate in these working-class communities is very high. Social organization has not been able to transcend ethnic differences and create a cohesive community. The only places that may superficially unite people are the shops in the neighborhoods and the mosque at the Friday communal prayers. In the daily rounds the only identification for a stranger is his *gabila* (tribe) or village. In time, ethnic communities may form. If not, then ethnic *indaiyas* are set up, drinking houses that serve drinks only to a particular group.

Berta Women Versus Nuba Migrant Women

A Nuba woman, from the Western part of the Sudan, settled in a Berta village and three months later she raised a case against the villagers. It is traditional for the Sheikh of the village to grant available *juruf* land to new settlers in the village. The Nuba woman received *bilaad* (vegetable and farm land). She and her daughter worked on the *bilaad*. One day the daughter went to the land and brought home a bundle of straw which she found there. The mother realized that it did not belong to them and planned to return it as soon as she finished her work. In the meantime, the owner of the bundle came with his women. He asked for his bundle back and before the Nuba woman could offer an explanation, he insulted her, called her a thief and other names. She was quiet and did not respond. The next morning the sister of the man in question came and sat quietly facing her but soon started to provoke her, calling her a troublemaker, and an impure, loose woman.[7]

At the People's Court, the accused people kept interrupting the Nuba woman, calling her a liar, telling her how many other people did not like her, that she has taken the *marisa* (local beer) making business away from the Berta women, that she was luring men into her house, that although she was a stranger and a guest in the village she was not behaving like one, and that she antagonized village folks. The judges, having heard the two sides, sent the litigants away before they discussed the problem. In making their decision, it was clear that they felt the Nuba woman was at fault and behaved disgracefully with the people who took her in as a guest. The accused and the Nuba woman were called and the judges warned the latter that she should be careful and stay out of trouble. They said she must be grateful to "these Berta people," the owners and original settlers of the land, who have accepted her and given her a home and *bilaad*. They said she should learn to accommodate herself to their customs. To the Berta people the judges said that they are to be hospitable to strangers and welcome them, try and understand them, and accept them as one of their own.

Immigrant Murder

After a prolonged fight, a woman from the Western part of the Sudan killed her husband. The man worked as a mine laborer in the Ingessena Hills but the marriage payment was not settled between the husband and the woman's previous in-laws. The woman was previously married to a *magnun*, a "madman," and had a son by him. To remarry, her father or "husband-to-be" had to repay the original marriage payment. Though her "huband-to-be" had promised to do so, he only paid half the amount to the first husband's brother, took the wife and son and left for the hills to work in the mines. The problem of the unsettled marriage payment continued. The woman's father was arrested for not having repaid the *mahr*, and the woman was forced to return to her village in an attempt to solve the problem. She then moved to Khartoum and found a job in a factory. Soon her second husband appeared, having heard what had happened and where his wife had gone. He convinced her to return with him to the hills, again promising to repay the debt soon. He never did and marital friction continued between the two. To make matters worse, she had no one to visit or talk to in the Ingessena Hills. Her only acquaintance, a relative, stopped visiting her because of the household troubles. Her husband, angry at the behavior of his wife and his in-laws, began to spread vile gossip about her. She reported this to the police but having been pressured by her husband before the case was heard she withdrew her complaint. When the husband stopped providing her and the child with food, she became desperate. A quarrel broke out late one night when she asked for some food. Before she was hit, she threw a stone at her husband and killed him.

The case was heard at the Resident Magistrate's Court and the woman was given seven years imprisonment. The details of the case are clear. Many migrants to the two towns are uprooted and cut off from their villages, kin-ties, and social activities. They are faced with inhospitable people with whom they establish only a working relation. At most they meet in the evening at the many ethnic drinking houses *(indaiias)*. Being in a new town, social recreation is absent and other forms of interaction are not available. To many, the immediate family becomes the most important factor and in this case the nuclear family was not stable. The couple was being pressured by the woman's family, insisting that the marriage payment be completed. The second husband resented the alienation, the distance from his village, the local people, and the work situation. Leaving the village and being employed somewhere else places a tremendous burden and responsibility on an individual. People back home have high expectations of money flowing to them and rightly so on account of being related. Here, murder concluded the story of the labor migrant who left his home to earn a better salary. This is not the story of all migrant laborers, but eventually many will visit one of the courts. Economic attraction is not met by local social acceptance and adjustment.

Fellata Agriculturist and a Land Claim

This case was heard in the Roseiris People's Courts. The Fellata Abu Shaib could not speak Arabic well and a translator was found. He claimed that he lived in the Sudan for 35 years and that he was born in the Sudan. He had no nationality papers to prove this.

The Sheikh of the village gave Abu Shaib a plot of land to farm. Abu Shaib left the village and his father rented the land to another Fellata for LS5 a year. The father said he made it clear to the man that he would take it back when he returned. The son came back and the Fellata farmer refused to give the land back. He claimed that he actually bought the land from the father of Abu Shaib, even though the land was apportioned to Abu Shaib himself. The new Fellata farmer said he had paid money for the land. But according to the father of Abu Shaib, the LS5 was rent and not the sale price of the land. The Fellata was adamant and refused to move from the land. He argued that when he first got the land, he worked very hard since the plot was forested and the soil rough and rocky. He claimed he worked the land for one year which, according to the law, made the use of the land rightfully his. Each side had witnesses. For Abu Shaib and his son, the Sheikh of the village swore on the Koran that the *teen* (land) belonged to Abu Shaib. The Sheikh said he had given the land to Abu Shaib years ago. The land was cleared at that time, before Abu Shaib's father rented the land to the Fellata. The document which was written for the Fellata by another Fellata clearly stated that the land was to be rented for LS5 a year. The Fellata's witnesses did not oppose the accusation brought in the land dispute. One of the witnesses, who had written the note at the time of the initial negotiations, could not contradict his own writing. The second witness, though not very sure, swore that the Fellata was on the land 12 years but that he was given back his land rent money when he was removed from his land.

In making the decision, the two Judges agreed that the Fellata and his witnesses were in league against the indigenous inhabitants, and that this was one of the many ways in which land was being taken away from the poor local farmers. The economic condition of the inhabitants is deteriorating and land is rented to new arrivals at incredibly low prices. The land in question (if it could be sold) was worth LS800 and the Fellata claimed that he bought it for LS5. The original rural population is being displaced from its traditional lands by migrants, state farms, private mechanized farms, and companies. The judges ruled that all three Fellatas were scheming to take the poor man's land, and that once they got a farm, they would continue to ease out other subsistence farmers. The court decided that the LS5 should be given back and the use of the land returned to its rightful owner.

This type of case where land is slowly appropriated by those who are economically better off is a quite common. Once a farmer loses his land, through indebtedness or otherwise, he moves out of the village to the nearest town or mechanized farm in search of work, leaving behind his wife and children.

Immigrant and Imam

A Fellata claimed that he was hit with a deadly weapon. He said he went to his *bilaad* and found some men cutting his sugar cane. He asked them for an explanation saying the field was his and that he had rented it from an Imam, also a local farmer. Having heard him the men left the farm. He remained and cut 30 sugar cane plants. He left briefly and when he returned he found the three men and the Imam from whom he had rented the land. He kept quiet but later asked the Imam about the illegal action. The Imam replied that the land belonged to him even though the Fellata had rented it. The three other men called him names including a slave and son of a slave, which is a punishable offense. Then two of the men picked up a stick, beat the Fellata until he was unconscious, and left him lying on the ground.

The accused men denied the charges, though the Imam, being a religious man, confessed to the beating, saying that it was in self-defense. The three men complained that the Fellata would not allow them to eat some of the canes, that he was being greedy. They were fined LS3 each or one week in jail and were warned not to trespass on other people's farms, whether they are Fellata or not. Hitting a man with a stick is against all social norms and the law was violated. In contrast to the previous case, the Fellata had in fact rented the land and when requested he refused to share his produce. As a result the Imam took back his land and refused to rent it again.

Displaced Farmers

Land is available for cultivation in the Sudan. When land is distributed, the government appoints the *majalisa* or *mashaikh* (rural councils or village leaders) to divide the apportioned land among the villagers. When the original owner of a garden came back to the village after seven years, and trespassed into the new owner's garden, he was taken to court. He lost the case because in his absence the village Sheikh gave the use of the land to another person, who paid his annual land fees to the appropriate authorities. Land belongs to the state *(dawla)* unless it is registered. One can use land that is unregistered and/or not in use by others at the time. If a man has been using a farm or garden and then stops cultivating it for a number of years, the land can be used by others with the permission of the Sheikh.

In this case a man allegedly trespassed into a garden, which he had used a long time before. He had left the village and the use of the land had been given to a man who paid the annuual land fees. The man worked on the land for three years before the previous owner came back to reclaim his garden. A committee was set up to assess the conflict, and it gave the first owner the use of a second plot of land, an area which he had in the past. Despite that, he trespassed into the other garden creating damages to the crop. The court fined him LS5.

Nonetheless, because the state owns the land, it can also displace the subsistence farmers in order to implement large, mechanized farming schemes. The displaced farmers have to be allocated to a new area. Yet due to the fast rate at which mechanized farms are increasing, there is a question about where these subsistence farmers will be put in the future. The possibility of holding a share in the scheme should be considered as an alternative to displacing the farmer.

Intratribal Fights

At one of the watering points, dug out during the time of the British for nomadic use, a branch of one of the many Rufa'a al Hoi groups was watering its cattle and resting while the animals drank. In the meantime, another branch of the same nomadic group came towards the water hole and proceeded to lead the animals to the water. For fear of the animals mixing, those who were there first asked the latecomers to wait until they could round up their cattle and leave. The request was not accepted and the second group allowed their cattle to proceed towards the water hole. The cattle rushed to the water and caused a mix-up. The two groups fought with each other, and three people were killed. Since the two sides were related, they had a joint mourning ceremony for 40 days and then each entered a case in front of the judge. The case was not resolved during our time in the field, having been postponed until further witnesses and evidence could be found.

Though the two groups were socially and culturally related, being members of the same descent group, the competition for pasture land and water created by the demand for more mechanized farms has resulted in an ecological disequilibrium. This state of affairs cuts across kinship ties, tribal identity, group cooperation, and sharing of scarce resources.

Nomads and Mechanized Farms

A nomad and a few animals were found near a mechanized farm, but not on the farm itself. The nomad was taken to court by the farm owner and the judge fined the nomad LS50. Although there was no damage nor did the nomad trespass onto the farm, the fact that animals were found near the farm and could have damaged the produce was sufficient for the judge to fine the nomad.

There exists a general mistrust and antagonism towards nomads and in whatever conflict the blame is usually placed on them. Today, there are cases where a nomad is accosted, beaten, and robbed by someone claiming perceived damages which were caused at some other time.

Nomads and Villagers

Two Rufa'a al Hoi nomads rode their camels towards a village. A fight broke out and the Sheikh took the nomads to court, accusing them of hitting one of the village men with a sharp instrument. Yet the nomads were hurt too. At the People's Court hearing, it became clear that when the two nomad brothers got down from their camels, the Sheikh and his brother hit them and robbed them of LS42. When the Sheikh failed to convince the nomads that they should settle the fight peacefully, he reported the case against them hoping that because nomads are in ill repute, the police would not believe their story. In this case, the Sheikh and his brother were found guilty and fined LS15 each and had to return the stolen money. The judges rebuked them for their behavior, especially because Sheikhs have a respected position in the village and should set the moral standard for villagers and transients.

Nomad Talef (Trespass)

Three nomad boys were herding their cattle near a mechanized farm and the farm owner claimed that their cattle ate LS3,000 worth of grain. The herders said that they were outside the farm. A committee was set up and assessed the damages. Though the animals were caught outside the fields, the boys were arrested and presented at a police station in a remote area outside Damazin. The local authorities requested LS1,000 from the boys' families and promised to call off the case. Money was collected from different members of the nomadic group and was supposed to be paid to the farm owner so that he would withdraw the case. The money was kept by the appropriate authority (in Guli village) but the owner did not withdraw the case. The Sheikh of the nomads then hired a lawyer. It turned out that the lands where the grain was damaged was government land, and cultivation should not have been practiced there. The farmer's agriculture was illegal. Illegal cultivation, embezzlement of the funds, and the incredible amount of grain which was supposed to have been consumed by a handful of animals, were all issues in this *talef* case. The nomads are beginning to use their personal ties in the administration and among lawyers to challenge provincial development programs, which are not concerned with their welfare.[8] The case (like most other nomadic cases) was postponed for lack of information. Given the nature of the nomads' way of life, more time is given to the collecting of magisterial information, thus delaying the cases for months or years. Most nomad cases are heard just before the rainy season or after harvest time.

In general, one of the arguments the nomads offer in court is that their cattle get loose during the night and wander into nearby farms. In 1977, one of the nomadic groups let their cattle loose in the Agadi State Farm, a government-owned mechanized farm. When the authorities discovered the damage and caught the cattle, the cattle owners claimed that the animals got lost during the night and wandered into the farm, and that since it was dark they could not look for them. The court charged them with *talef* and they were given a minor sentence because they had families to care for, and because the animals were lost. Each person was fined LS60 or 6 months in jail. The money was collected and given to the State farm authorities.

Similarly the owner of a mechanized farm found some animals grazing on his land. He asked the herder why, and the classic reply was that it was too late, the animals were lost, and that by the time he had found them, they had consumed 50 sacks of *dura* (sorghum). In court, the nomad was charged with trespass and destruction of the grain. He was found outside the "Arab kilo," the nomadic route, but because the committee which assessed the damages could not prove that indeed 50 sacks were consumed, the nomad paid only a LS5 fine. The fine was intended as a lesson to the nomad, that he should not be found outside the boundary of the nomadic route. Today the sentence would be harsher given the increase of these incidents and the tremendous loss the farms incur annually.

Cases of the above type are very common. Nomads camp near large and small farms and cause damages to both. Animals are known to "get lost" on harvested farms, or the herdsman and the animals wander into a farm on a dark night and in the morning find themselves in a predicament which is only solved in courts at the penalty of high fines. Some nomads deny that the animals are theirs, especially if the fine is higher than the cost of the animals. Nomads are also known to come to the courtroom and deny that they had even seen the owner of the scheme, or that they had ever gone near that place. Many times there is no substantial evidence even though some animals have damaged the fields.

Law, Courts, and Development

Independent new states opted to change the old colonial legal system to one more rational or modern, and more suited to their perceived condition. The issue was not to replace traditional values by Western models for action, but to respond to new challenges in the field of economic development. Thus, local planners hope that economic advances will continue without too much effect on the social structure and values of the people, and that economic progress and the social structure would co-exist without inherent contradictions. Looking at the legal system is one of the ways of evaluating the impact of economic and political changes in society, especially with respect to rural inhabitants whom the development planning aims to benefit.

The major problem of development is the speed with which plans are drawn and decisions are made, yet hardly any local input is called for. When projects are implemented, the land improves somewhat, and production on mechanized farms is slightly higher or the same as that on subsistence farms. Villages are vacated and population disperses, some people migrating to the overcrowded cities, while others are employed as wage laborers on mechanized farms.

In most colonial regimes, including British-held African areas, there was a difference between the legal machinery applied in "civil as opposed to criminal matters, and between the laws applied to the residents of the traditional rural sector and the Westernized elite of the urban areas." (Rosen 1978:5.) Thus, during the colonial era there was an increase in "tribalism" -- emphasising differences rather than similarities among people. When the leaders of the newly independent nations took control of the country, they wanted to use the instrument of law to achieve national objectives and social equilibrium. To do so, the multi-faceted legal system had to be unified. The state then had gone through a transformation, first from traditional life to colonial rule and then to independent nationhood. The result was a conflict of cultures and legal systems. (Obeid Hag Ali 1970:152.) Nonetheless, the single united legal structure was, and is, seen as the strongest cohesive force that would allow social change in the country. Similarly, though subject to political pressure and restricted in action, the institutions of law may provide an index for a regime's political tendencies, a mirror of intent and accomodation, a vehicle for national unification. (Rosen 1978:28.)

The legal system in the Sudan has altered aspects of society and introduced new relationships in place of the older, more traditional ones. Contrasted to the rule of custom in the past, today the unitary system does not allow procedural manipulation in the application of the law. Thus, changes in the concept of the family, loyalty to the tribe (*gabila*), region, and other changes in values are caused by economic, political, and social policies of the national government. These changes are manifest in court hearings brought about by the country's development policies.

Max Weber stated that one can best analyze structural change in a society through the judical system and the concept of law, but that in itself, as a permanent and unchanging institution, law will not bring about economic and political changes, rather in time, the latter will will affect the structure of law. "Except as a vehicle of overt coercion, the legal systems of developing nations will probably play only a supporting role in economic development." (Rosen 1978:22)

It is evident from our data that the growth of specific kinds of social disturbance in the two towns and the surrounding rural villages are a result of the changes introduced into the Province. The courts are swamped with unheard cases and the prisons are overcrowded with the accused awaiting trial. *Talef* and *taadi* cases are heard daily in the two courts. As more projects are introduced the number of land-related cases increases as well and traditional disputes give way to graver clashes, even murder. The courts cannot solve these problems in the province since a vicious circle is created and remains an unresolved fact of life. A sentenced person may pay his fine, serve his prison sentence, while similar criminal cases are still being heard in the courts. One can predict by month and season the kind of cases that will exercise the courts. At the end of every month there are cases of civil disturbance, drunkenness, and theft. Seasonal clashes occur between the nomads and agriculturist because of the bi-annual migration routes and the damages cattle cause during planting and harvest time. Other seasonal clashes occur with labor migration to the two towns at the time of harvest; problems arise between workers and the farm owners. With the increasingly mobile population seeking work on large farms, and with the presence of a unified legal system, the application of abstract and not custom oriented law, makes interdistrict migration possible, an inconceivable phenomena during colonal times. The nature of the family is also affected. Men travel seeking work in other villages, town and provinces. Women and children are left behind in the villages, but in time they too leave in search of jobs, and their home becomes a ghost-village. On the other hand, many subsistence farmers lose the right to use their lands as a result of development, rising cost of living, and other economic pressures.

There are many unregistered cases in the rural areas. Lack of travel funds to report a case in town, a 3 to 5 hour drive, court fees, and waiting time in towns, add to the existing problem in the villages. During one of the three-day Islamic feasts, 7 small subsistence farms were damaged by the nomads. None of these cases were reported. But the larger companies and mechanized farms have the power to present their cases in the courts. Though the older court structure was hierarchical in nature and a remnant of the colonial administration, nonetheless, a movable court helped in cases of this kind. When a case was heard, damages were paid for and order restored. This was possible because the Omda had a powerful and respected role among his people. The nomads used to pay the damages due immediately, mainly because they were represented on the Native Customary Law Courts. It may be too early to assess the full legal impact of rural development, but a trend is being laid down at the present time. This trend does not bode well for the future. The unified legal system does not respond to the problems experienced by the Province. Although some of the older courts have been dissolved, their ability to resolve conflict survives in the new system of People's Courts. But the different courts (civil, local, and Islamic) do not articulate with each other very well. The courts exhibit only too well the problems, raised by development and occasioned by economic and cultural changes. There is an increasing distance between local society and values, and the demands and values of development. The legal system cannot integrate and resolve these disparate problems and no longer gives expression to the culture of the whole society. At the moment it merely reflects the extent of disarray in the Province.

Notes

[1] See Rosen 1978; Verholst 1968; Fallers 1968; Akolawin 1971; Mustafa 1971.

[2] Rosen 1978:5; Mustafa 1971:2.

[3] It must be reiterated that the Civil and Shari'a courts are separately structured and administered.

[4] Once the rainy season has stopped and the river insects have died, the nomads and their cattle enter the Blue Nile Province (November-December) heading towards the southern parts. They camp in the south until May or the beginning of the rainy season when they travel up north to avoid the mosquitoes which harm the cattle. The rich clay soil becomes saturated with water, making travel very difficult for man and animal.

[5] Of course at the time of the nationalist movement, political prisoners were considered to be heroes by society.

[6] *Dia:* Blood money in exchange for the dead person.

[7] Implying that Nuba women are not circumcised.

5

Administration, Officials, and Development

Mahgoub El-Tigani Mahmoud

Social organization and cultural values are not the property of "indigenous societies" alone. Administrative officials, development project personnel, and officers of the courts also constitute social groups and relationships with their own values and organization. Admittedly these groups are not independent of the wider society. Nor are they a part of the local societies they administer. More important, all development projects are implemented (if not planned) in the context of local administration. All development effort has to be applied sometime, somewhere in a locality, and has to rely to a greater or lesser extent on officials who help or hinder the process. All development projects are directly affected by local conditions, including officials and merchants, and especially the local people. Dr. Mahmoud asks several questions: What kind of society did the officials and administration build in Roseiris and Damazin? How is this society linked to national politics and administrative history? What is the hierarchy of offices, how does the system function, and what are the values that order and reveal this society? How are officials connected to other parts of the society both locally and further afield?

Dr. Mahmoud's study ranks as one of the rare glimpses into the day-to-day world of local and regional administrators. Neither development economists nor anthropologists have shown much interest in the culture of local level officials as a

*This chapter was compiled and edited by Ákos Östör and Lina Fruzzetti from several of Dr. Mahmoud's writings: an unpublished MA thesis for Brown University (1980) and a long report on the team field research (1979). Dr. Mahmoud approved the manuscript and he wishes to acknowledge the assistance which Lucia Tezba, Yousif El Mek, Sherk Al-Sinat of Roseiris, and the people of the PSE gave to him.

group. Here we have a field study that is complete in itself and complements the studies of courts, markets and development projects in this volume.

The administrative system reflects the historical impact of colonial rule. This is best seen in the society of administrators who are drawn from different regions and groups of smaller scale societies. The system also reflects the vicissitudes of post independence political changes and the various regimes' efforts at nation building. The wider considerations of history, nation, tribe and ethnic social structure as well as merchants and markets, local societies and courts come together with the social relations and cultural values of administrators to create the context of development.

A.O. and L.F.

The word *muazzafeen* (singular *muazzaf*) designates public service employees and government officials in general. It was introduced after independence to replace the British colonial term "civil servants" which in turn replaced (in 1927) the term *effendia* which has been current since the beginning of Turkish rule in 1821. During Condominium times (pre-1956), the top ranks of the administration were occupied by British officials with Egyptians on secondary levels. By 1920, Sudanese holding the lowest-ranking jobs of junior clerks, junior accountants, elementary school teachers and Shari'a Qadis (Muslim judges) comprised 36% of the administration.

The colonial government established a centralized system with the Sudan divided into provinces, and the provinces divided into districts. The British Governor-General of the Sudan acted for the Condominium powers. A British governor and his assistants, district-commissioners, were named to every province. The district-commissioner had the power to carry out all government functions. Being representative of the colonial administrator, he was loyal to his superiors in Khartoum amd his social ties with the people were strictly formal in his position as ruler.

Sudanese junior administrators were much closer to the people. Some were sons of tribal chiefs and Sheikhs, administering their own groups. Being under supervision of the district-commissioners, they became an important agency in administering the country and maintaining the system. They had more education, wealth, and social status than the rest of the indigenous population. The British relied on them and they were loyal to the British. Their status was respected and in turn they helped their families with income and used their positions to perform services for kin and acquaintances.

In 1938, the General Congress of Graduates was set up. As members of the educated class, Sudanese officials (mostly college graduates) aimed to work with the Government in developing the country by increasing their participation in planning and decision-making. They were also interested in national unity. The position of these officials affected their posture in the Congress: in the Omdurman Graduates Club, the faction of the more senior officials worked closely with sympathetic British officials who supported the setting up of the Congress. The Sudanese were interested in Sudanizing the higher posts in government service to ensure better promotions and terms of service for graduates.

The administration differentiated the ranks of civil servants with respect to pay and authority. Sudanese junior officials were placed at the bottom of the ladder however, they had a significant and effective role in the national agitations after the 1939 Treaty with Egypt and in the earlier White Flag League of 1924. The British were aware of this. After 1924, with the Egyptians as rulers gone, the graduates suspect, neo-Mahdism feared, and a combination of the two in the cause of Sudan for Sudanese foreseen, the administration was to call the forces of tribalism to its support against its former allies. It therefore hastened to dismantle the Sudanese elements in the bureaucracy in order to devolve powers upon tribal authorities (Bakheit 1965).

In the years after the 1939 Treaty with Egypt, Sudanese officials tried to achieve more influence in public affairs. The administration thought of them as "one small group," yet it tried to mobilize them as the elite to counter a growing Egyptian interference in the Sudan on the platform of "Sudan for the Sudanese."

Officials had also taken an active and effective part in the striving for independence and national unity. Out of their writings, discussions and associations, the Sudanese nationalist agitation emerged into political movements and parties. Since independence, *muazzafeen* have participated in the National Unity Party, the Umma Party, the Communist Party, and the other political parties until 1969 when the new military regime banned all parties. *Muazzafeen* trade-unions, established in the 1940's, endeavoured to protect and improve living standards and collaborated with labourers' and peasants' unions organizing a successful strike in 1964. Assisted by radical army officers, the trade-unions contributed to the overthrow of the earlier military regime that ruled between 1958 and 1964.

In 1969, the new regime of Colonel Nimeiry (the May Revolution) emphasized the role of the military in administration and development. Hence, the civil service was politically mobilized and the Ministry of Public Service and Administrative Reformation was established to improve public administration and the conditions of service. The *muazzafeen* are represented in the State's legislative and political systems. They have representatives in the People's National Assembly and the Sudanese Socialist Union (SSU).

The *muazzafeen* played a major role in the April 6, 1985, popular uprising which overthrew the May dictatorial regime and abolished the People's National Assembly and the Sudanese Socialist Union (SSU). After the April 1986 election, a transitional military government was replaced by an elected government led by Prime Minister Sadig El Mahdi. The number of officials continues to increase. In 1901 the number of classified employees was 935. By 1956 their number had increased to 12,127. In 1975, the ILO Report stated that the "central government ministries have about 120,000 employees (including workers) in all grades, while provincial and local governments employ another 130,000." The armed forces add over 50,000, so that total employment in Public Service numbers more than 300,000. This represents well over 5 percent of the total labour force, broadly defined, and more than half of modern-sector employment -- the numbers have quadrupled since independence in 1956.

History and Organization

For most of its history the relation between central governments in Khartoum and provincial administrations was centralized, with little regional participation in decision making. The modern provincial administration of the Sudan was set up during the pre-independence colonial epoch (1899-1955). As Bakheit (1965:144) wrote,

> Like early medieval governments in Europe, the provincial administration of the Sudan as it existed in the middle of the nineteen twenties, busied itself mainly with the primitive functions of collecting taxes, petty litigation, and keeping order. The great bulk of its work was judicial and fiscal. At the head of each province, the Governor, representing the Governor General, was the supreme executive, financial, military, and judicial authority (except in private cases under the *sharia*), and the sections of the government departments supplying specialized service in the province were also under his direction. The District Commissioners...held under the governor's direction similar supreme authority over their districts. Under the District Commissioner and Assistant District Commissioner, Sheikhs and Omdas acted as agents in the assessment and collection of taxes, providing labour, catching offenders, enforcing government regulations; but no executive power or jurisdiction had been vested in them personally or *ex officio*. They were acting in every thing for the District Commissioner; and their reward was court fines and a fixed percentage of the tax collected.

Soon after the Sudan gained independence in 1956, a military regime replaced the parliamentary system. The Provincial Administration Act of 1960 determined the composition of province administration, government representation, and the province council. It also held that the representatives of the Government "shall be responsible to the Supreme Council of the Armed Forces for the good government in the province and shall be head of all government officials within the province and responsible for coordination and reporting on the activities of Government units" (Section 6-2).

Section 18 determined that "the Province Council shall be competent to make decisions on policy and make local orders; make decisions levying taxes and rates assigned to it or fees for its licenses of services; pass the annual budgets of the Provincial Administration, and approve the annual budget of Local Government Authorities in the Province, including the development of budgets of all Local Authorities." Hence the Act secured the central government's domination over provincial administrations, which could not participate in decision making. However, many Sudanese continued to raise the question of autonomous regional government, and after the revolutionary uprising of October 21, 1964, various groups participated in the struggle for regional autonomy.

The advent of the May 25, 1969, regime heralded the Declaration of June 9, 1969, granting regional government to the Southern Sudan. In 1971, a conference held in Khartoum stressed, for the first time, that the provinces would not be ruled from Khartoum. During the same year, the People's Local Government Act of 1971 repealed the earlier act of 1960.

Section 5 of the People's Local Government Act entrusted the People's Executive Council (PEC) and the Provincial Commissioner (PC) with authority over financial and administrative matters affecting the province, especially taxation. The PEC could delegate authority to People's Councils at regional, town, and rural levels. To achieve further decentralization of services and decision making, the Charter for National Action 1971, chapter 5, offers

> the citizens...great opportunity for exercising genuine democracy by active participation in government, resolution, implementation, and supervision. Popular and official activities combine to serve the needs of the masses...The power of local government bodies which are democratically elected..must be supreme over the executive organs.

Decentralization refers to the process of increasing participation in decision making by Local Government Units in accordance with the policies of the Central Government. Section 15 of the Act gave the PEC the power to delegate authority to regional, town and rural councils, even in some administrative and financial matters. Each council has a certain degree of discretion in decision making and implementation.

The PEC could also delegate power over any aspect of its jurisdiction, such as education and health services, on a horizontal basis. This meant that when a "provincial directive" was signed to establish or perform services, it applied to all councils regardless of their hierarchical position. Through this procedure a more direct and effective communication was established between local councils. Hence, the lower councils representing the vast majority of the population, found an opportunity to communicate directly with the PEC. As a result, they could make a real attempt to

FIGURE 5.1

THE ADMINISTRATIVE SYSTEM

```
          PROVINCIAL COMMISSIONER
                     |
          PEOPLE'S EXECUTIVE COUNCIL
                     |
             REGIONAL COUNCILS
          ┌──────────┴──────────┐
  RURAL COUNCILS           TOWN COUNCILS
  Village, cluster, and    Quarter, Industrial,
  Nomads' Councils         and Market Councils
```

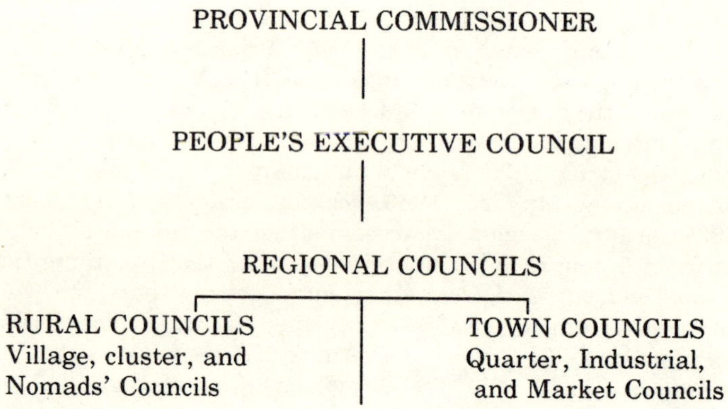

monitor bureaucrats at both the provincial and regional levels of administration. But senior officials pointed out difficulties of coordination due to the lack of hierarchy between the PEC and lower councils.

After a short experiment of active participation in decision making, the central government introduced a hierarchical rule that no council should be permitted to overrule the council superior to it. Eventually the quarter and village councils were put under town and rural councils, respectively. The Regional Council was then created to connect lower councils to the PEC. The chairman of a regional council was empowered to address the PEC on behalf of all lower councils in the system.

The PEC is the most prominent body in the administrative system. It has financial and administrative powers and is the highest supervisory council. Village councils were not entrusted with financial authority, but they could discuss the problems of their areas and bring these to the attention of the rural council which, in turn, could submit them to the Regional Council. Coordination between provincial councils is handled by the Commissioner of the Province (CP) who is the chairman of the PEC. But this task was actually left to the assistant commissioner who represented the CP. So the Regional Council lost its role as a coordinating council. Moreover, an assistant commissioner can be elected chairman of the Regional Council itself, if all the members of the council concur. People's Councils are elected, but the SSU screens both the electors and the candidates.

In the relation between government agencies and the provincial administration, the latter supervises all local units of government agencies, with the exception of Central Agencies. The latter are directly administered from their headquarters in Khartoum. But their managers can be co-opted by the PEC. The agencies include the Armed Forces, the Judiciary, State Security, and the Ministries of Irrigation, Transport, and Communications.

Muazzafeen act as secretaries and legal advisers for the People's Councils. They are also charged with the task of carrying out the councils' decisions. The senior administrative officer in a region is the assistant commissioner. Many officials are dissatisfied with their current position compared to their policy-making status prior to the enforcement of the 1971 Act. Although the records of council meetings are supposed to be written and kept by the secretariat, junior officials actually perform this task.

In the election of People's Council at least 25% of the membership is reserved for women. No more than 1/3 of every council's membership is reserved for PSEs selected by the CP in accordance with Presidential Decrees. The number of members, except for the PEC, must not exceed 24 for each council. Council committees act on behalf of their councils throughout the year. These cover finances, services, and public utilities, which are primarily managed by the Central Committee headed by Chairman of the Council. Administrative officers act as secretaries for the Central Committees of the councils. In the Provincial Administration Headquarters, the Executive Director, who is the top administrative officer of the province, is Secretary of the PEC. He may issue directives to the administrative officers as "institutions," but not as individuals, on whatever concerns the councils.

The Executive Director and the Assistant Commissioner of the region are synonymous with the Governor and the District Commissioner under the colonial administration. These administrative officers seem to maintain a stronger position than the elected members of the People's Councils. Thus, while the PEC directs the People's Councils in the provinces, the Assistant Commissioner and administrative officers mediate the actual implementation of delegated powers to the councils.

Many people, including chiefs of indigenous groups, merchants, intellectuals and previous political leaders, are not closely connected with the People's Councils due to their political opposition to the May regime. Consequently, the People's Councils include many who are not well-versed in political and administrative matters. Financial deficits and the shortage of competent administrators create difficulties in the enforcement of the People's Local Government Act. The Act produced a complex system of People's Councils which confused large sections of the population. This made participation difficult for many illiterate and less-educated people. It seems that there is a divergence between the Act's intention and its actual implementation. Local governmental bodies are not, in fact, "supreme" over the executive organs. Thus the experience of People's Councils has not brought active participation for the vast majority of people.

The CP is the representative of the state in the province and is responsible for general supervision of government agencies and their coordination. He is Treasurer of the PEC and Chairman and Secretary General of the Sudanese Socialist Union. During his stay in the province, the CP is busy the whole day in meetings of Boards and Committees that are created almost daily. Many of these include the political and administrative officers of the province. Hence authorities overlap, and one official may be entrusted with three or more chairmanships. The CP presides at many Boards and Committees whose members he selects personally.

In the Blue Nile Province, the CP acts as the Chairman of many Committees and Boards, for example, the Council of Adult Education, the Council of Social Affairs, the Provincial Security Committee, the Committee of Market Stability. Similar responsibilities may be referred to other officials by the CP. Because they are continually engaged in meetings, office work is seldom performed. Meanwhile, the CP and his aides do not delegate their executive powers to middle or junior PSEs, hence problems accumulate. We often observed members of the People's Councils, merchants, owners of agricultural schemes, bureaucrats, and leaders of nomadic and indigenous groups crowding the CP's office, waiting for his decision on their problems.

The Executive Director is the Deputy Commissioner of the Province. He is the Secretary of the PEC and acts *ex officio* for the CP. But his jurisdiction is not clear, except during the CP's absence. For the most part, officials and representatives of the People's Councils cling to the CP's status as the boss and as the most responsible official. For many of them, the Executive Director has an ambiguous rank in the administrative hierarchy. He is not a member of the Provincial Security Committee, but leads its meetings whenever the CP is absent. In fact, the CP has more authority than the colonial governors, and is authorized to override any decision by the People's Councils, including the PEC. He can appeal to the central government to dissolve the PEC and to elect a new one. He is directly connected with the President of the Republic in ruling over the provincial administrative and political systems. In one case the CP disallowed a decision of a regional council allocating land to some nomad groups and the land was given to a big farmer.

Some *muazzafeen* and members of the People's Councils view the authority of the CP as a means of ensuring responsibility and efficient decision making. But, in fact, it is not very efficient and deprives People's Councils from active participation in decision making. Instead of channeling hierarchy, satisfying public needs and supervising government units, the People's Councils tend to advance the interests of a few members at the expense of the majority. As in the colonial epoch, bureaucratization of state power produces favoritism and maladministration, despite the intention of the People's Local Government Act to advance popular participation.

The PEC consists of sixty members (and an additional 14 reserved appointments): 34 elected as geographical representatives; 13 allied forces (police, prisons and army); 13 representing administrative units; 9 reserved *ex-officio* and 5 coopted officials. The first PEC elections were held in 1974. Few people were allowed to participate: in the 1975 elections, there were

Administration, Officials and Development

350 voters for the geographical seats in Roseiris and 298 in Damazin. In the 1978 elections the figures were higher, but still low in relation to the population. Thus People's Councils may not be very representative of the people.

The provincial administration is selective in its handling of elections. In one case, a defeated merchant complained about the proceedings. This was immediately attended to by the head of the Elections Board. In another case, defeated candidates of an indigenous group made a similar complaint. They received no reply for months and were ignorant of the rules in their favor which are stated in the Statutory Law. Mutually beneficial relations between senior officials and merchants explain the courteous behaviour of the Elections Board in the first case. In the second, the indigenous group is in an inferior position, and its relative remoteness from officials and merchants accounts for the apathetic attitude of the Elections Board.

Although the PEC elections can be contested by every citizen eligible to vote in accordance with the Councils' Ordinance, candidacy has to be approved by the SSU. Councils other than the PEC are represented by means of selection from rural and town councils. Members of the latter councils elect members to the Regional Councils. Supervised by the Executive Director, the Secretariat of the PEC is composed of junior officials who perform clerical tasks and record and follow up the decisions of the Council. But the enforcement of these decisions is under the control of the Executive Director. This is only true, however, when the CP is present in the Headquarters. When the CP is absent, the Executive Director takes over his office while the work of the PEC is carried out by junior *muazzafeen*. Similarly, the Central Committee of the PEC acts for the Council during its absence. The Committee has only five members, mainly senior officials. The PEC should meet regularly in the different towns of the province to help with decentralization, yet when senior officials leave Damazin the administration grinds to a halt since power is not delegated to junior officials.

We observed in the course of our work that there is little trust between People's Representatives and *muazzafeen* in the PEC. The officials know that People's Representatives are legally entrusted with the right of criticizing government policies and practices. However, officials believe that the elected members of councils do not meet the professional standards of administration. Conflicts arise in the discussions of the councils' annual budgets. The government emphasises budget cuts to reduce deficits in the balance of payments, while the People's Representatives ask for more services in health and education. Senior officials point out that in discussing the new budget People's Representatives are only interested in the "economic returns" of the budget. They do not care for the "social aims," which require funds to maintain services and to establish new schemes. Officials also stress increasing revenue by reducing expenditure. But many representatives voted against the expansion of the secretariat as proposed by the administration. Some representatives protested against the reduction of the education budget. The CP and the Executive Director tend to keep proposals within limits stated in directives from the Central Government. Most important, senior officials act in the meetings in a patriarchal way. They impose what they believe to be a learning process on the elected representatives. The latter are mainly farmers and small traders, but the geographical representatives include businessmen and merchants whose numbers increased in the PEC recently. This is due to the political conditions which were created after the 1978 announcement of National Reconciliation between the May regime and the National Front, composed of the Umma Party and the National Unionist Party. The new alignment was felt in the elections of People's Councils which took place immediately after the reconciliation. Many candidates for membership of the councils were old protestors against the existing regime. The composition of the PEC reveals that officials along with merchants and businessmen constitute the largest section of membership. *Muazzafeen* hold the higher offices of Chairman, Secretary, Representative of Administrative Units.

The Roseiris Council of the Central Region consists of six rural and town councils. The Roseiris Rural Council has twenty-two village councils of which four are considered as quarters' councils. Every Chairman of a town or rural council is paid a monthly gratuity for five years' chairmanship. A council is to lay out general policy to the administrative officer who is both executive and consultant. Members of the regional, town, and rural councils are mostly small traders and junior *muazzafeen*. Middle *muazzafeen* are also elected as members to town and rural councils. One such heads the Roseiris Rural Council. He was purposely elected by the people in his area to use his position in the Roseiris Education Office. In addition, he declared, "Roseiris is my home and I am interested to serve them."

Sometimes there are hostile relations between the members of the councils. Many commented that members are too caught up in office work or in market business. The Chairman of the Roseiris Rural Council complained that he couldn't pursue his proper work in the Education Office. "Members of the council are not quite conscious of the job," he said, adding that members often attempt to make use of his position in the office. Yet he believes that his work in the Council should offer "equal chance" to all citizens in the area in terms of education and other services. He felt disappointed because there is little or no chance for the decisions of his council to be approved in the higher councils. For example, many decisions were taken with respect to improvement of health and education in the Roseiris rural area, but the Regional Council disapproved these due to shortage of funds.

Many members of the Roseiris Rural Council are not as educated as the Chairman. Some consider only their own advantage, as the Chairman declared. But the Rural Council is aware of the people's needs for services and economic development. The membership of these councils is not necessarily representative of all the people in the region. After the

National Reconciliation was promulgated, the interest of many merchants, intellectuals, and skilled workers (who were members of parties and organizations in the opposition) was directed towards the PEC and the National Assembly rather than the lower councils. In the meantime, significant parts of these groups continue to stand in opposition to the administrative system. The majority of nomadic groups and indigenous people in the area are also not properly represented in the councils. Some junior officials and merchants in Roseiris privately believe that a new system with a concern for ways to promote participation and decision making by the vast majority of the people should alter the existing hierarchical relations in the administrative set up. It should release the potential of the people to administer their own affairs, assign sufficient funds to enhance services, and open up a viable path for democracy.

The councils also have many material and logistical problems. They are short of buildings and office space as well as committed PSE staff. For example, the Central Regional Council of the Blue Nile Province occupies buildings reserved for the Roseiris Rural Council. Administrative problems of the councils have produced difficulties in financial and administrative relations. Government units in the People's Council call for more facilities and financial aid to supplement funds received from headquarters. Because of the failure of the Assistant Commissioners and the Regional Councils to satisfy their needs, these units stress their own jurisdiction apart from the Regional Council.

The expansion of provincial administration did not help many government units to function more efficiently. The large number of People's Councils, which are actually controlled by officials, created tensions between the heads of government units in rural areas and council personnel. Because there is a shortage of funds and expertise, the heads of government units resent the People's Councils and ask for direct relations with their headquarters in the provincial administration.

Another problem is the particular position and role of administrative officers, who oppose the authority of elected leaders of People's Councils. The domains of authority are not clearly defined between the two groups, nor are they explained in the People's Local Government Act or the Council Ordinances. The Charter for National Action (1971) gave elected leaders authority over the executives (the administrative officers) and the PSE's. Although administrative officers should work as secretaries for the councils, they are also entitled to advise council members to abide by regulations. Still, the limits of such advice are not clear. Hence, administrative officers, led by the Assistant Commissioners, compete with elected members of the councils even in minor decisions such as announcements of meetings or celebrations.

As previously noted, the absence of trained personnel and experienced political leaders has affected the administrative efficiency of the PEC. This has given officials a major role in administering the councils. They propose, direct, and decide the agendas and minutes for all Council Committees. They also distribute quotas of commodities, and act for the Councils to approve or disapprove petitions for trade licenses, which constitute a major source of revenue for the provincial administration. During the rainy season, difficulties in transport and communication make meetings of the Rural Councils impossible, thus giving the administrative officers unrestrained control of the Councils' work without consulting the elected members. The officers prefer to report to the Chairman or Central Committee of the Councils whenever possible.

The Political Framework

The Sudan Socialist Union, SSU, is the regime's political organization. The General-Secretariat of the union is in Khartoum. In every province there is a Provincial Secretariat of which the CP is the Secretary-General. He has five Assistant-Secretaries who are responsible to him for the supervision and leadership of the SSU. The SSU is deemed to be responsible for state policy, the leader in development programs, and the supervisor of government services. Its teachings and principles are promulgated as basic to the country's future. Membership is open to every citizen regardless of religion or social background. It is made up of hierarchical committees where every committee is empowered with some degree of political supervision. Recently elections replaced unanimous selection to "section," "region," and "provincial" committees. CP as Secretary-General is the chairman of the Provincial Committee whose membership includes CP's Assistant-Secretaries who must be elected according to SSU practice. Election rules regarding these appointments are not seriously followed. Candidates defeated in the elections to the Provincial-Secretariat were nominated to be Assistant-Secretaries. These supervise the sections of development and services, popular organizations (parents' councils, cooperatives, village development committees, women, and youth groups) professional and trade-unions, administration, and organization.

The Sudan Women's Union (SWU), and the Sudan Youth Union (SYU) have their own organizations which are supervised as independent associations by the provincial secretariat. It is possible to hold office in more than one committee of the SSU. The Provincial Secretariat exercises formal supervision over all other associations in the province. The SSU projects its existence as "the organization leading the march of...people and....includes all revolutionary working masses."

The SSU is the highest arbiter of government authority. It "guides" the provincial administration in policy, development programs, and public service. The relation between the SSU and the provincial administrator is meant to be complementary. The CP is the head of both.

The SSU consists of *muazzafeen*, in addition to workers, farmers, and merchants. Women and youth are also represented. Since the establishment of the Blue Nile Province, leaders of the SSU nominated by the CP and approved by President of the Republic continued to lead despite their failure in the elections. Some of the leaders and officials have previous political backgrounds. Yet they consider themselves to be "new leaders" to maintain their prestigious position in the SSU. Thus, they are loyal to CP rather than to the political organization.

Leaders of the SSU maintain contact with the Central Government in Khartoum. Assistant-Secretaries make frequent trips to meet the political elite of Khartoum. In contrast, even senior officials in the administration are discouraged from making such contacts. Although the SSU budget is separate from the provincial administration's budget, the SSU uses the equipment of administrative units. Given the limited resources of services, communications, and transport, the administrators of the province are dissatisfied.

The majority of SSU leaders are officials. In the absence of competition in free, direct and secret elections, SSU leaders are nominated by the CP. Leaders and members of the Provincial Committee and of all the other committees are also appointed without any real participation in political activities. For example, a few members of a section committee declared themselves to be secretaries for existing vacant posts. Announcements of meetings are postponed for months. One member said he never saw the committee of which he had been a member for three years...except for the opening session. Most important, some members and leaders of the SSU still maintain their allegiance to the previously banned political parties.

Merchants are also active members in the provincial administrative councils. They also contribute money to the provincial secretariat of the SSU. But they are secretly committed to the banned political organizations. After the National Reconciliation took place in 1978 many merchants expected political liberalization to follow. But the May regime refused to part with the single-party system. Smaller traders are also leery of the SSU. One of them, however, holds several leading positions in the SSU. He is Secretary of a Regional Committee, representative of his region in the Provincial Committee of the SSU, and is also representative of his region in the PEC.

There are few links between leaders and members of the SSU. Leaders assign dates for meetings to resolve tensions in the lower ranking committees, but these are seldom held. In contrast, the *muazzafeen* pass problems upward because they are not able to make decisions, since there is no delegation of financial and administrative powers. In the SSU the leaders enjoy a wider span of decision making, but they are authoritarian. Most important, they do not acquaint the CP with viewpoints and criticism from the lower committees. They are primarily concerned with their image as competent leaders in the sense that they can surmount tensions, but they merely surpress opposition from the lower committees. In the end a

FIGURE 5.2

SSU ORGANIZATION

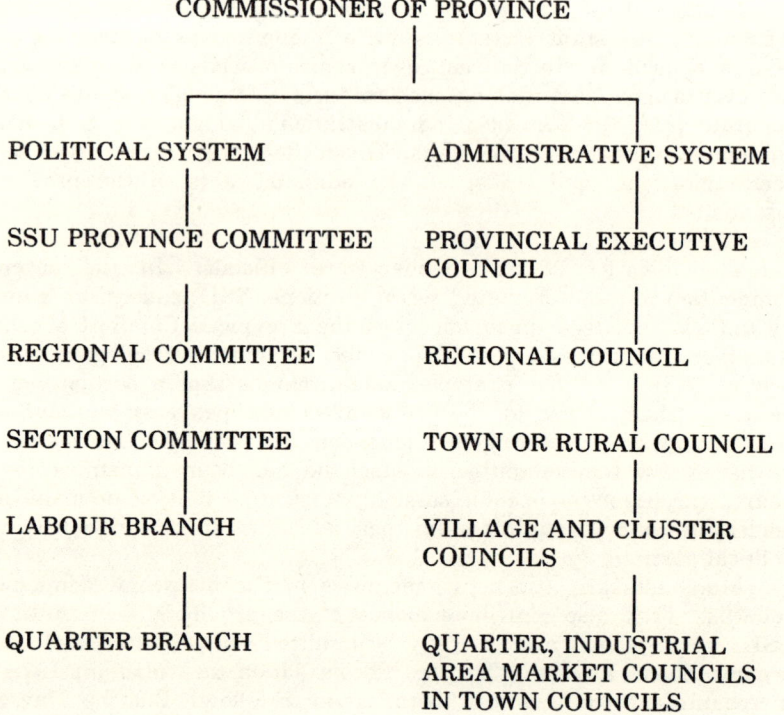

few members of the committees in question refrained from criticism or abandoned their membership. As some of them said, "the leaders of the provincial committee were not elected by the people; they were selected by the CP. Therefore, they cannot challenge him with our criticisms."

Administration and Politics

The Charter for National Action states that, "the Socialist Union... should be capable of exercising political, economic, and social leadership from the base in the village to the summit in the political power. Its authority and popular supervision over the executive power must be ensured."

The incumbency of senior officials often overlaps in the administrative and political systems. According to regulations of the SSU, joint meetings should be held between political committees and People's Councils in the province. All proposals should be submitted to the SSU Provincial

Administration, Officials and Development 115

Committee and to PEC. After discussing and approving proposals of development in the province, the CP submits them as a part of the annual budget to the central government in Khartoum. The submission is made before the beginning of the new fiscal year in July.

In practice, joint meetings between the Political Committees and the Administrative Councils are rarely held. PEC meetings are not attended by SSU Provincial Committees. Most important, there is a lack of definition of roles, responsibilities, and boundaries between SSU and the Provincial Administration. It seems that the only well-defined role is that of the CP who is the political and administrative head of the province. Consequently, if the CP is absent, no other administrator or political official can fill his position. Assistant-Secretaries are not entitled to represent the CP either in administrative or political organization. The CP tries to adjust conflicts between his assistants in the SSU and the Provincial Administration, and attempts to maintain the status quo in his headquarters. High officials in the political and the administrative systems compete for the CP's support. Administrative officials feel superior to their political counterparts and believe that the political leaders are opportunists of inferior experience and do not have a significant role. On the other side, the political leaders believe that their position is higher since they are concerned with wider issues. At the same time the political leaders, in an effort to control administrators, try to cultivate close ties with the officials in the administrative system.

The Secretariat-General of the SSU in Khartoum directly controls the provincial secretariat in Damazin. For example, the Provincial Administration Headquarters allocated financial aid to the Social Welfare Office in Damazin with the consent of the provincial secretariat of the SSU. Yet the Secretary-General of the SSU in Khartoum transferred the funds in question to SSU headquarters in Damazin. In another case, a regional manager of a government agency in Damazin stated that an SSU leader once required the services of an official of the agency for an extended period without consulting the manager. The People's Town Council in Damazin witnessed many conflicts issuing from interventions of the SSU Provincial Secretariat.

The strategic goals of the SSU are the enhancement of equality, economic development, and participation by the people in decision making. How far is this implemented? Some Ingessana youths became leaders of the Sudan Youth Union in the SSU Provincial Secretariat. They were also members of the SSU section in the Ingessana Hills. They held a conference of the SYU and extended the services of the Adult Education Office to their people. But they also criticized the merchants in the hills for selling *dura* at higher prices and for expanding illegal cultivation in the unplanned areas of traditional agriculture. The merchants, who led the political section of the Ingessana area SSU, were supported by the Ingessana elders against the Ingessana youth. The conflicting parties raised complaints against each other to the CP, who transferred the case to the SSU Provincial Secretariat. The Provincial Secretariat rejected the youth leaders' complaint against the political leaders, but the youths were not satisfied. A meeting was held with the Assistant-Secretary for popular organizations in the Provincial Secretariat. The youth leaders criticized their leaders in the section and urged that their section be converted into a regional committee to enable more Ingessana youths to participate. They also urged that their district be up-graded to an administrative region according to a previous decision of the CP. The Assistant Secretary disapproved of their criticisms, since, according to the rules of the SSU, such problems must be dealt with in their own section. Furthermore, he told them that decisions of the CP to convert the Ingessana district into an administrative region were subject to approval by the SSU Conference in Khartoum, and refused to discuss the accusations against the merchants. At that, some of the youth leaders attempted to gain support from the Secretariat-General of the SSU in Khartoum, but they failed and became frustrated. Finally some resigned, while others remained content in their role as "political leaders" in the Provincial Secretariat.

Muazzafeen Society

About 65% of the officials in Damazin and Roseiris hail from the Blue Nile and neighboring provinces, with about 40% belonging to the *gabilas* inhabiting the Blue Nile Province. These are the indigenous "Arab" groups such as the Rufa'a and Kenana, and the northern groups such as the Ja'alyn and Shaigiya who have migrated to the Blue Nile in the past. Few belong to the original inhabitants of the area such as the Hamaj, Berta, Ingessana, Kadalu and Funj. Although their numbers are increasing, the employees from these groups still mainly occupy the lower ranks. For public service employees the qualifications include a high school diploma, as specified by the Central Establishment Office in Khartoum. Since more than 40% of the *muazzafeen* are newly appointed and since efforts have been made to employ local applicants, many new people have joined service in Damazin. However, many of these do not have high school diplomas as required and are not qualified according to the high standards of the central administration. Some have not been trained at all and even upon joining they are not provided with orientation courses. Although the offices are often equipped with modern computing machines, the people do not know how to use them. Many of the high posts of the administrations remain unfilled, especially in the finance and accounts sections. This slows work, burdens senior officers, and confuses areas of jurisdiction. Office work is poorly organized and files pile up since there is no shelving and storage is haphazard. Officials claim they are overworked, facilities are inadequate, and there are no incentives for efficient performance.

At the higher levels the educational qualifications have increased remarkably. Many *muazzafeen* have university degrees, and some are holders of post-graduate degrees. Other changes are in demographic structure: those under 40 and those unmarried are now in the majority.

Most officials are Muslim and many belong to the *tarigas* represented in the area. They also follow the Shari'a laws in daily life. They try to apply these precepts to their work and believe in punctuality, helping the public, and praying. Some give discourses in the mosques. But the practice of the Shari'a is rather liberal. Some officials see room for change in marriage relations, women's status and other matters and see the Shari'a as changeable. But since Islam is permanent and unchanging they also see social reform as a way to secure the place of religion in society. These more "radical" *muazzafeen* view their colleagues who disapprove of changes in the Shari'a as traditional, conservative, and fundamentalist. The disagreement often leads to heated discussions further slowing work in the offices. A smaller percentage of officials believe that religion is a personal matter and should not be involved in public affairs.

Most officials live in nuclear families, and polygamy and divorce are rare. Very few of the men are married to *muazzafat* (female officials). Many married *muazzafeen* are still economically dependent on their family. Married life is also approved by religious teaching. Large amounts of income are devoted to family expenses and to visiting relatives in other parts of the country by officials who insist on making full use of vacations and holidays. Most junior oficials visit home on family and religious celebrations. Marriage, circumcision, or death in the family lead to requests for leave, loans, and contributions from colleagues. However, a new trend is visible in which unmarried *muazzafeen* who live at home are expressing their desire to escape family obligations which are becoming a heavy burden, given the prevailing low salaries.

Ties with kin, affines, friends, and colleagues affect the *muazzafeen's* performance in office. In general, parents and siblings (father *aba*, mother *umma*, brother/sister *ahu/ukt*, father's brother/sister *amm/amma*, mother's brother/sister *khal/khala*) are the closest relatives *(ahal)*, and relatives by marriage *(nasaba)*, are less important. Obligations depend on personal relations. Kinship conflicts may occur and divorce is always a possibility. The indigenous groups such as the Berta and Hamaj do not make a distinction between kin and marriage, and kinship relations suffuse the whole *gabila*. This is true of relationships in the office as well. But the importance of friendship is increasing and colleagues often become the closest person for many *muazzafeen*.

Colleagues, those one studied with at school, worked with in the past, or work with now, often demand and get special consideration in the office. These relations extend to neighbours in the quarters *(hara)* where *muazzafeen* live. These circumstances may lessen conflicts among junior officials, but have little to do with relations between junior and senior *muazzafeen*. Here the ties of kinship are the most important.

Officials and traders use their kin relations for their own advancements in all matters of administrative hierarchy. For example, traders find it difficult to receive payments from the Regional Councils. Junior officials must prepare several papers and a senior must approve the payment. Many regulations hold up the whole process, but kin ties speed it up considerably. Junior officials use kin relations in securing promotions, vacations, and transfers. Official equipment (cars, telephones) are used by juniors to help their relatives, and regulations are ignored or violated for the benefit of relations and friends. The railways are a prime example. Officials are entitled to several free or reduced-charge tickets a year and these have become an index of how close family relations are. They involve a whole system of relationships between official, family, and railway personnel. The Sudan Railways Corporation sustains heavy losses as a result.

In informal association also *muazzafeen* tend to follow the a pattern set in the office. *Muazzafeen* with shared professional experiences tend to have less conflict in their work and tend to cooperate in administrative situations. Conflicts arise especially when several departments have to cooperate and there is a perceived difference of status between the departments. Officials also belong to trade unions of which there are many in the different agencies and parts of the provincial administration. They pay dues but seldom meet to discuss their problems. The unions are not very effective in improving their members' standard of living. Senior *muazzafeen* regard them as troublesome. Union leaders tend to defer to the senior officials and neglect to press legitimate claims. Demands for change in administrative structure and function, relations between senior and junior officials, salaries and office privileges, and relations between unions and the political organization are regular trade union affairs, yet they are not always pursued with diligence and commitment. Local unions are supposed to wait for directives from Khartoum yet the members in Damazin and Roseiris often act before receiving them. In the 1978 accountants' strike, the local officials struck before they received word from their leaders. Local members believe that their leaders are conciliatory to senior administrative and political officers, so they retain the right to strike apart from their leadership.

Senior and junior officials are mistrustful and dissatisfied with each other. Senior officials are uninterested in their junior officers, while the juniors feel the seniors are too bureaucratized and arrogant, and they complain that office regulations are not enough to assure good office work. Nevertheless there are informal relations between juniors and seniors. They pay house visits, invite each other to feasts, and evening drinks. These relations are significant for office work as well. Some problems left unresolved during the day are discussed freely over drinks at night and may be worked out to mutual satisfaction. On the other hand conflicts may also arise during the night, in which case hostile reports get written the next day. A minority of officials are therefore against mixing office and social relations in any way. The Damazin Muazzafeen Club is frequented by senior officials and wealthy merchants but juniors stay away.

Markets and Development

In 1970 the regime embarked on massive nationalization and confiscation of foreign and local enterprises. But, "the private sector still holds dominance in the fields of trade and industry. According to a 1971 industrial survey the share of the private sector accounted for 73% of the total number of industrial establishments, 42% of total industrial employment, 47% of total industrial wage,..... and 40% of capital investment in agriculture....But one of the main characteristics of the private sector industrial establishments is that they are dominated by small size units" (The Six Year Plan: 137). Table 5.1 shows public and private sector investment during the period 1968/1971-72: we may note a considerable decline in the private sector.

In 1971, the May regime crushed a pro-communist coup and set up a presidential single-party system. Thus the Charter for National Action (1971) was amended to foster new political and economic policies. The charter aimed

> To speed up the process of liberation, the resolution will continue broadening the public sector and strengthening it as the leading sector of the economy...This sector was broadened by legitimate nationalization which was not meant to be a punishment for foreign or local capital. Nationalization was taken up as a lever of socialist development and a factor in creating a healthy atmosphere for speedy growth... The Revolution, however, does not put the public sector at loggerheads with the private sector, nor is it a substitute to it. They both complement each other. The private sector has a historic role to play. In order to play it, it is provided with all necessary legitimate guarantees. (Charter for National Action, 1971: chapter 3).

Eventually, foreign and national capital were asked to participate in development. The Industrial Investment Act and the Agricultural Investment Act were issued with special emphasis on incentives and concessions to the private sector. Also, the Six-Year Plan of Economic and Social Development 1977/78-1982/83 aimed to help the private sector to "invest and mobilize its savings." Political changes were made by the regime to facilitate private investment in the economy.

Officials have close personal relations with traders in the *suq* (see Chapter 2). To procure food and other commodities *muazzafeen* rely on merchants, just as other people do. But because of their official position they are able to facilitate the merchants' sometimes troubled relations with the provincial administration. The latter, of course, depends on traders and markets for its own supplies, spare parts, and equipment. Many people believe the merchants' safes hold more than the government's bank. Close ties between merchant and official are to the mutual benefit of both. Senior *muazzafeen* tend to establish credit and installment relations with a big

TABLE 5.1

PUBLIC AND PRIVATE INVESTMENT

Year	Private Sector Amount (In LS)	Public Sector Amount	Total
1968	56	25	81
1969	55	31	86
1969/70	64	32	96
1970/71	63	27	90
1971/72	10	66	76
TOTAL	248	181	429

trader *(tigar)* for their own personal purposes, and the trader in turn gets the orders for the needs of provincial administrative units. Through their relations to the officials, the merchants demand and get immediate payment. Under ordinary circumstances payments are often delayed and bills have to pass through many offices of government corporations and agencies directed from headquarters in Khartoum. Cash is always in short supply. However, personal relations cut through the regulations, and in the link between official and merchant the informal rather than the official relations count. This personal interaction also helps merchants vary prices in their dealings with administrative units since People's Councils and other provincial units do not use a uniform system in awarding contracts. Informal relations can secure orders for merchants on an individual basis, at an advantageous price.

The cost of living is considered to be high for *muazzafeen* in Damazin/Roseiris. Senior officials are well-placed through their ties with big merchants. For them supplies and goods flow without interruption throughout the long months of autumn scarcity (May to October). However, junior officials face hardships during this season when the rains disrupt all movements and may form corporatives to secure their basic household necessities and needs. Even though the cooperatives' office of the provincial administration supports them, the cooperatives themselves lack capital. The provincial supply office provides the cooperatives with a set percentage of goods such as tea, sugar, cooking oil, flour and grain, upon cash payment. But the cooperative structure is cumbersome, being built on local, regional, and national cooperatives. Prices increase at all levels, so by the time goods reach the officials they are either level with open market rates or slightly higher. Still, officials believe in cooperatives because these were set up for them to be directed by them in an egalitarian manner. Thus cooperatives are compatible with the cultural and Islamic values of Sudanese society. Junior *muazzafeen* tend to sell or barter their goods to merchants for cash or other goods. Also, high officials and big merchants cultivate their ties and relationships to mutual advantage. They can be found spending time together in the Damazin Muazzafeen Club, visiting each other in office, store, and home. In these and other ways, merchants have access to restricted wholesale commodities such as sugar, oil, and flour.

Big merchants supply the provincial administration and government agencies with building materials, food stuffs, and office furniture. They bring essential items such as sugar and flour from Khartoum. They also own mechanized farms and rent houses to officials, and the administration. They even provide cash loans to the province when cash runs too short to pay officials, and contribute funds to the celebration of national holidays and religious festivals. Thus big merchants are essential to the functioning of the provincial administration. They are also active in the elective offices of local government and of the SSU. Merchants and officials comprise 2/3 of these various councils and political committees. Officials tend to become merchants upon retiring from the provincial administration, and some own merchanized farms and pursue trading activities even while members of the administration.

Senior officials enjoy a higher standard of living than the lower ranking *muazzafeen*. But their expenses create strains: cars, houses, and good education for children are costly yet expected of senior administrators. Their life style has further repercussions: officials find they have to maintain certain standards to meet the expectation of honour and respect. High office status demands a style of living that induces respect but the costs of this cannot be secured from salaries. Hence, the attraction of business deals and relationships in the market. Both officials and merchants need good connections in Khartoum and senior officials can facilitate the business of particular merchants through government contracts and the supply of controlled items such as gasoline. Calling on their contacts in the central administration, officials can make things easier for particular merchants. The latter may in turn give special consideration by accepting installment payments for supplies and services. Officials may also counteract the role of elected councils and act unilaterally in the private sector. In this case, the maze of regulations can be used to justify the actions of *muazzafeen* even in opposition to the wishes of committees and trade unions. In these matters, seniors tend to back up the decisions taken even by junior officials.

The role of officials in development administration is highlighted by the problem of the nomads. About 58% of the population of the Blue Nile Province are nomads. Their animal wealth and cultural values run counter to the aims and assumptions of the new provincial administration in

Damazin. The latter favors the expansion of mechanized agriculture and this directly threatens the nomads' way of life. Periodic conferences are held between nomads and officials to discuss various issues. One such conference was called in 1978 by the nomads and several groups such as the Kenana and the Rufa'a participated. However many invited officials did not turn up. Those who came spoke generally and enthusiastically of the advantages of a more settled way of life. Modern grazing, intensive husbandry, and animal related industries were explained by the top veterinary officials. However, senior officials of the labor, police, agriculture, cooperatives, and other departments did not attend. Though the labor department did not attend, it complained that the nomads did not follow procedures in organizing their union, and that their "ignorance" of bureaucratic regulations was not an acceptable excuse. The nomads loudly demanded water, land for settlement, modern amenities, and improved style and means of living. The secretary of the union declared that "nomads are no longer a tribal group. They live in villages and take interest in changing social and economic conditions of living. They are eager to harness their natural wealth for the betterment of their lives." Yet the nomads feel threatened by the extension of mechanized farms which increasingly encroach on what they regard as their customary grazing lands. Although they take some of the mechanized farms allotted to them as compensation, most of these development plans directly interfere with their animals' grazing lands. In addition the schemes also remove from the land the indigenous inhabitants who are rainfed, subsistance farmers and/or part-time nomads. The extension of mechanized farms is not always planned and is often illegal. Furthermore the owners enclose water holes, reduce passage ways of animals, and encroach on grazing lands. Altercations between nomads and farmers escalate quickly to armed feuding (see Chapter 4). Expansion of mechanized farms in the northern part of the province and the shortage of grazing lands is becoming acute. Officials are deeply involved in the allotment of mechanized farms. Some of the larger development projects are planned from Khartoum but local officials decide on most farms under 1,000 *fedans*. The mechanized farms proliferate, while the provision for passage ways and nomads' land remain unfulfilled.

Junior *muazzafeen*, among whom the nomads are very well represented, display a keen understanding of the nomads' position. They point out that the nomads need to be told of the provisions available for them and to be guided and helped by the various agencies and departments. Even senior officials (especially those related to nomads) will point out that development administration is impossible without a solution of the nomadic question. But most officials claim that this is an issue to be solved and decided by the central government. Great waste results from armed protection being provided to the farms against the nomads. However it is difficult for the administration to admit a rightful place for the nomads in the current framework of development. Government agencies are incapable or unwilling to give a role to nomads in development since the provincial administration is oriented towards the central government, and the latter has little understanding of the different roles nomads' perform. Thus even sympathetic officials find it difficult to do anything for the nomads. Any such attempt puts them at loggerheads with the Commissioner and the central government. At this point there is almost a total lack of contact between government and nomad with the former relying on directives which are not implemented and the latter resisting pressure and manipulation. The result is a danger to peace and to the future development of the province.

Relations in the Office

The sytem of transfering officers from province to province forms the core problem of *muazzafeen* life. Transfers are important for they create changes on both personal and administrative levels in the offices. They may also create deep social and psychological conflicts as well as failures in administration. Transfers are handled by senior officials in the headquarters of the central government, and the provincial administration has little say officially. Nevertheless decisions are rarely made without prior contact with senior *muazzafeen* in Damazin. Junior officials accept their new postings since they cannot start petitions to stay in their present position and oppose the transfer before taking up new appointments. The scepter of disciplinary boards and held-up pay are strong deterrents, since the last salary payment of the old post is only given upon joining the new one. Junior officials complain of stubborness, strictness, and arrogance of the senior officials in the handling of transfers, and too often bureaucratic regulations are honored above social and other considerations. At the same time, the system is haphazard, replaced and transferred officers do not show up, and posts are kept vacant for long periods of time. In general, a transfer is obligatory in the public service and vacancies have to be filled with qualified personnel. Although the *muazzafeen's* own wishes are to be considered, there is no provision for the adjustment of administrative and social requirements, and juniors complain that the system is applied mechanically. Officials are entitled to a statement of transfer preference only after completing two years of service, but even after that, short-term deputation to other units or branches is mandatory. Orders for such postings may come through pressure from merchants, politicians, or other officials.

There is a conflict between the functioning of transfers and the *muazzafeen's* own desires. Paramount to the latter are family considerations. Administrative regulations place great emphasis on transfer lists and on complying with transfer orders. However mediation through relatives and various interest groups results in more amendments to transfer lists than do formal petitions. Also, there is passive resistance: in a recent case only one of 40 transferees arrived at Damazin and that one was originally from Damazin. It is advantageous to keep officials in or near their places of origin, since staying with their families creates better working conditions for *muazzafeen*. Yet senior officials do not condone excessive concern with the family. They hold that the power of superior status should not be questioned. However, nepotism and favoritism are the result.

Junior *muazzafeen* argue that good performance rests on good will, and assert that it is for the sake of their families that they go through all the frustrations and difficulties of their jobs. Juniors complain that senior officials have a say in their own transfers and lose their privileges only if their relations with headquarters deteriorate. But junior officials use every subterfuge in pressing their case not to accept a transfer. As a result of unwanted transfers, absenteeism is rampant and various legal ways (such as sick leave) are exploited to the full. Lower-ranking officials are unanimous in their desire to see the transfer system democratized.

Promotions are another bone of contention. Promotion lists are issued by the Establishment Office in Khartoum and approved by the Minister of Public Service and Administrative Reform. The criteria are seniority, educational level, and recommendations on the basis of previous service. Promotion lists are secret and boards make their selection from among competing juniors, but many feel that decisions are based on secret reports of officials not necessarily in the strict lines of formal evaluation. Personal impressions are important so junior *muazzafeen* offer many services to their superiors in the hope of good reports (whether these are solicited or just sent in on initiative).

Office regulations govern the relations between senior and junior officials. Only the seniors' assistants among the junior *muazzafeen* are supposed to have contact with the seniors. Nevertheless, contact is maintained, but has to be pursued with strict adherence to authority and hierarchy. Senior officials are adamant about following the regulations concerning intra-office relations. Yet, "over-stepping" is widely practiced. This practice refers to junior *muazzafeen* making decisions that can only be made, according to regulations, by senior officials. Juniors often make direct contact with other offices for the benefit of their own unit, a practice that is always met with the disapproval of senior officials. Even if the action is for administrative efficiency, it being against the rules is enough to raise the ire of senior administrators. In theory, the hierarchy in the relations between offices and officials is to be strictly observed. Yet, senior officials routinely overstep the authority of the Executive Director in their dealings with the CP. The ED is supposed to be the go-between the CP and the heads of provincial units, but senior officials claim that officers can dispense with hierarchy in the name of speed and efficiency. This, however, does not extend to the actions of their juniors.

6

Village Development Projects: A Case Study

The great Gezira scheme with its massive structure of administration and tenancy was a mainstay of Sudan's export economy and has influenced all thinking on subsequent development.[1] But the big schemes have long been plagued with problems and clearly they are neither the only, nor the best answer to the problems of the country. Unfortunately, a more recent alternative, the smaller scale rural development project is also facing a host of problems. Very little is known about the local level prior to and during any encounter with development. In this chapter we examine a relatively small, so called integrated rural development project, in an area which has not been studied before, but one that has long participated in the wider systems of the region's culture, economy, and society. Here too, however, the lesson is the same, the targeted villages and social groups are not a self contained society in themselves -- merchants, officials of Roseiris-Damazin, and planners in Khartoum and abroad (including those who would develop the Eastern Sudan) are as relevant to the discussion of a project as the social organization of villages.

The rural area of the province consists of clusters of villages. A number of households make up a cluster. The unit of production and consumption is the household. Upon marriage, men are expected to set up separate households, but such households can remain within the father's compound. For purposes of production, though not necessarily consumption, newly established households are separate units. Three to seven households can be found within a compound. For our purposes, a household or family consists of a man and wife, children, and at times, the parents of the man.

We will use family and household in the above senses, keeping in mind the importance of a layered system of relationships. Lineage, tribe, and even large households divide into smaller units. Such fissions occur along the lines of work and production, the new units retaining cultural ties to the larger group. Kinship sentiment and other ties of relationship remain intact. In daily village life, families who farm separate plots keep close ties with their affinal and consanguineal relatives.

Members of a household share implements and agricultural produce. The availability of extra labor is crucial for the organization of small farms. It is difficult to work a farm for a small family especially in the case of young childbearing women, since the cultural norm does not expect a mother to participate in farm labor. If *nafir* (communal work) is called, it is not necessarily the kinship-based organization which is called upon but the members of the village.

There is a strong sense of familial ties among rural people. People in the Blue Nile Province more or less follow the Arab model of patrilineal descent with authority vested in the men of the household. Women are relegated to the private sphere, a thatched roof hut with a *rakouba* (an attached shelter made of straw and mud). But as we noted in Chapter 3 the majority of women can not be kept away from the public arena. There is a prevailing ideology that women are to be protected and separated from the outside world, a picture close to that given for Arab women. Contrary to the expected norm, in addition to household chores and duties, women take part in various income generating activities as co-workers with their brothers, husbands, or sons.

Sharing farm labor and active participation of women on the farms are not the kind of information a male farmer would acknowledge. To the outside world, rural women are far from being simply householders. It is important to note this discrepancy between ideal and practical images of male and female relationships. We saw in Chapter 3 how development efforts have bypassed women and concentrated on the work of men in the households.

The village has one voice that includes all the people in all matters, and any decision about change is discussed before it is instituted. Each village has a separate rural council and its own spheres of economic, social and political activities. The village is marked by its geographic boundary, and this serves to delineate also the village as culturally constituted. Villages in the eastern Sudan differ from those in the north.

Traditionally, at the top of village hierarchy sat the Sheikh who was in turn responsible to the Omda.[2] On the village level the Sheikh was the voice of authority. The dissolution of Omdaship and other forms of traditional rule leaves the Sheikh still in control, but the authority structure has taken on the characteristics of incipient *class* formation. The merchant and the appointed officials further afield can, in principle, overrule the Sheikh and other locally elected politicians. Unofficially the merchant holds the highest position because he has the only economic power in the village. He owns the local shop and caters to the villagers' needs. The villagers depend on him for daily basic needs, and approach him for credit. As the economic agent, the merchant provides credit and dictates the political and social mood of the village.[3]

The new voices in the village are the merchants, teachers, and nurses. These are not necessarily local inhabitants. The recent shift in power relations place economic and educational factors over the traditional social hierarchy.[4] Villages today operate under two systems of hierarchy, formal and informal. Outside agents of change work with the formal structure, since economic development in whatever form comes down from the top, the government, to the grassroot political representative in the village.

Objectives of the Project

In discussing the goals and impact of the Blue Nile Integrated Agricultural Development Project (BNIADP) we are mainly concerned with the social and cultural patterns of rural communities before they undergo development. This case should be salutary since social science research was to be a central feature of the project, and extensive studies and surveys were undertaken before the project plans were implemented. Project goals were discussed in the light of the sociological findings, and methods of intervention were to be tailored to the conditions encountered in the project area. We give below an outline of village organization and structure, the occupation of the inhabitants, and the age, health, and educational level of adult men and women.

The project area is about 60 km southeast of Damazin. There are only fair-weather tracks, no permanent roads to the area. There are some 2500 families in 8 villages, belonging to various social groups in the project area (see Figure 6.1 and Table 6.1). Figure 6.1 shows the village layout characteristic of this area. Note the prominence of the *dokan* (village store), the school, and the clinic in the middle of the village cluster. These three centers attract villagers who gather around daily, gossiping and discussing market prices, local, and national news, and make decisions concerning village welfare. The size of the project area was not determined precisely since the terrain and the scattered nature of the settlements made it necessary to concentrate on families rather than territory. Figure 6.1 gives an idea of the area: a rectangle about 20 miles wide and 30 miles long. Table 6.2 shows the *gabila* (tribal) affiliation of villages: the Berta are the most numerous, followed by the Jebelawin, Funj, and Hamaj. These groups are the original inhabitants of the region. Table 6.1 lists the number of households and the average family size by village, the highest number per household being 8.41 and the lowest 5.41.

BNIADP was an interdisciplinary development project designed with three major objectives. First, to introduce appropriate technology into the area for the enhancement of the lives of the residents with specific emphasis on a side-by-side comparison of alternative systems of agricultural production. Second, to undertake sociological, anthropological, and economic studies about the technological impact on traditional farming. Third, to develop a trained cadre of locals and Sudanese government officials capable of designing and implementing similar development projects.

The project was designed to produce and test a system for comparing development approaches in the traditional agricultural and livestock sectors of Sudan. The beneficiaries of the project were to be the small producers in

TABLE 6.1

NUMBER OF HOUSEHOLDS AND AVERAGE FAMILY SIZE
BY VILLAGE

Villages	Number of Households (a)	Average Family Size (b)
Abu Gumai	225	8.41
Dan Dan	61	6.42
Dan Dan Azaza	117	6.41
Shaera	66	5.41
Abu Shenina	177	5.47
Esseil	88	7.31
Illyas	128	5.61
Kharen-Kharen	138	7.33
Total	1,000	N/A

(a) Census Data
(b) Derived from panel family data

a selected rainfed area of the Blue Nile Province. A series of integrated rural interventions on behalf of the small producer along with partial mechanization and improved agricultural practices were applied in different parts of the project area. This was to help develop a viable system to compare and test the application of farm machinery to the traditional farms of rural Sudan.

A series of micro-interventions was used to stimulate the social and economic life as well as influence the regional infrastructure. The primary goal was to increase the production of 2,500 traditional farming and 3,300 nomad herding families in the area. Assistance in improving the economic condition of farmers and herders was to lead to building up the provincial government's planning and design capabilities for the traditional sector of the province. This would become possible through the development and verification of an effective systems approach to small farm and livestock improvement in the traditonal area.[5] The agricultural component of the GOS Six Year Development Plan (1977-1982) was taken into account during the planning of the project, hence the emphasis was placed on improving the traditional agriultural sector and the lot of small producers.[6]

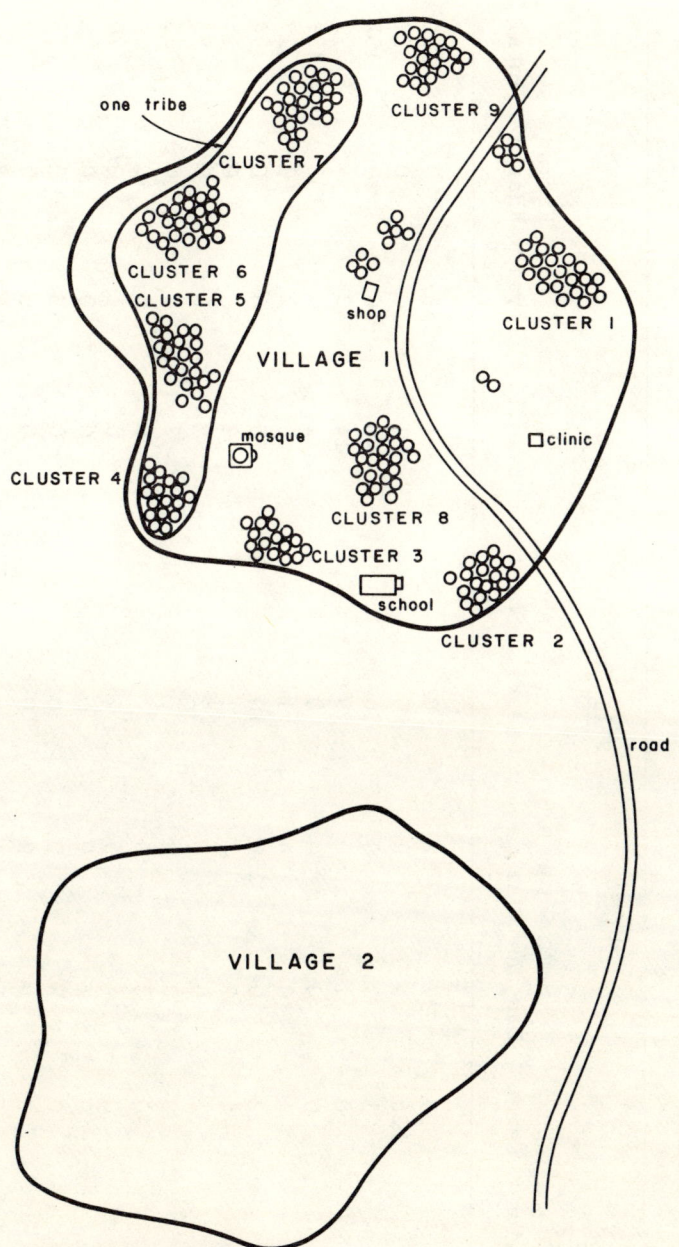

Figure 6.1 Village clusters

TABLE 6.2

TRIBAL AFFILIATION OF HEADS OF HOUSEHOLDS AS DETERMINED BY CENSUS

Tribal Affiliation	Villages							
	Abu Gumai	Dan Dan	Dan Dan Azaza	Shaera	Abu Shenina	Esseil	Illyas	Kharan Kharan	Total
Berta	39	37	48	0	11	1	46	0	182
Hameg	126	0	0	0	4	1	0	0	131
Jebelawin	1	0	0	36	75	40	0	0	152
Fung	0	2	0	9	14	14	49	4	92
Ragreg	0	0	0	0	6	1	0	132	139
Fellata	4	0	4	1	0	6	2	0	17
Hausa	12	0	56	10	1	15	0	0	94
Dongalawi	0	2	1	1	8	0	3	0	15
Gaalien	34	0	0	2	8	3	8	0	55
Mahas	0	0	2	1	10	2	0	0	15
Merfab	0	0	0	1	0	0	0	0	1
Yagubab	0	14	5	0	0	0	1	0	20
Sardia	0	1	0	0	7	0	0	0	8
Hadara	0	3	0	0	9	0	13	0	25
Dowala	2	0	0	0	1	0	0	0	3
Other	7	2	1	5	23	5	6	2	51
Total	225	61	117	66	177	88	128	138	1,000

Results of the Research

Occupation, Education, Age, and Health

The main occupation of rural people is farming. In the project area, most people are subsistence farmers although many have more than one occupation, combining farming with fishing, carpentry, and mechanics. Tables 6.2 and 6.3 show the breakdown of the project area's professional activities as well as tribal affiliations. Presently, few farmers who cultivate the traditional plots of 7 to 10 *feddan* per household can subsist on farming alone. Especially after the harvest in December/January, many migrate in search of work. For some, outmigration from the village for 3 or 4 months is an established pattern. Yet additional income generating activities do not conflict with farming. Farmers return to their *dahari* before cultivation begins. Some of the more popular and renumerative forms of income generating activity are rope or charcoal making, tailoring, and working as a mechanic or driver. Fish consumption has increased recently. Refrigerated trucks drive to Abu Gumai hauling the fish away to district and city markets. The influx of Hausa and Fellata migrants to some of the project area villages have introduced fish to the local diet. In some Hausa dominated villages fishing is the primary occupation.[7]

In the Sudan farming is not a lowly profession and to work the land is in itself highly regarded. To farm one's own land is an honorable, culturally approved profession, and the farmers expect their children to take up the same occupation. However, since today's small plots are not enough to subsist on, children of farmers seek alternative means of livelihood. The physical labor invested on the land is not enough to compensate, nor to warrant a farmer to continue tilling the land. Though a mass exodus of farmers has not taken place, the option to migrate is becoming a viable reality for many rural farmers.

In the past, production from a subsistence farm was sufficient to meet the daily consumption of a rural family. Farmers would not conceive of buying grain, they grew all the grain they consumed. Because of the recent rise in daily living expenses and the introduction of consumer goods into the rural areas a rural household has to supplement its income.

Not all the people in the Blue Nile Project area can remember their own age or that of their children. Nonetheless, girls tend to marry at an early age, soon after they achieve puberty. It is not uncommon for a man in his late 50's to marry and acquire a third or fourth wife who is barely 16 years old. Tables 6.4 and 6.5 show the age structure for heads of households and the level of educational attainment per village. Historical facts are used as markers to estimate one's age, and these dates may be the coming of the British to the area, the rise of the Mahdi, the building of the Roseiris dam, Sudanese independence, and the like. The average age of men is approximately 42 to 43 years, and 34 for women. There is usually a 10-year age difference between wife and husband.

The younger generation has a higher level of educational attainment

TABLE 6.3

PROFESSIONS REPORTED BY HEADS OF HOUSEHOLDS BY VILLAGE:

Villages

Profession	Abu Gumai	Dan Dan	Dan Dan Azaza	Shaera	Abu Shenina	Esseil	Illyas	Kharan Kharan	Total
Farmer	219	61	116	66	164	86	122	132	966
Hunter	3	2	0	0	0	2	0	0	7
Carpenter	0	0	0	1	0	0	0	0	1
Merchant	4	1	1	2	5	3	5	2	23
Tailor	2	0	0	0	0	1	1	0	4
Teacher	3	0	0	0	1	0	0	0	4
Blacksmith	1	0	0	0	0	1	0	0	2
Driver	11	0	0	0	0	0	0	0	11
Ropemaker	0	0	0	0	0	0	0	1	1
Cook	13	0	0	0	0	0	0	0	13
Unemployed	16	0	1	0	4	2	3	3	29
Other	14	0	2	7	16	4	13	5	61

TABLE 6.4

NUMBER OF HEADS OF HOUSEHOLD BY VILLAGE BY AGE CATEGORY

Category	Abu Gumai	Dan Dan	Dan Dan Azaza	Villages Shaera	Abu Shenina	Esseil	Illyas	Kharen Kharen	Total
20 & under	4	3	8	0	4	2	3	4	28
21-25	22	1	8	9	13	7	6	12	78
26-30	43	9	13	7	32	14	20	28	166
31-35	26	9	10	6	19	14	16	16	116
36-40	29	8	17	13	21	11	18	19	136
41-45	24	7	14	6	16	11	8	4	90
46-50	21	4	13	5	19	3	10	11	86
51-60	29	7	18	12	13	19	21	18	137
61-70	16	7	11	4	17	7	17	15	94
Over 70	11	6	5	4	23	0	9	11	69
Total	225	61	117	66	177	88	128	138	1,000

TABLE 6.5

NUMBER OF HEADS OF HOUSEHOLD BY VILLAGE BY LEVEL OF ATTAINMENT FOR BOTH RELIGIOUS AND SECULAR SCHOOLS

Type of School and Attainment	Villages							
	Abu Gumai	Dan Dan	Dan Dan Azaza	Shaera	Abu Shenina	Esseil	Illyas Kharan	Kharan	Total

Type of School and Attainment	Abu Gumai	Dan Dan	Dan Dan Azaza	Shaera	Abu Shenina	Esseil	Illyas Kharan	Kharan	Total
Khalwa									
1 year	12	0	7	2	1	0	2	1	25
2 years	4	0	6	0	6	1	2	1	20
3-5 years	17	2	11	3	6	5	7	2	53
6-10 years	4	0	16	5	11	6	4	0	46
more than 10	1	0	18	6	1	6	2	0	34
no response	187	59	59	50	152	70	111	134	822
Total	225	61	117	66	177	88	128	138	1,000
Secular School									
1 year	1	0	1	0	4	1	1	0	8
2 years	5	0	0	2	4	1	0	2	14
3-5 years	16	7	3	5	22	4	8	9	74
6-10 years	7	0	2	0	4	0	2	1	16
more than 10	2	0	0	0	2	0	1	0	5
no response	194	54	111	59	141	82	116	126	883
Total	225	61	117	66	177	88	128	138	1,000

than the older generation. There are two types of schooling available in the rural areas, formal and informal. Informal schooling tends to be concentrated in the Koranic *khalwas* where religious learning and guidance predominate. Again, it is not remarkable to find that the elder generation spent more years at the *khalwa* than the children. Girls and boys begin to attend *khalwas* at about 5-7 years of age. The Koran is memorized and recitation is also taught. Boys can continue to attend Koranic schools, but girls stop attendance after puberty. Post-puberty girls, from the age of 12 on, assist in the household chores or start their own families.

Formal education is available in each village. It may extend up to the end of the elementary level; for high school, students have to go to the two towns. One of the two surveys showed that about 7 male heads of households have received a primary level of schooling and more. The elder generation prefer *khalwa* education and for men there is no limit to *khalwa* attendance (see Table 6.5). This is not true for wives, even those who are young. Many wives and mothers in their early or late 20's lack any formal education. Being girls, they are kept to help on the farm, working the *juruf* and *abala* lands as well as domestic chores. The most productive women are in their 20's; a woman raises a family and assists her husband in farming.

The preference is for large families. It means additional hands to work the land, which in turn increases one's income. Men are encouraged to contract more than one marriage. The sucessful households are those where the head of the family has more than one wife. One can see a logic emerging in the rural areas: large fields and large families lead to an increase in one's income and to an increase in prestige and status in society. Such expectations hold true irrespective of the level of education or even the health and age of the people involved.

Agricultural production seems to dominate the primary concerns of the villagers. Children are kept away from school if they are needed to assist on the farms. If a family has a choice, girls are removed from schools first, but prominent families demand a higher level of education for their children than poorer ones. Because of poor or erratic attendance, schools in the villages are not performing adequately. There are no incentives for the parents or the students to continue with formal education. What is most immediate and of utmost urgency is the labor needed on the farm.

Rural inhabitants are in poor health, suffering from local ecological diseases, malaria and schistosomaiasis. Hence the poor school attendance, especially during planting. Low income proves prohibitive to procuring the necessary medicine to combat illnesses. Illiteracy is very high, with women having the highest proportion of illiterates in village. Income is low and continues to decline. Average annual income of a rural household in 1978 was estimated at LS195 and in 1980 LS310.59.[8] Subsistence farmers depend on agricultural production and can supplement their income only after the harvest of their crops (see Table 6.6).

TABLE 6.6

TOTAL ANNUAL EARNED HOUSEHOLD INCOME IN 1980

Villages	Mean	Median	Maximum	Minimum
Abu Gumai	291.0	200	6,000	3
Dan Dan	303.0	195	2,000	28
Dan Dan Azaza	209.5	165	1,066	17
Shaera	522.9	347	5,500	25
Abu Shenina	337.0	216	6,300	9
Esseil	362.6	250	2,300	11
Illyas	308.7	175	4,900	11
Kharen Kharen	150.0	75	3,500	–

Land Use and Food Production

Land in the Sudan falls under two categories, registered and unregistered. All unregistered land belongs to the government, the distinction between the right of use and the ownership of land being quite clear. The use of agricultural or pasture lands falls under unregistered lands. In most of the Sudan land ownership has to do with use and falls within the jurisdiction of the villages. However even land in use can be reclaimed by the government, under the Government of Sudan Land Regulation Act, unless the land was registered prior to 1972. The issue of land ownership in the project area is not any different from other parts of the Sudan. Because of the Land Act, land disputes are over village landholding, and not over ownership, sale, and inheritance. The village Sheikh allots lands for use in the village.

Traditionally each village owned its own farming lands and in some cases the *juruf* land along the river bank (see Figure 6.2). The responsibility to allot land for cultivation lay within the jurisdiction of the Sheikh. Village farmers could expand their land holdings, opt to clear a new plot, or work lands not in use. Newcomers to a village sought from the Sheikh the right to use farm lands in the village. Land was granted to a newcomer after consulting the other villagers. In the past, due to the abundance of farm lands, land disputes were minimal in the native and civil courts. Given the present expansion mechanized farms and the curtailment of nomadic pasture land, land-use disputes are increasing at a rapid rate.

In discussing agricultural development in the Sudan, we emphasize the different and special use of land by the rural farmer. Agricultural lands are not all used solely for farming of cash or subsistence crops. Land *(teen)* is divided into three separate categories and all three can be found in different parts of a village. Taking the project area as our example, we find that land is divided into *dahari, juruf,* and *abala* lands (Figure 6.2 illustrates types of rural land use). Land is used for both crop cultivation and nomadic cattle grazing. This dual form of economic activity, though part of traditional Sudanese rural life, is rapidly changing. Changes in the agrarian system, the use of land, crop production, alternative system of farming, and the use of labor in the rural areas also affect the types and uses of land. A brief description of rural land use and family structure will help in understanding current changes in agricultural practice as a result of rural economic development.

Dahari or *bildaat* are farm lands devoted to sorghum and sesame cropping. These plots surround the village, a distance of an hour's walk from the houses. *Dahari* lands are used for a period of 5 to 7 years after which newer plots are cleared for farming. The slash and burn method which is practiced on most of Sudan's rural subsistence farms is also undergoing change. With 5 to 7 *feddan* plots, working a new *dahari* is not taxing to the farming household (1 *feddan* = 1.04 acres).

The use of *dahari* lands can be passed on to one's children though not as a form of inheritance. A man's children have the first right to use their

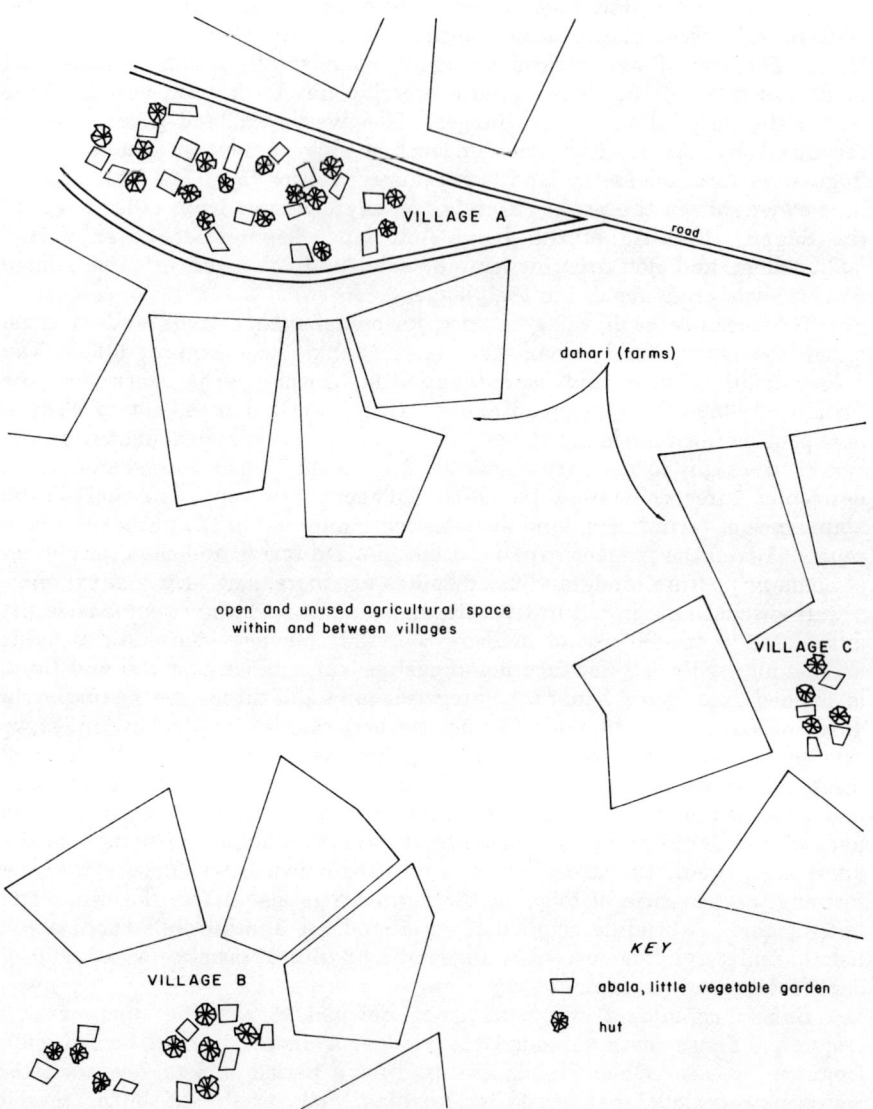

Figure 6.2 Rural Land Use

father's land before it is passed on to communal village use. Some of these plots are clearly demarcated, though others are not. Farmers have enough space to expand or cultivate a new plot. There is an unstated understanding regarding the direction a farmer can expand his fields or clear a new plot, without infringing the rights of village farmers or farmers from adjacent villages. In the Blue Nile Province, villages are well scattered and thus *dahari* expansion did not use to pose a problem. Culturally *dahari* lands are considered to be the responsibility of men. Though women are active laborers on *dahari* lands, they are considered to be assistants. Sesame and sorghum (*dura*) are two crops cultivated on the *dahari*, with *dura* the consumable crop and sesame the cash crop. Ocasionally other crops are also cultivated on *dahari* lands.

The major part of rural household labor is invested in *dahari* lands since the household maintains itself through products of such land. The family as a unit: men, women, and children, begin to clear the fields in the months of April and May. Using a *saiif* (sword), bushes are removed and trees and grasses are cut. Soon after the second rain the farmers begin *dura* and sesame planting. Although farmers will not divulge the exact planting date, an approximate time may be given. Farmers do not cultivate as a group and the family as a unit prepares the land before seeding begins. When the crop is a foot high, after about 4 to 6 weeks, women will assist their husbands in the first weeding, locally known as *mur*. There are three or more types of weeding: *mur*, *kadeb*, and *hash*. Weeding is a time consuming and very difficult activity. Without a family, a farmer will call for *nafir* to assist him and supply his work mates food and drink during work days. He will also hire wage laborers if any are available. Because the villagers do not plant their fields on the same day, it is possible to assist each other in various stages of the cultivation cycle, especially weeding. The work invested in a new plot is locally known as *duwerta*, followed by *umbahate* when the trees are cut down, the stumps being left in the ground.

Dahari lands (also known as *bildaat*) do not necessarily compete, in terms of labor needs, with *juruf* activities. *Juruf* lands are the strips of land along the Blue Nile. After the rainy season, at the end of October, the river waters recede, leaving fertile alluvial lands on the banks. It is prestigious to have use-access to such lands and in most cases such use is kept within the family. Land litigation in courts mostly concerns *juruf* lands. Vegetables are grown on the *juruf* from February to April, providing additional income to the household.

Abala lands are the women's sole responsibility. These are small plots next to the house.[9] Work on *abala* plots occurs simultaneously with the activities on the *bildaat*, but *abala* receives more attention once the women are done with their farm and household duties.

Different crops are grown on the three types of rural land. *Dura* (sorghum) and seasame are the primary crops on *bildaat*. *Bildaat* are rainfed lands, and crop planting depends on indigenous calendrical calculation. Corn and various types of vegetables are grown on *juruf*.

tomatoes, cucumber, eggplant, peppers, okra, squash, and melons. Women grow corn, okra, and maybe squash on their *abalas*. The labor input on *dahari* begins with land clearing, planting, weeding, followed by *dura* or sesame threshing on the farm or at home, and finally food preservation and storage.[10]

Though *juruf* lands tend to be closer to the village than *dahari* lands, the labor invested in vegetable gardens is tremendous. For two to three months both men, women, and children are actively working on their *juruf*. Unlike the *dura* farms, *juruf* lands need constant protection against nomadic cattle which often stray into the gardens, not to mention bird pests, and the rising theft of local produce. It is not uncommon for a *juruf* owner to camp on his land to protect his produce.

Rural cultivation is not the sole responsibility of men since women and children are active in agriculture. So far, labor on subsistence farms has not been attached to gender, and family members act as a producing unit for household consumption and for the market. Women's role on the mechanized schemes remains periphereal to the management and responsibilities of the large farm.[11]

Belonging to a tribe (*gabila*), village, and family establishes the standing of an individual. The fabric of village life, where members have similar economic and political conditions, had been more equal than is the case at present. Families harvested an equal number of acres per household. *Nafir* (communal, unpaid labor) was used instead of hired wage laborers. Today, in the project area one can find wealthy families in villages which have large *dahari* holdings and which employ paid laborers. Most villagers still depend on *nafir*.

The physical strength of a farmer or the number of people in his household would dicate the amount of cultivable acreage per house. Although the lands of a village are enough for the number of households in the village, individual household possibilities for expansion could create a problem in the future since land is not equitably distributed. Land scarcity in the Sudan is not an issue, but villages have been known to move to new locations because the slash and burn method of farming depletes the nutrients of the land.

The traditional village farmers have a system through which land is used, labor is assigned according to sex and age, and household priorities are ordered. Time spent on planting, harvesting and post-harvesting activities is used according to an age-old pattern, making it a problem to introduce additional acreage for cultivation, unless subsistence farming is radically changed.

Expenditure, Credit, and Indebtedness

Social spending, spending on social occasions in contrast to household expenditure, is similar to other parts of the Sudan. Total expenditures of a household incorporate such spending, especially on the major life cycle rites, demonstrating the close ties between families and the lineage. There are times when expenditure on social affairs exceeds agricultural expenditures (see Table 3.3).

It is evident from numerous surveys that farmers in the Blue Nile Province cannot increase their income solely from agricultural produce.[12] Given the condition of the small plots, the use of primitive implements and an inability to pay the annual debts, the area has remained one of the poorest in the country.

Since the 1970's efforts have been made by both the local government and donor agencies to improve living conditions in the province. It is through the analysis of the AID/Sudan Government project that we question the value, effects, and methods of such development goals. With an annual income of about LS100 a year, any additional economic expansion of the existing infrastructure would improve local conditions. In terms of health, rural farmers are in a poor condition, being afflicted with malaria, especially during rainy season.[13] It is commonly held in the Sudan that farmers are unwilling to complete their work and lack a positive attitude to work. This is an urban view and has no actual foundation. Our research has shown contrary results; agricultural work is often augmented by off-farm work. In fact, the need to improve economic conditions and to hold onto the profession of farming are a primary choice. Unpaid debts and the continuing decline in economic terms have discouraged farmers, forcing them to migrate from their villages to urban areas or abroad in search of work. Though not now at an alarming rate, continued migration can in the long run affect not only the rural but the national economy.

Lack of an organized form of rural credit forces the small farmer to borrow from the local money lenders and merchants. Banks cannot use *dahari* lands or thatched roof huts as collateral. Based on the traditional form of lending, the *shail* system continues to spread in the rural areas. There are no government controls on *shail* since mutual trust, shared beliefs and values, and personal friendship form the underlying "collateral" of the loan. Each village has a shop (*dokan*). The merchant buys his goods from the Damazin or Roseiris market. District merchants in turn receive their supplies from cities. Similarly provincial banks extend cash loans to the merchants who, in turn, perform the same services for their village merchant clients.[14] In the village, *shail* replaces banking arrangements. Interest on loans is collected, the repayment is in kind.

In late March or early April, before the beginning of the rainy season, village merchants procure their loans and supplies. Before planting, rural farmers need cash to purchase seeds, improve (or buy) agricultural implements, and provide other household needs. The sesame produce is mortgaged since *dura* is not a crop which can be used as *shail* repayment.[15] Rarely is borrowed cash returned in the same form, unless one deals with relatives. Normally *shail* is extended as cash, or a farmer may be given an expense account in the merchant's shop.

One must remember that the merchant is the major commercial power in the village. Loans are small in volume and each case is individually assessed, depending on previous experience, work pattern of the individual, the extent of the farm, and most important, the *irfa*, the relationship between the merchant and the farmer. Those farmers who are successful have a better chance for loans. Few farmers have access to cash outside their village merchant. Having repaid last year's debt, a farmer takes a new loan. When the sesame plants are about 10 weeks, a merchant can decide on whether or not to extend the credit. *Shail* disadvantages the farmer since he takes a risk, but if the crop fails the merchant does not recover his debt. Cash loans are tightly controlled by resident village merchants. These merchants are related through kinship and *qabila* (tribe) and see themselves as a class-like group.

The development of the area poses threats to the existing structure of control and marketing of agricultural produce. The village hierarchy (merchants, nurse, teacher, and Sheikh) are threatened since village ties to the provincial town are changing. The likelihood of a surplus crop and improved transportation to the town introduce new marketing control mechanisms and competition, taking away the monopoly and purchasing power of the old village hierarchy. Thus if a farmer does not sell his crops to the village merchants, his loan possibilities will also change. Previously, a farmer in the project area borrowed for 3 reasons; agricultural operations, household expenditures, and expenses incurred for social occasions. We already noted that agricultural financing is not the sole purpose of *shail*.[16]

The first two months of the agricultural cycle are the most important since it is the time when the bulk of the work is accomplished. The rainy season starts as early as May and lasts till November. Between May and November most village farmers return to their *dahari*. *Nafir* is undertaken during the weeding period especially for the first two weedings, *mur* and *kadeb*. Inability to call *nafir* and provide the *dura* plants with both *mur* and *kadeb* weeding can ruin the crop. At times a farmer resorts to paid labor, the cash being borrowed from local merchants. Rural farmers are ready to accept agricultural changes which would relieve them of existing obstacles, the use of outdated farming implements, and the ever increasing indebtedness to money lenders.

Nomadic Transhumance

Prior to the inception of most planned agricultural schemes, the people in the rural area practiced rainfed subsistence agriculture along with semi-pastoralism. Developing the irrigated agricultural side of the economy meant the introduction of social and economic changes along the rivers. Irrigation schemes are located along the rivers, areas which earlier supplied dry season grazing for the nomadic herds.

Grazing lands of the nomads have been affected by the growth of irrigated schemes but equally important is the increased mechanized rainfed cropping. Mechanized rainland farming curtails available rainland grazing, forcing the nomads to move closer to the rivers, losing access to seasonal grazing lands. The irrigated schemes along the river have the alternative of incorporating the pastoralists as agriculturists, or facing the constant threat of cattle entering the farms.

Many nomads who have been squeezed out of their wet and dry grazing lands have opted to give up their traditional work for farming. On many of the irrigated farms tenants were recruited from local nomadic groups. A choice had to be made, a choice which changed the life of the nomad. Presently many schemes contain a large number of local nomads. Although the majority gave up the herds, some kept a part of their animal wealth and retained ties to their former way of life. Thus one finds a high and increasing density of livestock on the schemes. Nomads refuse to completely give up their way of life and this has an impact on the future of the schemes. With the exception of the new Rahad scheme, no irrigated scheme has made an effort to fully incorporate livestock into the project (see Chapter 7).

In the past, there existed a somewhat complementary relationship between the nomad and the subsistence farmer since land was plentiful for both. The relationship between the pastoralists and the irrigation scheme tenants today is more complicated. Some of these ex-pastoralist tenants are discouraged by the low yields and low income of their tenancies. Nonetheless, these "pastoral agriculturists" clearly see that their future as pastoralists is uncertain. Agricultural expansion, in irrigated schemes and mechanized farming, has curbed the dry and wet season grazing rights of nomadic groups. Agricultural expansion, a government priority, is competing with nomadic activities as the basis of livelihood. Pasture lands are depleted, given the increasing number of livestock in a limited area. Traditionally, nomadic groups followed an annual timetable of migration and grazing. Today, the available grazing land is limited and some passages are closed, adding to the increasing number of clashes between the different nomadic groups, not to mention those between nomads and subsistence as well as modern agriculturists. Competition over land and water resources has led pastoralists to encroach on nearby subsistence and irrigated farms.

Though many pastoralists have given up their herds and joined schemes, we must not be deluded that the low income from the new profession will keep them committed to farming. A nomad as a tenant farmer has been able to succeed only because he still owns a small number of animals which he sells from time to time to supplement his agricultural income or to pay wage laborers. The successful ex-pastoralist might use cash income to increase his herd. That perhaps is one of the pastoralist's aims. "This goal is not part of an investment strategy, to convert income or increase of the herd into other values, but is maintained for reasons of prestige: the more animals a man can boast about, the more important he is" (Horowitz, 1979:20).

Joining an agricultural scheme can have a number of divergent aims. Though it is encouraging to find some pastoralists on the schemes, while others go back and forth between being farmers and herders, it is the possibility of off-scheme interests that keeps them on the schemes. Off-scheme ventures differ from one scheme to the other, but an example is the maintenance of small numbers of animals on the scheme. Such ventures have made it possible for the ex-pastoralists to shoulder the burden of "...fluctuating yields, inadequate loans and low prices, and thus, the pursuit of off-schemes interests has enabled the labor upon which the schemes are predicated, to continue to exist" (Sorbo, 1980:3).

The issue of the nomads is not resolved and their role in development is unclear. Yet one has to deal with their existence as a viable economic group. Expanding the agricultural sector at the expense of the nomadic groups is not a solution. Many propositions have been presented for the settlement or the incorporation of the nomads into the national economy (see Dyson-Hudson, 1980). An immediate plan should be adopted to preserve the grazing lands in order to alleviate the ecological crisis in the area due to over-grazing. We agree with Sorbo's recent suggestions (1980) about the measures to preserve the nomadic way.

Accomplishments and Failures

The project started in November 1979, and the contracts of the American technical and managerial staff were to terminate within a five year period. The Americans would leave behind a trained core of Sudanese cadre who were to run the project. The infrastructure needed for the operation of the project, vehicles and housing for the staff, tractors for the mechanized portion of the area, tools, warehouses, offices, and workshops would continue to be available.

In terms of actual performance, the project area's 2,500 families should begin to see the benefit of improved farming at the end of five years (1979-84). From the agronomical side, the work of the experimental demonstration farm would introduce improved seed varieties to project farmers along with a planting and intercropping plan for mechanized and non-mechanized areas. A 20-40% increase in income was anticipated for the rural farmer who adopts improved agricultural practices, participates in village cooperatives, and heeds managerial advice.

The project goals in the provincial town were completed on schedule, but the construction of the physical facilities took more than three years instead of the anticipated one and one-half years. On the agronomical side, farmers were not taught the uses of newly tested agricultural procedures which emphasised new ways of cropping, especially of non-traditional crops. Agricultural development was to be accompanied by the introduction of cooperative credit on a village level. By June 1982, 44 farmers had applied for loans and joined the local cooperatives, and approximately 1,300 *feddans* have been measured for mechanization.

At the beginning of implementation, the training expatriate and Sudanese counterpart staff felt that the credit and cooperative component of the project was so crucial that without it the work could not proceed. Mechanization was introduced in three or four adjacent villages also on a cooperative basis. Time was spent in teaching the cooperative members in each village about rules and by-laws drawn up for their societies. The proposed credit and loan plan suggested for the project area was close to the traditional *muraba* system. Interest was not charged to the individual but a percentage rate based on the farmer's profit was calculated according to his average yield.

Previously, production societies or *j'amaia* were a part of the rural social organization. These groups are formed on the same principles as *nafir* (communal labor). The basis of such organizations is not cash but a shared system of values and beliefs, kinship and tribal ties or just the fact of belonging to the same village. In Illyas, the flour mill *j'amaia* is a classic case of such an organization -- money was collected and in part donated by outside politicians. An annual fee was paid by the villagers for maintenance and wages. Introducing elaborate cooperative and credit by-laws to the villagers under the new plan and completely by-passing the local hierarchy and not making a success of the new system leaves the farmers at the mercy of those who control village society. Yet, having available credit from a second source can in the long term limit the power of the merchant.

The expectations of the farmers from the project diverged somewhat in terms of goals and achievements. Responses from the eight villages point to an improved standard of life. The people hoped that the project will improve transportation, education, provide additional employment, and perhaps encourage the settlement of the nomads. All along the villagers have been eager to help with the implementation of the project. Increase of the rural households' income by 20-40% was also the villagers' goal and expectation. Cooperatives to perform and manage local activities were expected to be set up on a village level, since the inter-tribal cooperation in the villages was not a problem.[17] Many villagers were asked where would they invest the additional income. Building better housing, education of children, improvement of diet and health, adequate clothing for families, and expanding business were some of the answers. The agriculturists wanted to see an improvement in their production and better marketing facilities. The nomads wanted more attention, more pasture lands, wider passage-corridors for travel, and veterinary services for their cattle. Women wanted to improve their working conditions, the marketing of their goods, health care, and a better role in the development process.

These were the goals of the AID project and of the local people. Some were taken up by the planners and implemented -- others were set aside. The project's progress and performance have been very slow. Most of the effort was spent on housing construction for the Sudanese and expatriate staff in the provincial town. Many of the Sudanese counterpart staff were not "seconded" on temporary assignments from their place of work to the project on time, affecting field implementation. By the third year, with the exception of sociological research, hardly any activity took place in the field and project activities tended to concentrate on urban development. For a rural development project, the turn of events has not been appreciated by the local community, not to mention the Sudanese government.

The project's overall progress depends on a number of interrelated components. In the first two years, lack of additional Sudanese staff to complement the expatriates, last minute hiring of untrained staff, lack of living facilities in the project area, problems in securing gasoline, duplication of work, and overlap of responsibilities delayed the completing of plans. Some of these were short-term problems and easier to solve than others. Most seriously, up to 1982, there was no provision for viable and practical planning. This state of affairs effectively blocked all progress. Lack of communication between different sections of the project added to delays. Each separate department had a clear indication of what it intended to do in the following few months, but there was no sense of direction to the work nor an awareness of how the parts fit into a rational whole. It was the consideration of the separate parts which seemed to make sense to the project staff, but not the interconnectedness of the whole effort.

The agronomical section of the project included two experimental farms in 1981, one in the field at Abu Gumai, the other a demonstration farm in Damazin. No tractor or other form of intermediate technology was used on the village farm. All the farm labor was done traditionally, using hand tools. Improved varieties of sorghum, sesame, and a type of legumes were used. Two *feddans* were planted with sorghum, sesame, cow peas, and a legume known as *lablab*. Improved seeds were distributed to some of the families.

The farmers in general were very receptive and did not object to using the improved seeds. Their preference was for *Gadam al Hamam* and *Dabar*, which apparently have out-performed the local hybrid variety by about 70 percent. Though the local variety is resilient to local pests, the improved seed tolerated conditions equally well. The yield of sorghum was 3 to 5 sacks per *feddan* and 2.6 sacks for sesame. These results do not sound as high a yield as one might expect, given that the average yield per *feddan* on a subsistance farm was the same for sorghum and sesame. By comparison, the yields from the Damazin demonstration farm were 6-8 sacks per *feddan* (cumulative average) for sorghum, the figures for sesame were not available.

The economics of fallow land and intercropping were central issues which concerned the agronomists. The main issues were economic, not cultural. Ways to introduce a "growth approach package" in a socially acceptable manner were not considered to any extent. Regarding the question of land use, it seemed feasible to go with maximum use of the land and not adopt the fallow land concept that is practiced in the rural areas, where a plot is allowed to remain uncultivated for a number of years so that it can regain its natural nutrients. Legumes would be planted in an inter-cropping basis to help the land regain nutrients and at the same time offer the farmers a marketable crop. Legumes have been introduced on an inter-cropping basis on the two experimental farms with hopes of introducing them on the subsistence plots. Here a positive economic argument can be made, especially since the farmers can use some cash. Secondly, the farmers need not move their villages when their lands become unproductive, since the legumes will solve the land depletion problem.[18]

On the cooperative scene, though the scheme is sound in theory, it is difficult to foresee the impact of the laws and rules of the society on the village membership, the leadership of the society, and the smoothness of the day-to-day performance of the cooperative. The co-op was set up differently from what the villagers expected. The villagers had many views and some misunderstanding about the nature of the cooperative society and what it will provide. The drafted by-laws will create difficulties for the villagers who are not accustomed to a cash repayment system. The cooperative society in each village will be tied to the central "mother" co-op for the whole project. Project cooperative meetings will include representatives from the different village cooperatives. Each village co-op will handle its administrative work for the different functions of the society such as seed purchases, marketing, mechanization, credit, and vegetable and fishing consumer shops. Credit is extended to cooperative members only, and the society has its built-in mechanisms to supervise the use of funds and repayments. There are still many misconceptions, nationally and locally, about cooperatives and their function. The educational process, specifically associated with the project for cooperatives, may, in time, help the farmers to adopt a more positive view.

The local notion of *j'amaia* will be replaced by the cooperative. The question of responsibility and control of funds tend to cause the downfall of many new cooperatives in the country. The *j'amaia* (a loosely defined group for a purpose) is a voluntary association which can be formal or informal. The germ of the cooperative idea is not new to villagers since there have been *dahari* and flour mill cooperatives in some of the villages within the project area. However, given their history in Sudan, cooperatives tend to last two to three years before they fold up and some of the members become involved in court cases due to embezzlement and other corrupt practices. In the project area the principles of *j'amaia* were to be followed, giving one vote to the households that join, members being responsible for the functioning and continuity of the society. Outsiders will not be brought in to run things. The shared responsibility of work and management will rest solely on the villagers, who will make their own decisions about their needs for village and personal development.

Imposing the by-laws of the co-op society will pose problems, since village lands are not pooled into a cooperative, and co-op members have to use mechanized service on their individual plots. If a number of the farmers want to pool their land, they can do so and share in the fees and expenses. The cooperative society will serve to attract new members and extend credit services to them. Members may continue to plow a small plot or to increase their farm *feddans*. But these practices do not coincide with the idea of contiguous farms making the maximum use of tractors.

The project introduced an extension agent to work with the women of the area. The extension agent works closely with the coop and credit division, extending services to the wives of the coop members. Using results of the women's survey, the extension division aims to expand the locally available income generating activities, such as poultry, vegetable gardens and handicrafts. The extension agent, the only woman on the project other than the anthropologist, agreed to the proposition of incorporating women into membership of the farm cooperatives in the villages.[19]

In 1984, the project came up for renewal and its expatriate phase was terminated on schedule. No evaluation of the results has been made to date, although this is expected.[20] However, we can make a general assessment on the basis of the available data. The project was delayed so often that the year of research, initially slated to go hand in hand with implementation, was already finished before the field intervention began. As a result, the research component was detached from the subsequent phase of intervention and the socio-economic findings were not integrated with other aspects of the project. There was no feedback mechanism for anthropological research to inform the subsequent developments. When the anthropologist was on the site, she was increasingly called upon to guide project activities through the administration, *suq*, and local societies, rather than to participate in decision making.[21] Housing for officials was situated in the province headquarters and not on the project site. There was constant friction and misunderstanding between the different sections of the project, with little coordination of effort. The most successful aspect was the research itself, but even this took place in isolation -- without any links to the other parts of the project. But at least the work was carried out. The agronomic cooperative and other aspects of the work were constantly delayed, so that by the third year of the project, little visible impact was made in the project area. The staff (both expatriate and Sudanese) was slow to gather, there were frequent changes in personnel, and there were many transfers. The findings of the research team were not incorporated into an effective plan of action. The same was to be true of other project undertakings later on. The staff that was to implement the project was very different from the initial team. The greatest difficulty seems to have been the recruitment and maintenance of a competent, committed project staff in the field consisting of Sudanese and expatriate experts working together with a reasonable understanding of the project aims and methods. Even more difficult is to ensure that the efforts applied in the different directions called for by the project will remain linked to each other and that the integrated nature of the work is not jeopardized.

There are many lessons to be drawn from this experience. Here was a well-designed, well-thought-out plan for development. It gave a pride of place to research before implementation to create an effective feedback loop. Yet the results were indifferent. We knew the socio-cultural condition of the rural area before development. We knew the values and expectations of the rural people. Yet this information remained as it was collected, a phase of the project carried out by people whose work was set aside when performed, just as the builders left after the housing was completed, and the expatriate staff had left once they trained crews for tractors and other machines. Hence even the right kind and right amount of research was not enough. The delays and separation observed in the phases of design, recruitment, and initial implementation proved to be an accurate forecast of the project's later fate. It is too much to expect a magic transformation in a project still struggling with basic problems of staffing, logistics, and organization half way into its life cycle. In this case no amount of honest, careful pre-implementation planning could stave off disappointment.

Change in this case was imposed on the villagers from above and from outside. This was as true of AID as of Sudanese participation in the project. The infrastructure for operating the project was incomprehensible to the villagers. This applies to the officials' housing and the project buildings (most often in Damazin) as well as the hardware in the project area. The same is true of the project administration. The local people anticipated the project with a mixture of welcome, high expectations, and deep suspicion. But immediately the local leadership was by-passed by the project staff in an effort to democratize the participation and assure the distribution of agricultural benefits. The process, though well-meant, assures the opposite outcome. The ties that hold the villages together are challenged, and kinship, tribal, and locality ties are cut across by the effort to organize cooperative and other groupings alien to indigenous society. Women are left out and their position is likely to worsen as a result of the development process. New forms of cooperatives replace existing organization of communal effort (such as *nafir*) because the latter are non-cash based. Competition is introduced since incentives are held out and greater production is rewarded. Men are enthusiastically incorporated into mechanized farms and women are ignored, even though all agricultural work is shared between the sexes. As a result of being unable to earn more cash, women's position deteriorates within the family. On the subsistence farms women contribute 80 percent of agricultural labor. On the new mechanized farms, women are expected to help out without renumeration whereas the male head of household is paid cash. Markets in grains and cash transactions are introduced into the village and the cash is used to purchase luxury goods. Innumerable surveys in East Africa point to the conclusion that increased cash income in a family does not result in more spending on nutrition and health. Consumer goods are accumulated and elder males acquire new wives. Due to the loss of independent earnings, an inimical effect on the position of women is inescapable.

Notes

[1] See chapter 7.

[2] For an organizational account see Chapters 1 and 4.

[3] *Shail:* a system of local borrowing and indebtedness. Cash advanced as loan is repaid in kind after the harvest.

[4] It is not accidental that the *dokan* and the clinic are well-built structures, centrally located in the village.

[5] However this feature was to be added later.

[6] See Appendix 2: Methodology of the Survey

[7] Although the indigenous inhabitants of the Blue Nile Province once held fishing as taboo, today fishing has become an alternative profession for those living along the river.

[8] The average median of the eight villages in the project area.

[9] Usually not more than 1/10 of a *jeda'a* (1 *jeda'a* = 5 acres)

[10] Traditionally there are two types of storage in the village: *suweba* or *matmura*. The former is a cylindrical structure built above ground, the latter is dug and the hole is sealed after the grain is poured in.

[11] Unlike subsistence farms, irrigated and mechanized land is not community (village) owned, rather it is state or privately controlled and organized. Farmers on state schemes are paid employees of the government or the private managing agency.

[12] Women's personal income is partially used to pay occasional household and social expenses (see Chapter 3).

[13] The research survey showed that the health of the people in the project area is poor: they complain of malaria, dysentery and malnutrition.

[14] See Chapters 2 and 4 for a detailed account of town merchants and administration.

[15] In 1979 *shail* prices ranged between LS2 to 3 per *kantar* of sesame. After harvest, sesame was sold for around LS7.5 per *kantar*.

[16] See ESRC Report no. 7, October 1979. Khartoum, Sudan.

[17] The only problem was a Fellata group which insisted on a separate, tribal-based cooperative society for themselves.

[18] It is too early to discuss the social implications of the maximum use of land and the practice of giving up the custom of leaving land fallow.

[19] Note that the anthropologist so far has not been asked to carry out the evaluation of the project.

[20] A final report has just been issued by Experience, Inc. By 1985 approximately 13,000 *feddans* were planted under the mechanization program.

[21] It is instructive to contrast this with our experience on the Abyei integrated rural development project (Southern Kordofan Province). We coordinated a limited social survey in cooperation with the Development Studies and Research Center (Khartoum University) and the Harvard Institute of International Development (see Hassan et al. 1979). This survey also preceeded the intervention phase but unlike the Blue Nile project Abyei subsequently persevered with the research effort with different personnel. The Abyei project folded after a few years of uneven effort with even more disappointing results than the Blue Nile project. Ironically, while HIID prided itself on its research effort, it failed to translate its findings into the desired results and could not cope with the technical and other non-research aspects of development. It was unable to recruit and hold competent project staff at the level of implementation.

7

Agricultural Schemes: Tenants and Institutions

Having explored the general issues of development, the specific systems of court, market, and administration involved in the effort to develop a region, and having taken a close look at a small scale development project, we now turn to the more established, as well as the newer, large scale, state owned agricultural development schemes. What are the historical and contemporary models of development? What are the social effects and performance of existing schemes? How do these schemes function and have they fulfilled what was expected of them?

The Sudan is a vast country but except for the White and Blue Nile basins it is sparsely populated, with about 80% of the inhabitants depending on agriculture for their livelihood. Forty percent of the GNP and 90% of exports come from agriculture. Modern mechanized and irrigated agricultural projects exist alongside traditional rainfed subsistence agriculture. This dual system dominates Sudan's economy and competes with a rapidly declining pastoral economy, which was once a thriving business and a way of life.

The backbone of Sudan's economy is the Gezira scheme. Devoted to cotton production, Gezira holds a central place in Sudan's development plan as the model of agricultural progress. The Suki, Managil, Guneid, and Rahad projects, to mention a few, are built on the pattern of the Gezira scheme.

Post-independence Sudan is committed to bringing more land under cultivation by increasing the acreage of irrigated agriculture. Irrigated agriculture is central to Sudan's economic planning. Sixty percent of all agricultural exports comes from cotton, the Sudan's main cash crop, grown on irrigated schemes.[1] Out of the Sudan's 16 million cultivated *feddans* 25% comes directly under government ownership. Contrary to the ILO report and recommendations, Sudan continues to expand agriculture by bringing more land under cultivation, without intensifying cultivation on existing cropped land.

The policy of expanding agricultural practices and model farms means a duplication of success or failure, an increase or decline in production, the

153

possibility of social disruption, and the creation of obstacles to progress.

The Role of the Gezira Scheme

The Gezira scheme is one of the most renowned agricultual projects in Africa and the Middle East. Built by British colonial power around the turn of the century, this scheme has been both a successful economic venture and one which many other countries have tried to emulate. In Gaitskell's opinion it is "...a remarkable example of development achieved by combining the entreprenuerial spirit of private enterprise with the paternalistic spirit of colonial government" (quoted in Barnett 1977:3). Presenting the historical background will be useful for our discussion of development, especially since the Gezira scheme has provided the model for other development ventures in the Sudan.

Many factors combined to bring about the establishment of such a scheme in the Sudan. At the turn of the century the British Government decided it should not be burdened by the expenses of its many colonies. This, combined with a growing need for cotton for the textile industry in Great Britain, pointed the way to the introduction of large scale cotton cultivation in the Sudan. In this way the Sudanese Government could finance its own expenses from the proceeds of cotton sales. Furthermore, it would be less expensive to import cotton for British textile factories from the colonies than from the countries which imposed export tariffs on raw cotton. The scheme was set up as a combination of government and private commerical enterprise with local involvement. Already in 1904, before the construction of the scheme, inspired by the British and the success of Egyptian cotton growing, cotton production begun at the Zeidab Pilot farm, making cotton the country's priority in agriculture.

The scheme was planned and executed in the light of the economic needs of the two countries in an attempt to resolve the financial difficulties of both. With the Lancashire mills in need of cotton, the British Cotton Association pressured the British Government to finance the project. To provide water for irrigation, work began on the Sennar Dam in 1906. In 1925, the dam was completed and the scheme commenced operation. The Gezira Scheme started as a tripartite partnership between the British Colonial Governmment, the concession companies, and the tenant farmers. The colonial Government was responsible for building the dam and financing the irrigation system, the Sudan Plantation Syndicate was in charge of the scheme itself providing the managerial services, and the tenant farmers, who had no say in management, cultivated the cotton.[2]

Economic production prior to the opening of the Gezira Scheme was organized along lineage and tribal lines with communal lands being shared by all members of the group. The leader and the head of the tribe *(gabila)* or lineage (or other organizing unit) made decisions regarding usage of pasture lands and cultivation areas. The decisions of where to plant and graze had to be made on a yearly basis. By rotating pasture and cultivating lands, the tribes avoided overgrazing and allowed cultivated lands enough time to regain nutrients. *Nafir* (communal labor) and family labor were used for agricultural activities. If a person extended assistance, he received communal help. Instead of being paid wages for agricultural labor, the people shared the fruits of the land. During the early 20th century the economic and political organization of tribes were closely connected. A tribe shared the use of the land communally. The concept of private and individual ownership was nonexistent. Land could not be sold or bought; one only had the use of the land. The right to use the land could be (and in some parts is still) inherited by one's children, but land was never sold. Thus economic production was embedded in political, social, and cultural factors.[3]

In some parts of the Sudan, villages are still organized along the lines described above. But in other areas, villages have undergone changes similar to those introduced by the Gezira Scheme with new concepts and new demands, new standards of living, new wants, and new needs. These changes were brought about by and depended upon a new source of wealth (cash) and contact with the new culture of a consumer society (Taha 1977:20). Today the tenant farmer on the scheme is supplied with seeds and services for cultivation and irrigation. Previously, his labor had no economic or market value except for himself. Now, he produces a commodity which is sold in the market for cash. In turn, he becomes a member of an economic class. Instead of just producing crops for consumption, he now produces cotton, a cash crop for the world market. As a rational man in economic terms, the new farmer has no direct relation to his erstwhile social and political unit, lineage, or tribe. Previous ideological considerations are now irrelevant in terms of his livelihood or in regard to what he produces because he is now responsible to a board that decides the costs, profits, crops, and the number of *feddans* to be planted. He is responsible to the scheme's syndicate and not to the leader of his tribe. Economic considerations now override all matters that were important in the past and as a result the old political and economic structures have been weakened. A modern western type economic power structure has replaced the old system and in part strengthened the economic unit of the nuclear family. Though the old kinship bonds (based on lineage, clan, or tribe) have been weakened due to new demands and migration from traditional areas in search of work. The basis of the family so far has remained unchanged even though the extended family has disappeared. Tribal identification still means something for the farmer but it only serves as an identity for the individual rather than being the main organizing unit.

The creation of the scheme altered the traditional social organization of the rural areas. Before the start of the scheme, land and labor did not have economic value. "Value as a term applied to labor implies that it is a saleable commodity which can be the subject of calculative determination" (Voll 1975:190). Land was communally owned and men worked their small subsistence farms for their own families. Crops were not produced for sale in the market; production was purely for immediate or household consumption. Most farmers planted *dura* (sorghum), the staple diet, at the onset of the rainy season. Some combined pastoralism with agriculture.

The terms traditional versus modern/mechanized agriculture in the Sudan simply refer to using agricultural machinery instead of employing the methods of indigenous farming. The bases of farming have changed; the additional inputs of modern farming incur higher expenditures for the farmer, tenant, and government. Due to the push for increased agricultural production, mechanization was introduced at different times and for different types of schemes throughout the country. Gezira, Rahad, Managil, and Guneid are a few of these schemes. Given Sudan's unique and still existing problem of labor shortage, mechanization of the cash cropping areas has served to alleviate the problem. There are guidelines for selecting qualified tenants with nationality as a prominent factor, since non-Sudanese are not accepted. Age, occupation, marital status, size of family, and ownership of tenancy in other schemes are the other important considerations.[4] Whenever possible, preference is given to local inhabitants, other subsistence farmers or nomads who live in the neighboring areas, and lastly other qualified Sudanese. Scheme managers are known to travel long distances recruiting tenants, who are then settled in residential units on the scheme. Resettling local inhabitants is easier than moving different tribal groups from other parts of the country. Added to the problems of reorientation and adjustment, intertribal tensions at times lead to conflict in many newly settled villages. Resettling tribal groups in one area with previously no symbiotic relations between them, has proven to be a cause of tension.

Seasonal need for labor is greater for the small nuclear family units displaced from their original residences. Larger families and early marriages prevailed in the older schemes. Tenants hire laborers to work their land, however the low yields do not warrant further capital investment, and incentives remain low, adding to the continued decline of the national economy. Demographic consequences of multiple marriages and large families, though unheeded at present, will become a cause for future concern. A survey has shown that tenants in Managil do not work their tenancy after the age of 45 years, leaving a growing number of adult male workers unemployed. Hence the necessity of larger families. Before the scheme was established, a large percentage of the present tenancy acreage was used as pasture land and subsistence farming. The state can reclaim fallow lands or even cultivate land for a national purpose, in this case for developing irrigated farms, such as the Gezira Scheme.

The scheme's best years were between 1925-50, when the profits from cotton paid for all of Sudan's foreign exchange. "The primary purpose of the Gezira scheme was unequivocably the creation of a source of a high level of output, revenue and foreign exchange" (Sarah Voll 1980:102). Presently, due to managerial and agro-economic problems the Gezira Scheme, once the backbone and mainstay of Sudan's economy, is operating at a deficit. Although many people have benefited from it, there is a growing disillusionment and discontent on all sides.

It is critical for the Sudan that the irrigated sector perform well. Economic and political stability of the country depends on the performance of the irrigated sector. Currently about 1/4 of Sudan's 17 million acres of cultivated land is irrigated.[5] Cotton persists in being the main cash crop followed by groundnuts, sesame, and gum-arabic. Irrigation in the Sudan began in 1917, under the British government, and gravity irrigation is still the dominant type. Since 1911 three dams were built and Sudan's GNP still depends on the cash crop proceeds from the farms watered by the dams. Presently all irrigated schemes are performing below expectation. Cotton is cultivated on irrigated as well as on non-irrigated but mechanized farms.[6]

Sudan's aim is to achieve higher productivity by re-arranging or revising the cropping pattern, and by selecting advantageous systems with incentives for the tenants on existing projects. Irrigated schemes in post-colonial times continue to operate on the basis of a tripartite partnership. Irrigated schemes are state owned and controlled, and tenants are still sharecroppers. Tenants, as state employees, continue to adhere to the Gezira scheme's system of management and capitalist farming, but the growing of cash crops on the basis of market speculation is not encouraged, as it is on the larger, food producing, rainfed farms.

The Gezira and subsequently all other schemes were built on a tripartite system. The scheme corporation supplies the tenants with land, irrigation and canalization systems, technical assistance, and supervision. Tenants on any state scheme are paid for their labor and in return the government supplies water, seeds, fertilizer, and insecticides. The tenancies are non-mortgageable, and the tenant's rights are a share of the profit after costs. The corporation also provides a mechanized infrastructure, and takes care of marketing the crops. After deductions of production costs, the proceeds go to the tenant. Deducted items include seed, land, rent, fertilizer, irrigation cost, and other services.

A major problem with the structuring of the schemes on the Gezira pattern is the relation between Tenant, Board, and Government. Cotton as a cash crop continues to dominate the agricultural scene on the tenancies despite the declining price of cotton in world markets. The bureaucracy insists that production of cotton remain the schemes' main goal, though it is neither the priority nor the need of the tenant. Therefore tenant incentive remains low. Attempts by the Nimeiry regime between 1969 and 1971 to lessen the impact of hierarchy in the Gezira and to collectivise production were sabotaged by the field staff and the management who refused to restructure the scheme. By 1972 the scheme returned to its original hierarchial structure. A class division was created between the tenants and the staff, with the staff reinforcing the distance in terms of operations and directives. Organizationally the schemes retain a rigid format, refusing to accommodate change. Also, diversifying to wheat, barley, or *dura* has met with difficulties both at the International Monetary Fund (IMF) and the Gezira Board.

On most schemes, the disillusioned tenant loses interest due to the high cost of farm operations, and, as a result, productivity declines. The conflict of interests is seen in the diachronous difference between "the partnership crops," mostly legumes, vegetables, and some grains, versus "the tenants crop" (cotton). The tenants are dependent on income from other sources to compensate for their low income from agriculture.[7]

The introduction and the expansion of modern agriculture on schemes such as the Gezira and others modeled after it (Rahad, Suki, Khasm El Girba) had a tremendous effect on the subsistence farmer. The presence of such schemes has encouraged labor migration.[8] Men leave the village in search of work on these attractive schemes, and in time, send for their immediate families, selecting against the extended and for the nuclear, monogamous family. On the scheme each farmer is given a tenancy which varies from 10 to 40 *feddans*. The size of the tenancy depends on the scheme and on the crops, with the majority cultivating cotton or other cash crops, such as sugar, ground nuts, wheat, or rice. The tenant farmer is responsible for producing the crop and has to work his plot with the assistance of family members, since he is discouraged from using hired labor. The nuclear family thus joins the production unit of the scheme. Now the farmer cannot depend on *nafir* (communal labour) or the extended family since the latter has broken up into small nuclear units. Since crops have to be cultivated when ready and one's nuclear family is small, there is often a need for other laborers. In many instances the tenant, though discouraged by the low agricultural productivity, does hire laborers and pays them out of his own funds.

The tenant farmer does not sell his whole crop on the open market. If he has 20 *feddans* he will grow cotton (or another cash crop) on 10 and on the other 10 *feddans* he may grow sorghum and wheat which he can market himself. Alternatively, he may cultivate garden vegetables for comsumption by his own family. The cotton and sugar cash crops, however, are collected and sold by the members of the syndicate. Once the joint expenses are deducted, the profits are divided three ways: government, syndicate, and tenant farmer. It is only after the profits are determined that the farmer is paid, the process itself taking a year or longer. In bad years the farmer receives no cash at all. Because the farmer has no control over either choosing or selling his cash crop he experiences, as Barnett put it, "individualization and isolation." It becomes apparent that a "contractually defined individualization of the nuclear family unit results from the tenant's relations to the means of production" (Barnett 1977:89). Each tenant is hired on an individual basis, the scheme hires a farmer by giving him a tenancy. The tenant cannot sell, mortgage, or give away his farm but can be fired if he does not abide by the rules. The tenant is isolated, he works alone and not in a group. The new farmer is thus alienated from the society of his tribe, village, or lineage and finds himself in a competitive world. On his part he produces the crops expected, yet he has no control over how and where they are sold. Some tenants expand their agricultural holdings at the expense of fellow tenants who undergo a process of "near proletarization" by being stripped of almost everything but their labour by the existing government policy for agricultural growth (Sorbo, 1980:4).

For many farmers on subsistence plots, the prevalence of lending and borrowing institutions *(shail)* makes it possible to continue their existing way of life. *Shail* is a traditional form of lending and it is practiced in the rural areas.[9] A farmer borrows from the village merchant or any other money lender who will then specify in what form he must be repaid. Paying back a merchant in kind is common and a farmer who borrows LS3 later may have to give the merchant a sack of *dura* which in high season sells for as much as LS10-12. The large difference in the amount of the loan and the value of the repayment is the basis of *shail*, since the risk of the deal is with the merchant. The borrowing and repaying are cause for the rather poor economic condition of the majority of farmers, especially farmers in modern agriculture. There are other kinds of loans *(dyn)* but not all are available to the tenant farmer, especially if he is not well known in the village. In his own village, a farmer may receive credit without *shail* repayment.

Shail is also practiced in the modern agricultural sector.[10] In the past, a subsistence farmer would give up his traditional job to seek employment on the modern farms. Such migration from one's own village was triggered by a number of accumulated catastrophies such as drought, heavy indebtedness *(shail)*, or decline in crop productivity. Producing enough for household consumption and for repayment of debt was possible in the past, but given the increase in the standard of living which has plagued the rural areas, farmers have fewer options.

On a modern scheme, a farmer's produce - cotton - is sold in the open market and is not used for his household consumption. Cash received from the sale of the crops is then used to purchase the grain needed for consumption. Instead of exchanging grain for cash (repaying *shail* in the rural areas) the farmer now produces cash crops for cash. If the system were successful, the tenant would not have to repeat a cycle of indebtedness similar to the one which he tried to move away from.[11] So we find that the modern farmer also needs to borrow and still depends on the farm management board.

Though some farmers regard the tenancy as a liability, they stay on the farms thinking that the next year they will make ends meet. The majority of them are constantly in debt, and as soon as they pay off one set of debts, others accrue. It is in fact the possibility of going further into debt which makes it possible for them to survive from year to year. The *shail* debt of most farmers is repaid in the form of *dura* (sorghum) or cotton, even though the repayment of debts in cotton is forbidden by the Syndicate.

In its efforts to modernize and to develop the agricultural sector, the Sudanese Government has ignored the traditional subsistence farmer. As elsewhere, in the Sudan it was "commonly alleged that traditional farmers would respond perversely or feebly to economic incentives. Hence, the argument ran, traditional agriculture should be largely bypassed as an unreliable, inelastic source of income" (Anthony 1979:18). Contrary to this view, recent surveys have shown that the traditional farmer responds to economic needs and opportunities.[12]

Old and New Projects

Managil

The building of the Managil Extension to the Gezira Scheme began in in 1957 and was completed in 1971. Prior to its inception, the inhabitants of the area combined subsistence agriculture with animal husbandry, growing *dura* and grazing their animals (goats, sheep, cattle, camels) in nearby fields and pastures. Water in the rainy season was ample for human and animal needs, but not during the dry season.

Before the opening of the Managil Extension, the inhabitants of Managil supplied the Gezira Scheme with most of its cotton pickers. Like other subsistence farm villages, after harvesting their own *dura* crop in December, the residents of entire villages in Managil migrated to the Gezira until the end of the dry season. As wage laborers, they picked cotton, pulled and burned the cotton stubs, and cleared the fields in preparation for the next planting. These wage laborers worked for the tenants of Gezira. Today, the Managil Extension competes with the Gezira main scheme for its labor supply.

The story of labor migration and the creation of newer schemes remains one of Sudan's problems. Scheme managements tap new sources of labor in different parts of the country, on the eastern bank of the Blue Nile and on the banks of the White Nile. Managil management, like those of the Gezira and other schemes, travel long distances to recruit labor in other areas for the cotton picking season. Laborers are recruited even outside the Sudan, from Chad, Ethiopia, and Nigeria but managers prefer to hire local labor from villages in the Managil area. Transportation costs are high and finding people to work on the scheme is becoming more difficult. With the number of agricultural schemes increasing, there are less and less people seeking seasonal employment and the competition for labor is becoming high. Most of the laborers brought from the outside leave in search of more profitable jobs in the nearby towns and cities, or seek work in the modern agro-industrial sectors. Labor shortages are expected to increase rather than decrease in the future because of the new schemes still being built.

The Managil Extension is controlled and managed by the Gezira Board. The scheme is divided into seven divisions or production units. A division is headed by an inspector and is further divided into 6-12 units known as blocks. Six to ten villages compose a block managed by a block inspector and two to three assistant inspectors. The village tenants are represented by their council at both the village and block levels. There is also another level of hierarchy, a group of tenants called *samada* (singular: *samad*) who supervise the agricultural operations of the village tenants. The production councils and the *samada* represent a link between the block inspectors and the tenants. Tenants are given 15 *feddans* to be used as follows: 5 *feddans* for cotton, 5 for wheat, 2.5 for *dura* and 2.5 for groundnuts. All 15 *feddans* are cropped.

New and larger villages were constructed and situated in sparsely populated areas along the main road network and near major canals. Inhabitants from smaller villages were grouped together in one village. In the new villages, education facilities and social services were provided to the tenants and other residents.

The Gezira system of net proceeds and sharing between Sudanese Government (40%), the tenants (40%), and Sudan Plantation Syndicate (20%), is used for the Managil Extension. In the early years of the scheme, the share of profits provided the tenants a good income. With time, the productivity of the scheme began to decline, and returns to the tenants started to fall. In turn, the tenants complained that their decreased income affected production. The Board decided to counter the decline in productivity and the management increased the tenant's share of profits to 47%.[13] The net returns are shared after all deductions are made but the tenants feel the procedure is still difficult to understand.

The Sudan and Egypt concluded the second Nile Waters Agreement in 1959. It enabled the Sudan to raise its share of Nile water by 18.5 milliard. Sudan proceeded to construct the Roseries Dam. Plans for the extension of irrigated agricultural lands were developed, building the Managil Extension of the Gezira Scheme. Unlike the Gezira Scheme with 40 *feddans* to the tenant, Managil has a 15 *feddan* tenancy. Small size tenancies were thought to be more manageable. They were to be handled by small families which did not in fact prove to be successful because of peak time labor shortages.

The Managil Extension intercropping pattern led to a 100% intensive use of tenancies. This gives the tenants an alternative crop for cash (groundnuts, fodder) as well as *dura* for household consumption. Agricultural production on the 15 *feddan* Managil tenancies compares very well with that of Gezira. The smaller tenancies produce more than the 40 *feddan* plots of Gezira. Our survey demonstrated that there was a direct relationship between farm size and productivity (Fruzzetti et al. 1979). The smaller the farm size, the more productive was the subsistence farmer. Higher agricultural outputs coincided with the farmer's ability to adequately control the farm's management as well as non-agricultural activities. The tenants in the Managil Extension receive 65% of their income from agriculture and 35% from livestock

Guneid

The Guneid Sugar Scheme is composed of 4 blocks with 10 villages per block, with a total of 37,500 *feddans*, divided into 2,500 farms *(hawashas)*. Each village contains more than 3 to 4 tribes. Prior to the early 1950's, as in the rest of the Blue Nile Province, the people in the Guneid area were cultivators on rainfed farms, inheriting the use of such farms from their fathers. *Dura* (sorghum) and vegetables were grown during the rainy season on an average of 2-4 *feddan* plots. They practiced slash and burn farming to build up land nutrients. Cotton cultivation was introduced to the villages during the 1960's and the farmers began to grow cotton as a cash crop instead of *dura* when the Guneid Scheme expanded and sugar cane replaced cotton as the cash crop.

As in all other schemes, the land surrounding the Guneid area was taken over by the state. When a state-controlled cash crop scheme was introduced, the growing of the household consumption crop, *dura*, was stopped. On becoming a tenant, the farmer, sharecropper or wage laborer, was alienated from his traditional practices.

The Guneid Sugar Scheme is modeled on the canal system of the Gezira. Up to the late 1970's, the 37,750 *feddans* of the scheme were irrigated by waters from the Blue Nile. In the late 1950's canals built to irrigate the cotton scheme were changed to irrigate sugar cane, without improving the existing pumps. Tenants found that sugar cane needed more water than the existing pumps could supply, adding to the annual loss in production. These problems pushed the administration of the scheme to take action. It abolished the cultivation of groundnuts and *lubia* (a legume), in order to control the spread of disease and to force the tenants to pay attention to sugar cane.

By 1979, the loss of cash formerly obtained from the sale of the groundnut crop, made it difficult for the tenants to buy *dura* or fodder for cattle. The inefficiency of the pumps and the resulting shortage of water continue to contribute to the decline in the sugar production. Depending on sugar cane as a cash crop, the farmers' income decreases as cane production declines, leaving them with less income to purchase basic subsistence needs. The poor condition of the canals, the silting problem, and water control all add to the decline in productivity. Tenants claim that about half of the required amount of water is delivered to their farms. In a surveyed village only 33% of the farms were well irrigated. The tenant farmers on the Guneid Scheme complained that lack of water affects the quality of the crop, in particular the thickness, the length, and the amount of extractable sugar in the plant. Also, inadequately irrigated crops are prone to disease. The scheme's infrastructure is lacking in supplying adequate water, electricity, and fuel. Some tenants blame inept management for the problems causing crop failures.

With the abolition of fodder crop on the scheme, the tenants' cattle suffer severely from poor grazing. Animal husbandry in the area is limited despite the importance of milk for the tenants' diet. Although there is a shortage of milk for family consumption, farmers are unable to buy milk since it is not sold locally. In the past, tenants were able to supplement their income from the sale of animals.

The scheme has contributed to the growth of a middle-class, but indirectly it helped to develop the rural area. The new emerging class is the farmer-worker (tenant-farmer), followed in number and importance by the merchant. Merchants bought shops and markets in the scheme and in nearby towns. Many laborers have come for work and settled at Guneid. The scheme houses an indigenous population, a mobile group of seasonal laborers, and newcomers, including people from Southern and Western Sudan, and West Africa. Low crop yield and labor outmigration add to the poor social and economic conditions which prevail on the scheme.

The level of education in the Guneid area is higher than the national level, and there are elementary schools even for female students, which points to a positive view of women's education. School attendance is encouraged by the villagers and many of the tenants attended elementary school. A recent study showed that younger tenants have a formal education whereas the older tenants tend to have a religious education. No tenant under 26 years of age has attended *khalwa* schools. Changing from religious to secular education could be a factor in socio-cultural change. Health conditions are similar to those on other schemes, with congested residential areas and narrow roads adding to poor sanitation. Cattle are kept on the grounds of each residence since other arrangements are lacking. Villages are surrounded on either side by canals which act as breeding grounds for mosquitos and parasitic snails. Village flooding is common during the rainy season. All the tenants suffer poor health and their health condition deteriorated since the building of the canals.

Suki

The Es Suki Scheme began operations in 1971, producing cotton and groundnuts. It is located in the Blue Nile Province, about 44 km northwest of Es Suki town. The first two or three years of the scheme were very successful with the highest yields in 1976/77, after which production began to decline. Irrigation for the project comes from the Blue Nile Waters with pumps located in Meina town. The water distribution network is modeled after the Gezira Scheme. In 1979-80 only half of the scheme's 85,000 *feddans* were under cultivation because there was not enough water.

The tenants in the villages covered by the research did not report any tribal conflicts. The Suki Scheme survey covered four villages, one from each of the four blocks which make up the total number of divisions in the scheme. The selected villages were Salma, Magam, Gumaiza, and Mahala, each inhabited by members of one or two major *gabilas* with a few other tribal groups. All the tenants of these villages had similar grievances; former nomads, who maintain tenancies but keep a large number of their animals with them on the land, complain about arrangements for animals and about the inefficiency of the managerial board.[14]

The tenants are in their most productive years between the ages of 30-45, even though presently this does not reflect the production outputs and incomes for the farmers. The inhabitants of the scheme combine traditional rainfed subsistence agriculture with pastoral activities. In the pre-scheme phase, the nomads were invited to settle and take up tenancies, and many opted to do so. Many of the nomads integrated their livestock into the scheme, and worked their tenancies at the same time. Family labor was divided between both occupations.

The working conditions on the Suki Scheme were perhaps the worst in terms of the tenants' hopes, expectations, and production. Some of the general complaints ranged from delay in water supply for irrigation, electrical power cuts, tenants' mistrust of the managerial board, and the inefficiency of the staff. Being so close to the Rahad Scheme (across the river) many dissatisfied tenants left in search of better working conditions on the more successful scheme.

The cotton and groundnut production of the Suki Scheme continues to decline. Helplessness and alienation dominate the life of the tenant. Land leveling and land preparation are not timely and the engineers are lax about work. There is inadequate spraying of the cotton crop and insufficient usage of fertilizers resulting in crop infestation with flies and other insects. In each of the first six years of the scheme, every tenant was given eight bags of fertilizer for his ten *feddans*. Presently, they receive four to five sacks, and even these are only three-quarters full, for the same area. Services needed for a successful operation of a tenancy are cut or not available at all.

Following the structural arrangements of other schemes, profits are divided three ways, the tenants receiving one third, the government one third, and the management one third. It became clear to us that the tenants had not been paid for their cotton for two or three consecutive years, due to the low world market prices and mounting production costs. Cash and grain had been advanced to the Suki tenant with costs deducted from the final accounting. Cash and *dura* advance were stopped as a scheme policy, forcing tenants with cattle to sell their animals for cash and those without to leave.

Tenants are caught in a dual bind: they lack a profitable cash crop and at the same time they are not extended a cash advance. Thus we are not surprised to find that tenants would grow *dura* for home consumption, rather than groundnuts for cash. Groundnuts do not fetch an adequate price on any market and they are costly to grow, requiring the same agricultural infrastructure and services as cotton which the tenants have to pay. *Dura* requires less time and effort, and costs are minimal. Nonetheless, scheme's board refuses to change the cropping pattern.

The overall productivity of the scheme has declined since 1976/77 due, to a large extent, to migration of tenants to more profitable schemes. Lack of an effective system of communication between the tenants and the Board remains a matter for concern at the scheme. Low income from agriculture does not meet the tenant's basic needs.[15]

The presence of the former nomads on this scheme warrants mention. When the nomads settled on the scheme and took up agriculture as their main occupation, some had a small number of animals and this proved to be a source of income, especially during low cotton production years.

Livestock holdings represent an important form of wealth for the "agriculturalist/nomad," animals being a source of cash reserve to supplement farming. But due to the presence of animals on the scheme, the conflict between the agriculturalist/nomad and the village/agriculturalist is increasing. The nomad-tenants allow their animals to wander onto other tenancies for grazing and they pay for the damages incurred. Nomads have cash and find it the lesser problem to pay the fine. But nomads complain about the shortage of land for pasture and the diminishing number of their livestock.

The clash between nomads and agriculturalists on these large irrigated schemes is more complex than in areas where subsistence agriculture is practiced. Here it is not the nomadic way of life which clashes with that of the agricultural farmer (in which case one is a *farmer* and the other a *pastoralist*). Each person encroaches on others' rights to pasture or cultivation. The clashes between the two are rather difficult to assess. Nomads who decide to settle on the schemes and take up agriculture as their primary occupation want to keep their livestock, balancing and supplementing their agricultural income through the sale of their animals.[16] Since livestock is the primary source of wealth, a nomad would allow his animals to enter his own tenancy, if necessary, to graze on the cash crops. The availability of fodder and water for his animals offers a secondary attraction for a nomad to work on the scheme.

Rahad

The Rahad corporation was established in 1972 and irrigation began in 1977. The scheme draws water for irrigation from the Blue Nile and power from the Roseiris Dam. Less than half of the project cost was covered by foreign donors, but costs have increased since the initial estimates. The Rahad was to bring 300,000 *feddans* under irrigation, housing a population of 100,000 in 46 villages. Expectations are high.[17] Village residential units are carefully planned by the scheme's board. The production relationship of the tenancy is monitored. The standard tenancy is 22 *feddans*, out of which 11 *feddans* are used for cotton, 8 for groundnuts, and 3 for fodder. There are also 1,700 horticultural tenancies of 5 *feddans* each.

The Rahad corporation supervises the tenancies under an inspectorate system, monitoring and evaluating production. Unlike other schemes, the Rahad incorporates a dual system of production, cash crops and horticulture. There is also more of a concern for the welfare of the tenant. But this does not stop the inspectorate from supervising the tenant within the hierarchial setup, and does not allow individuals to change tenancy.

The Rahad Corporation provides the tenant with the land, a canalization system, and technical and managerial supervision. In addition, the Corporation is responsible for the provision of mechanized cultivation and other production requirements. The management of the scheme markets the cotton and groundnuts. Only about 20% of the area allocated for fodder has actually been used to grow fodder, with the remaining 80% used to cultivate additional groundnuts. After the crop is sold, the management makes deductions for seed, land rent, irrigation (LS1.5 per *feddan* per watering), fertilizers and other services rendered from the tenant's share of proceeds. After cost deductions, the net proceeds go to the tenant.

In order to become eligible for a tenancy, a settler must meet specific, individual and familial requirements of nationality, age, occupation, marital status, and family size. No applicant for a tenancy is accepted if he has a cotton farm in any other area in the Sudan.

The Rahad took grassroots recommendations, and established coherent and socially ordered villages grouped together in such a way as to avoid the conflict or crisis so prevalent on other schemes. Those *gabilas* who were traditionally in conflict with each other were separated in the new settlements.

Rural villages outside the scheme follow the traditional model, each village has a council and a branch representative of the Sudanese Socialist Union (SSU). On the scheme the production council is the link between the scheme's corporation and the tenant, adding a third organizational voice to the decision making.

The Rahad scheme recruited and resettled tenants and agricultural laborers from different parts of the Sudan. It offers agricultural laborers the same social services, medical, and educational facilities. Generally a village has 250-300 tenants, located within walking distance of the farms. In the resettlement and relocation process of older villages the scheme management attempted to retain existing structures. This was the case with two older areas, Mafaza and Tinedbah, former market towns which maintain their old urban status. Those villagers who refused to transfer to the new sites on the project were excluded from tenancy. At the beginning of the first agricultural season, many of the Rahad tenants refused to settle in the new villages, thus violating the main condition for holding a tenancy, and many left their tenancies or neglected to work them. Such practices resulted in dismissal.

New schemes attract laborers from different parts of the country. The Rahad combines Sudanese tribes with many foreign workers. Tenants have to prove Sudanese citizenship but workers do not.[18] Agricultural laborers have a good working relationship with the tenants, and some tenants even have a partnership status *(sharaka)* with their laborers in the groundnuts and vegetable tenancies. The tenant provides the vegetable and groundnut seeds and free use of a vegetable garden. All other costs (excluding the partner's labor) are deducted from the gross proceeds and the remaining net proceeds are divided between the tenant and his partner. In a sense the tripartite scheme structure is replicated by a two-way partnership.

Like the other schemes, the Rahad needs seasonal laborers for the picking season. Tenants can recruit their laborers, and if they do not, the corporation will. At the Rahad laborers are treated much better than at other schemes, with good incentives and wages at competitive rates. Medical services, transportation, and housing are provided to the laborers, though the additional services add to the cost of cotton production.

Through organized campaigns in the Korodofan, Kassala, and White Nile Provinces, scheme officials bring in laborers, giving them LS2 as an incentive. These cotton pickers and their families are transported to and from the scheme, and housed and fed free of charge. Laborers live on the land of the tenant for whom they work. Though the daily earning can range between LS4-5, much of that is spent on daily needs (AID Rahad Report 1979). Nonetheless, seasonal income from schemes does in fact support the villages from where the laborers originate. Sudanese laborers are beginning to question their role in the production cycle. They supply the needed labor and yet they are not owners of the tenancy, nor are they allowed the use of the major social services on the scheme, such as education. The laborers fill a lower rung in the tripartite scheme relationship. Some schemes have permanent laborers, and still recruit seasonal laborers for the tenant in the Rahad. The distinction between permanent and seasonal laborers adds to dissatisfaction which surfaces at the crucial harvest time.

Two major actions recommended by the AID Rahad evaluation team are the introduction of sorghum cultivation and integrating livestock to the scheme. Nomad-tenants will maintain small livestock herds on their tenancies despite the eventual corporation's rules on the Rahad's 100% intensive crop rotation.

The construction and operation of the Rahad Scheme was supposed to have learned from the failures of past schemes, especially the Gezira. Taking that into consideration, the Rahad is expected to deliver the success story needed for Sudan's economy. Both the economic and social organization are a part of the scheme's production structure, seeing that the social participation and organization of the tenants are very low at the other schemes. Improving social conditions would increase the incentives for the tenants.

Widowed, female-headed households are not considered for tenancy on the Rahad Scheme, however women do the sowing, weeding, and harvesting on both subsistence and mechanized or irrigated schemes. In the Gezira widowed women can continue working their deceased husband's tenancy (see the ILO report vol 1). The Gezira and related schemes focus on the individual male farmer, allocating a tenancy to him and not to his family, although the nuclear family remains the unit of production. The status and responsibility of men increase as a result of "modernization", at the expense of women.

Through a brief history of the performance, success, and failure of the Gezira scheme and other large schemes, we may comprehend the scale of the problems the Sudan faces today. The arguments in favor of the country's push for agricultural progress did not anticipate the results affecting the culture and social structure of the area. The original blueprint for the Gezira, and hence all subsequent schemes, was drawn up by British rulers, seeking ways to raise funds in the Sudan to cover the costs of administration and, at the same time, assist the Lancashire Mills. The performance of schemes so far have caused cultural disruption, although this was far from being the aim of the planners. Our account highlights the economic and social arguments for the establishment of the Gezira scheme, which served as the model design for the later state farms. Given the government pressure to build more schemes, planners used the model of Gezira to create Suki, Guneid, Managil, and Rahad (to mention a few) to address the country's economic crisis. The emphasis has always been placed on an economic rationale. Thus, we experience once again a long standing problem, the failure to articulate economic development with changes in culture and society. The situation is serious; agricultural projects lag behind, but the pressure for growth continues. The hopes for growth through more land under cultivation and increased crop production persist in the midst of social chaos and cultural disorientation. Whose responsibility is the present cultural disruption and chaotic social situation, and who should address these problems? Where do the pressures for additional agricultural growth come from? We have learnt that state schemes are not manageable, and that the role of the farmer is inadequately addressed in the running of the schemes. Even when planners try to execute well conceived ideas for economic development, it may be impossible to integrate into preconceived analytic frameworks the processes and details of implementation, as well as the impact of the plan on different social groups.

Notes

[1] Irrigation is a very expensive venture costing on an average LS4.83 per *feddan*. The infrastructure for irrigation depends on the physical import of machinery, insecticides, and fertilizers.

[2] In 1947 a tenant's union was formed and in 1950 the Gezira Scheme itself was nationalized, to be managed by the Sudan Gezira Board (SGB). Tenants had a voice in decision-making through the formation of village councils which are known as production councils today.

[3] Presently *nafir*, maintenance of tribal and village lands, and the relationship of the farmer to the land have all changed.

[4] This is difficult to determine since we have no access to cross-check information.

Agricultural Schemes

[5] Blue and White Nile waters allowed the horizontal expansion of Sudan's irrigated lands.

[6] Salaam, M. Abdel, *The Institutional Development of the Sudan Gezira Scheme*, May, 1979, University of Reading, Department of Agricultural Economics and Management. Unpublished doctoral dissertation.

[7] In this case, labor migration is voluntary.

[8] *Shail* is a form of credit, where one's crop is mortgaged for cash and at harvest time the crop is given in repayment. Only this way can farmers get credit.

[9] A tenant in the modern agricultural sector who depends only on his tenancy will be driven into debt because of the scheme's low yields and "...because of the amount and the periodization of payments which he receives from the management" (Sorbo 1980:18).

[10] One may well question the value of economic change, from "traditional" to "modern" if the socio-economic evils continue to prevail in the system. Those farmers who opted to retain their subsistence farms have incorporated other income generating activities and managed to alleviate the *shail* more successfully than is possible for the modern farmer.

[11] Recent studies and surveys on subsistence agricultural farmers show that when compared economically to modern farms, they are in a better position. They combine agricultural activities with a number of other agro-related opportunities dividing their work time in accordance with their traditional cultivation cyle (Adams & Howell 1979; Barnett 1977; Fruzzetti 1979; Fruzzetti 1982; ILO Report for the Sudan 1978; Sorbo 1980).

[12] A Board member we interviewed gave the following figures: Government 36%; Tenants 47%; Sudan Gezira Board 10%; Tenants Reserve Fund 2%; Local Government 2%; Social Development Fund 3%.

[13] Tenant farmers' complaints differ drastically from those of tenant-nomads in regard to the Board of the scheme.

[14] The survey was done soon after the cotton harvest. It showed that the income from groundnuts is lower than any other income generating activity, even though it is a cash crop.

[15] See the ILO Report *Growth, Employment and Equity: A Comprehensive Strategy for the Sudan*, and the rejoinder to the report (Howell and Adams 1979).

[16] The demise of many other mechanized schemes is due to a lack of

balance between the maximum production output and the tenants' expectations and welfare.

17 Some of these immigrant laborers have managed to obtain Sudanese nationality, to satisfy the scheme's eligibility for a tenancy.

8

Culture and Development

In the course of our discussion we ranged from particular projects to large scale schemes, from markets and officials to judges and defendants, from villages to towns, and from women in production to traders in the *suq*. We devoted the bulk of the study to a series of case studies: law courts, markets, administration, and development projects in schemes and villages, each concerning an aspect of culture in the context of social change in the Blue Nile Province.

We did our fieldwork at a time when the Sudan was embarking on major development projects, in a place where the tensions and directions of this effort were clearest to see. Social science research and university involvement was increasing in the development process, yet there was no extended and systematic discussion, at any stage or level, of what "development" means, where, when, and for whom.

When we arrived in the Sudan our aim was to do a broad, long term, cultural study in a changing societal context. But immediately we were confronted with the pressing issues of rapid development and had to face the question of what our work could contribute. We took part in surveys, social impact studies, project research and evaluation, and research staff training and teaching. The present volume grew out of these activities as much as the wider theoretical concerns described in Chapter 1. A less fragmented time in the field would have yielded a different book, yet we believe that an orientation to symbol, meaning, and value is of significance even if we could not do as complete a cultural analysis as we wished. Hence some of the disclaimers in Chapter 1. Beyond these we are not at all reluctant to draw the appropriate conclusions from our study.

We criticized the accounts of development for failing to take into account particular situations, not just the issues of importance in a locality but the ways in which localities are tied to development agencies, donor nations and national, regional bureaucracies, markets, and courts. These factors have to be made a part of the theories themselves. Dependency theories blame the abstract world system too quickly while ignoring the in-between levels of development. In a different way modernization theories also assume too much in terms of the rationalizing behavior of the people in-between. These people are the merchants, judges, lawyers, and officials of our study.

Dichotomies such as tradition versus modernity, economics versus religion, real fact versus ideal value, and social basis versus cultural embellishment facilitate only one kind of development positing contending forces for or against change, with indigenous values and social formations ultimately condemned or at least marked for transformation. Hence the necessity of studying all cultural and social forms in a small compass in order to see the links among them. Community, tribal, and economic studies too often assume that they are faced with isolated domains rather than parts related in a whole. A critical evaluation of these dichotomies suggests that they cannot cope with the ambiguity and multiplicity of social formations, modes of living, and modes of thought in non-western societies today. No society can step consciously from tradition into modernity. In many cases pre-colonial social and cultural structures expressing values and meanings unchanged throughout the last two hundred years, exist in intricately overlapping relationships with planned national economies, bureaucracies, political parties, and urban classes. These multiple social, economic, religious, and political formations either succeed or fail to articulate, partially or completely, with each other within the newly created, overarching nation states. On our evidence there are more failures than successes.

The meanings of social relationships for the participants in such complex situations are not easy to discover, yet we think this is our task. In order to understand change we tried to apprehend the contexts, categories, manner and form of change. Simple-minded concentration on processes of change per se does not deliver meaning. Although claims about values and meanings are bandied about with ease in works of social science nowadays, these are notoriously difficult of access, resolution, and understanding. Once the separate concerns of our enquiry are unified as theories or hypotheses for the study of Sudanese societies, it is still open for empirical field study to establish the categories and data for analysis, and to determine the nature of the relationships between cultural, structural, and value considerations in the study of change. To what extent does this approach reveal conflict, contradiction, harmony, or integration within the various Sudanese social formations analyzed in terms of culturally constructed categories, values, and social structure? Do the different levels of society from "tribe" to "nation state" articulate with each other or are they in conflict? What is the nature of integration and/or conflict? Here too our understanding is helped by a systematic attempt to link values to cultural and social relations in order to understand the extent of change. Placing the focus of study on these issues, we may discover the meaning of change which studies more insistently concerned with change fail to achieve.

The specific features of the Damazin-Roseiris region illuminate the more general aspects of Sudanese society and the problems facing the

Sudan as state, nation, and government. The context of the current development effort is the overall shifting of emphasis by the Sudanese government and the international development agencies towards the concerns of rural society, agricultural production and agro-industries, and social justice, including the realization of a full human potential for all groups in Sudanese society, especially those in the most disadvantaged position. This shift is to be seen in the light of the failure of previous approaches to modernization and capital-intensive, purely economy oriented development. Changed emphasis does not, however, replace, let alone supercede, the continuing concern with returns on investment, foreign exchange earnings, GNP, and per capita income. Nevertheless the new concern with the rural poor is evident in planning, administration, and development aid, as well as in the political, social and cultural policies of national integration. Other contexts to be recognized are the attempt to build federated, regional states with a strong center in Khartoum (following the Addis Ababa peace agreement and the setting up of new regional governments) decentralization, the process of reconciliation, and the related expansion of authorized political activity to facilitate a broader societal participation in government and politics.[1]

Administration, Politics, and Development

During the past 200 years the Damazin-Roseiris region went through many political and administrative changes. It was a part of the Funj sultanate comprising several Mekships, and became a center during the Hamaj succession during the sultanate's period of decline. Under Turkish rule, Roseiris was a military-administrative center. During the Mahdiya, the region experienced considerable dislocation of population. Brish colonial rule it made it a district and after independence it became a part of a larger province. But in 1974 Damazin became the capital of the Blue Nile Province with newly redrawn boundaries. With an area of 142,000 square miles the province holds 27 percent of Sudan's population, has ample lands for cultivation, and is rich in resources.

A number of characteristics distinguish the province from the rest of Sudan. The Funj sultanate was the largest, most unified, indigenous kingdom in the Sudan. Many tribes, with diverse religious beliefs, were tolerated under the Meks' rule. Under British protectionist rule, the entry of immigrants from other part of the Sudan was forbidden. Hence the presence of a long-standing, homogenous population in this region in contrast to the Western and Northern Sudan.

As in the rest of the Sudan, land in the Blue Nile Province belongs to the State. Farmers have the right to use but not to sell land. The development of agricultural land began to take shape at the turn of the century, initially in the eastern and northern parts, where water and land were abundant. The later development of the Blue Nile farmlands along the lines of the Gezira Scheme drew on the early successes of the scheme, disregarding the subsequent chaos and confusion which were the long term result of implementation. The people of the province were not prepared for the encounter with developers and their designs for progress. They were unfamiliar with ideas of growth, change and the role of technology in farming. Since the 1960s, there has been an influx of investors and speculators with grand ideas, who were quick to grasp the opportunity provided by the availability of uncultivated arable land and a reliable water supply. In contrast to northern and western Sudan, the Blue Nile has the natural resources that invite exploitation by state and private ventures while the local inhabitants remain confused and uninvolved. To them any further development is of questionable benefit.

Throughout the 1970's and early 1980's the often contradictory aims of provincial government administration have been to equalize the economic condition of the tribes *(gabilas)*, solve the nomad-cultivator problem, improve animal husbandry for the nomads, save the forests, expand the lumber industry, increase mechanized agriculture and solve the attendant socio-economic problems, increase production, encourage tourism, and control the trade with Ethiopia. Government revenues derive mainly from forest products, taxes on animals, taxes on the movement of produce, sesame seed and oil export monopoly, and mining in the Ingessana hills. Separate development plans were drawn up for the Ingessana people (See Appendix 2) and for some of the villages of the Kurmuk and Geissan area.

The provincial government's budget is divided in two: the substantial part is for expenses of the departments, the other, a fraction of the former, is for local development. The major part of the development effort is centrally funded though ideally it is locally coordinated. There is a tendency to set up autonomous development authorities; scheme-based corporations that bypass the local administration. As we have seen, this creates as many problems as it solves. Furthermore, development is merely coordinated by the *mudriya:* it is directed and supervised by the Sudan Socialist Union (SSU). This, too, creates complications. Currently, the Blue Nile Province hosts several major schemes: the Suki agricultural scheme; the Abu Naama Kenaf scheme; the sugar, spinning and ginning factories of Sennar; the Kenana sugar scheme; the Faisal agricultural and livestock scheme; the Takamul agricultural scheme. Many others equal or bigger in scope are starting up or being planned (See Figure 1.1). In addition there are many local improvement schemes such as roads, rest houses, fisheries, clinics, schools and communications projects, as well as a stadium and a theater in Damazin and Roseiris, undertaken in connection with the independence celebrations and the President's visit to Damazin in 1978. The SSU is involved in all these efforts, especially in the attempts to improve services: educational, health, veterinarian, communications, water, and several self-help projects in the villages and the two towns.

In the 1970's many projects were put in around the two towns. Mechanized agriculture was being extended. Agadi was to reach 300,000 *feddans* soon and the total was expected to go beyond 1,000,000 *feddans* in each of the four sections slated for development. The vast schemes of the

Saudi agricultural and livestock company and the Triad livestock and meat producing company were planned at 1,000,000 *feddans* each. Sizeable tracts of land have been given over to major development projects aided by Yugoslavia, the United States, Netherlands, Korea, and the Sudanese Emigrants' Investment Fund. Mining in the Ingessana hills involved Chinese, Japanese, Kuwaits, and others. The Roseiris dam was to be heightened by 10 meters to allow irrigation facilities. Several irrigation schemes were planned. A number of generators were being added to the Damazin powerplant driven by the turbines of the dam. The dam was under the separate and central authority of the Ministry of Irrigation, without any local governmental role for the Damazin administration. The generators were dealt with by the Water and Electricity Corporation of the Ministry of Energy. None of the corporations was linked to the local administration, although departments of the *mudriya* often paralleled the work of local corporation officials and offices. To complicate matters further, the SSU had its own parellel organization for development, which was meant to be the vanguard of planning, direction, guidance, and thought.

Although parallel functions, unclear precedence, and hierarchy make for tensions in the relations between local administration, the SSU, and the autonomous corporations, there is a general *tenmiya* (development) ideology common to functionaries of all three, as well as the more educated, company-based commerical producers and traders. These are some of the new men brought into the political-economic process by the mobilization and changes achieved in the course of the 16 year rule of the May, 1969, regime. We should include in this group the older elites of the region, at least in the matter of attitudes to *tenmiya*. In this view, development amounts to education, Islam, mechanized farming, and human and animal health which benefit people, although the extent to which sections of the population should benefit is in dispute, and so is the desired pace, extent, and distribution of the process. In the almost universal perception by the new men, old elites, and merchants, the local people, subsistence cultivators, and tribals have to be pushed to be civilized since they are reluctant, even lazy. Furthermore, West African immigrants compete with the locals, to the disadvantage of the latter. They feel that development projects should be beneficial to them, since anything is preferable to existing destitution. They say wage labor will at least inject new wants and new consumption into the stagnating local society. Thus the development ideology links economic, political, and religious considerations even though methods and beneficiaries are disagreed about by the different proponents of the ideology. Industrialization is also seen as development, including the cotton ginning, asbestos manufacturing, chromite and other mining, cement manufacturing, meat, fish, agricultural and horticultural produce processing, all started or are being planned for the region. Also included in *tenmiya* (at least in administrative and political circles), are the town improvement of Damazin and the building of offices and housing for officials.

However, the ideology engages very selectively with the social composition of the region, since the social (tribal, ethnic, elite, class) aspects are so little appreciated. The effects of economic change and the response of the different sections of rural and urban society are merely assumed. It is accepted that the different elements and processes of development noted above will not have a uniform impact, yet the overall effect is still deemed to be beneficial. Officials appreciate that some schemes are tenant, others directly export oriented, and yet others are seeking profits for foreign investors. Yet, in the official view, the destruction of self-sufficient "primitive" ways of life and the transformation of owner-cultivators into wage laborers are "beneficial", in the long run, because these processes "improve" the material and social conditions of the whole region, introduce general standards, break down isolation and pull everyone into a visible center. It is argued furthermore, that the above factors create a uniform pattern of work and improve the position of women, since "the men too will have to work". But no training, direction, and guidance is provided for the course of the development process. Younger officials point out that the already sophisticated worker will benefit while the "tribal," including the "nomad," will be degraded.

The "civilizing" mission of officials and merchants can be linked in part to the increasing effects of Arabizing and Islamizing influences and processes, and in part to increasing trade, migration, and the general impact of outside forces on the local communities. Although expectations are high in every quarter, the precise social and political consequences of development cannot be predicted. At best, we can point to the possible results of change which include the disintegration of local social systems, including values, without the assurance that changed practices and institutions with their concomitent new values will replace what has been lost. Detail is necessary for planned change, yet planners are impatient with the imponderability of everyday social life and the enormous variety of probable consequences attending intervention. It is, as if in recognition of this, that the people of Damazin/Roseiris often speak about being *taban:* tired, weak, in a state of decline. *Taban* is a general term referring to a falling away from a previous, ideal state -- a loss of values and a decline of ethics. This despite or perhaps because of the efforts of developing and modernizing the region.

Changes are affecting the *suq* as well. But the oft repeated, dispairing question of planners and officials, "why don't the merchants look ahead and use the mechanisms of the market" is misplaced. The *suq* manages with what is given. The present systems of distribution and communication cannot be relied on, so, at best, merchants muddle through rather than plan. Doing with what there is, the *suq* constantly rearranges existing parts of the system in preference to introducing new practices. This way of doing things *is* inventive, and merchants are not against innovation, because abruptly introduced new elements may break the links among the parts of the existing system.

Merchants regard their way of life superior to farming and agriculture.

This is a society-wide valuation. It is linked with notions of free market *(suq hurr)*, meaning a freedom to trade and to set prices and supplies locally or in trading with other markets, without any meddling by government and officials. The idea is that the "benefit" (profit) a merchant receives should be left for traders to enjoy and not given to the administration. Traders pride themselves on being their own person, free to pursue customary trading practices no matter where they are placed in the *suq* hierarchy. Other values they adhere to are respect, trust, fate, and reputation. These all play a role in the local way of handling supplies, money, capital, and credit. The intrusion of government agencies, corporations, and larger, outside trading companies makes for havoc in the system. While merchants complain bitterly about officials and government interference, they don't resent the activities of the big trading companies. Traders argue that there is room for big and small in the *suq* and that one kind of trade will not harm another. In the indigenous conception the market is a hierarchical system with many interests accomodated within its wide reach. The big companies rank above the local merchants, so as long as the latter can sell to the former both should find a place in the scheme of things and need not threaten each other. Local traders feel that since they have links at their level, in terms of contacts, respect, trust, and history, they cannot be squeezed out. They do not see that time is on the companies' side: in the long run it is the latter which will be able to stock more produce and choose the right time to sell.

The *suq* faces another challenge in view of the relations between officials and merchants. Trade being prestigious and profitable, more and more outsiders with better contacts for loans and contracts in Khartoum form cooperatives and invest in mechanized schemes, with the aim of short term profits. Professionals, soldiers, and officials from towns and cities as far away as Khartoum are involved in these practices. Contracts for transportation pertaining to government projects are awarded by officials to particular scheme owners who, in turn, help officials invest in and run mechanized schemes.

The ideology of development is linked, at least among the urban, educated professionals and administrators and the old elites (including merchants and those educated in *khalwas*), to a belief in the enduring Sudanese, Islamic values based on family, clan, and brotherhood. The expectation is that economic change will not affect the locus, source, and survival of these values and beliefs (see Chapter 1). Technology is seen as a separate component, unattached to society as a whole, to be acquired and transplanted as a "good thing", without strings attached. In one sense at least, *tenmiya* transcends economics, since in the past the periphery was, at times, able to challenge the center.[2] So Islamic belief and practice, Arabic language, style of dress, public behavior, visible aspects of family life and property rights, together with trade, markets and patterns of exchange are seen to have a "civilizing," transforming role in the non-Muslim, subsistence-oriented, small-scale tribal societies of the Sudan. These are strongly held beliefs in the Sudan today. Increased production, technology transfer, and the like are seen as added components in the process as perhaps faster, but not radically different, agents of a transformation already underway. In the past Islamic universalism, justice, law, and tolerance in addition to the principles of fusion in pre-colonial segmentary societies of the Sudan allowed the emergence of centralized, over-arching polities.

Mudriya and SSU relations are not only wary and tense, they are also overlapping. In addition to the Commissioner, several high officials hold dual appointments as Assistant Commissioners in the administration and Assistant Secretaries in the SSU. The latter screen candidates and supervise local elections. The *mudriya* is never without SSU men talking to the officials, consulting files and enquiring about particular procedures. Since the SSU parallels the function and structure of administration, it may act in a supervisory and directive capacity. This not only makes for resentment and rivalry, but also confusion and slowed-down, sometimes contradictory decision-making. The problem of hierarchy and the weak horizontal and vertical linkages are endemic to both institutions. The rungs of the ladder can be and are leapt over, and access does not proceed step by step throughout the system. Higher officials can reach the local councils directly, and sometimes, through extra-office links, lower levels can reach the top directly. The hierarchy is often perceived, at all levels, as a delaying and insulating, rather than a facilitating mechanism.

There is collusion as well as conflict between political and administrative officials. Both kinds of *muazzafeen* are imposed on regional societies and local people often do not distinguish between the two. Nevertheless both exert a direct influence on local society through the *suq* and the development projects.

Officials are a society unto themselves. *Muazzafeen* society has its own hierarchy, code of conduct, and bureaucratic norms and rules. Most officials, especially the lower ranks, are caught in the web of conflicts generated by their participation in office, family, and the wider society. Some are able to utilize kinship and *gabila* ties in the two towns. If they are serious enough, they can turn these links to tangible benefit with merchants in the *suq* or with owners of mechanized schemes. Nevertheless, almost all of them experience some contradiction between the demands of *awlad* (family), *gabila* (tribe), *tariga* (brotherhood), Islamic practices, and administration. Many of these demands are alien to the local society and the unique mixture of expectation and responsibility with which most officials have to live is incomprehensible to local people. Hence, officials live in a cultural context that shares only some of its aspects with the local society. The modernizing values of the bureaucracy are derived from outside the local cultural system and are linked to the national system of civil law, economic development and planning, and to the rationalizing attempts of administration. Many officials tend to resolve these contradictions in their several lives by trying to be men for all seasons. However, meeting contradictory demands is achieved at great personal cost, at the expense of either family, self, office, or the local society.

"Corruption" is one way of resolving these tensions. The individual is able to construct his own hierarchy within such a system, and he can rationalize his choices in terms of several systems of valuation.

Complications emerge most clearly in the way development projects appear on the ground in the Blue Nile Province. Major projects, especially those with foreign involvement, are agreed to in the Presidential Palace in Khartoum in concert with the highest political and administrative officers. Eventually, local government and SSU units become involved (as do merchants and other local leaders), but the extra local links of kinship and other ties remain and may be institutionalized by bringing the project under a completely separate development authority or corporation with direct responsibility to a minister or council of ministers. Since the projects come down from the top, the problems of local articulation remain an afterthought. Particular projects may make perfectly good sense for the Sudan as a whole and articulate well with other major undertakings in general or in relation to specific economic segments of the country, but in the areas where they are located, they fail to articulate with or distort in their impact whatever is already there (i.e., local societies in their economic, religious, political, and kinship aspects). Yet, at the same time the provincial administration is expected to help in the execution of project goals while the SSU is expected to monitor the direction and performance of major schemes.

National reconciliation has opened the way for participation in elections, and although the SSU had to approve candidates prior to the 1978 elections, there was considerable local involvement in the elections in the two towns and the countryside as a whole. We must note that the numbers involved here were very small. Elections for the Provincial Council were through local (rural and town) councils, and through the popular organizations of the SSU, such as the Nile land farmers', merchants', officials', and government workers' associations. Thus successful candidates could be elected by a few dozen votes. Larger numbers were involved in the election categories of professionals, merchants, and traders and in the races for geographical seats. But even these did not exceed several hundred. At the meetings of the Provincial Council administrators still take a pedagogic and training approach to the deliberations, and the discussions between appointed and elected members take the form of question-answer sessions, clarifications, and information sharing. Nevertheless the elections in the region were widely anticipated and the local people welcomed with ethusiasm this widening of participation in the political process. Many candidates entered, among them some who were ruled out previously because of their connections with the disbanded political parties. While several of the old elite were returned, especially in the legislative assembly, the new men failed to hold their ground in the provincial and local elections. This was, in part, due to the specific nature of the electoral process in the categories of occupation and administration, but merchants and local leaders did well in the less circumscribed rural councils. The ill-defined role of the SSU created some confusion and although some SSU men were elected to the various councils, there were no official candidates. The one party functioned as a channel of participation and although a number of SSU men were defeated many were reappointed to their party positions. As a result, however, elections to all levels of the SSU were promised, where the previous practice, especially at the higher levels, has been direct appointment as a reward for party services.

Subsistence Versus Modern Farmers

The contrast between two kinds of farming makes sense for our data from the Gezira and other schemes as well as the situation obtaining in the villages east of Damazin. The more recent projects such as the BNIADP attempted, so far unsuccessfully, to convert the traditional into a modern farmer without recruiting him into a scheme, relying instead on the introduction of new institutions and practices into the village and the local system of cultivation.

Traditional subsistence farmers can be compared to modern tenant farmers in terms of their position in the process of production, and in terms of the cultural contexts in which production takes place. Labor migration from the rural areas into the modern schemes is voluntary and the socio-economic attractions are as clear as the subsequent negative results.

The traditional farmer is engaged in subsistence economy, with an elementary farming technique, and an age-old system of slash and burn agriculture. His farm is about 8-10 *feddans*, cultivating about 2 to 3 *feddans* a year at a time. He takes few risks. Contrary to popular belief, he will accept farming innovations, seriously considering the alternatives. Since his agricultural production is not enough to satisfy the needs of his family, he must supplement his farm income from other sources.[3] He seeks employment in fruit gardens or he may work as a seasonal laborer on a large scheme. On the scheme, he is paid a minimal daily wage and a living allowance. If the subsistence farmer does not want to supplement his income through additional agricultural work, he can seek temporary employment in nearby towns and cities. He can plant whatever crop he wants to: the decision rests with him alone. If he decides to let some of his land go fallow for a few years, he can do this without fear of losing his right to the land.

In the modern agricultural sector the tenant farmer is employed at the inception of a scheme; he is a permanent resident rather than a temporary laborer. The tenant is given a number of *feddans* and is told what crops to plant. His position is different from that of the seasonal laborer in that his relationship to the scheme is of a long-term rather than a temporary nature. If he needs additional help on his tenancy, he hires migrant laborers. Tenant farmers and migrant wage laborers together form the modern sector of agriculturalists.

The modern farmer is under surveillance by a board; he can be evicted from the scheme if he fails to comply with its rules since he has no tangible rights over the land he farms. His crops are divided into those which are sold by the board and those which are under his own control. If he plants cotton, he has no right to dispose of the crop on the market. The cotton belongs to the government. After the crop is sold, deductions are made for water and land use, insecticides, and seeds. When all expenses have been deducted, the farmer receives around a 40 percent share of the profits. This figure may seem to be a sizeable return, but not all tenants receive it. Before a farmer is paid, further deductions must be made for the cash advances extended to him earlier in the year. Thus a farmer receives a much lower income.

Tenants on some irrigated schemes are allowed to cultivate specific crops, unlike schemes which are under a monocrop system, such as the Guneid Sugar Scheme. Additional crop cultivation (besides cotton, sugar, and wheat) is an added attraction for the tenant. These crops, such as groundnuts, are the prerogative of the farmer who in turn sells them on the open market rather than to a central board.[4] Given the tenants' depressed economic condition we question the social viability of capital intensive schemes. Still it it can be argued that the overall economic condition of the tenant farmer has improved, especially during the first years following the development of these schemes. Besides the tenancy which is given to the farmer when he joins a scheme in a tripartite partnership, social services and facilities are also provided. Some of these serve as part of the scheme infrastructure which adds to the attraction of modern agriculture. Educational facilities and health services are extended to all those connected with the scheme. However, in time, such social services deteriorate and add to the general malaise.

The three-way partnership between the government, scheme management and tenants is, when considered horizontally, egalitarian, but when viewed vertically, the relationship is very much hierarchical. The tenant as a partner is placed into a contractual relationship with the board and the state. The scheme's management is salaried and receives a monthly income, whereas the tenant has to wait for the sale of the cash crop before he gets back his labor costs. Given these social and economic conditions, what begins as an attractive opportunity in time changes, leaving the tenant the option of abandoning the scheme, or giving a higher priority to the non-cash subsistence crops. This has serious implications for the scheme and for the national economy.

Culturally, a tenant may view leaving as a defeat and may consider it a loss of prestige to go back to his old subsistence farm. The longer a farmer stays on a scheme, the more difficult it becomes for him to move out. If he does leave, he may move to a newer scheme, where the arrangements are slightly different. What has happened over the last few years is extensive "scheme hopping". This trend of tenants leaving one scheme for another is alarming. An older scheme is often allowed to run down upon the rise of a new one. In addition, as older tenants move among the schemes, their children leave the tenancies and agriculture for urban blue-collar work. Some farmers find that it is more profitable to be paid wage labor, especially on older schemes. As laborers, they are given a daily wage, wheras tenants have to wait out a long process before they are actually paid their accumulated wages.

Thus the farmer's life in the modern agricultural sector is very different from that of the traditional subsistence farmer. In most cases he does not cultivate in his home area, but has to leave his village, family, and tribe to work on a scheme. Rather than owning the farm, the tenant farmer is merely an employee, hired either by the scheme owner or the scheme board. The farm belongs to the scheme and not to the person who works it. As a migrant laborer, he sells his labor to a scheme in exchange for wages. After working for three to four months, he returns to his village. If he decides to extend his contract with the scheme, he sends part of his wages home to his family while he stays behind.

As part of the Sudan's national planning, almost all new development effort is directed towards extending existing agricultural projects by bringing more land under cultivation. Extensions to the Gezira Scheme resulted in more land under irrigation and in the promotion of tenant cultivation under state management. Recently, the state has been encouraging private mechanized farming schemes by extending credit to those individuals willing to take the challenge. Unfortunately, most economic planning is directed at the eastern part of the country where there are already a large number of highly organized development projects. A recent report by the International Labor Organization (ILO) questions the economic development plans of the Sudanese Government in the light of depressed economic conditions in the western and southern parts of the country. "It argues that traditional agriculture and animal husbandry are capable, in the long term, of better returns to investment than either mechanized rainfall or irrigated agriculture" (Adams and Howell 1979:506). The ILO feels that the traditional sector should also be modernized by making investments "in social and economic overhead capital programs... to achieve the technical and organizational advances necessary to improve the welfare of the poor" (Adams and Howell 1979: 513).

When the government of the Sudan envisions a "modernized" traditional agricultural sector it thinks in terms of "horizontal expansion:" the mechanization of traditional agriculture, the extension of land under existing systems of cultivation and the creation of links between traditional and irrigated/modern agriculture. But the government has been operating under the old pattern of development, emphasizing expansion rather than intensification and rehabilitation. Instead of trying to increase the yield per *feddan*, the government is increasing the total number of *feddans* under cultivation. By choosing quantity rather than quality, in the long run the land is endangered. It is clear that the problem with low yields does not reside in the number of *feddans* under cultivation but in the mismanagement of the schemes and the alienation of the tenant farmer.

Recent surveys by various funding agencies and individual social scientists have clearly demonstrated that large irrigation schemes yield high rates of return during the first few years but later are marked by low soil productivity and declining yields. All the large schemes have had low productivity curves and, as a result, there is little hope for an improvement in the life of the tenant farmer. As a result the agricultural sector's net contribution to government revenues has decreased over the last few years. Declining yields and poor economic performance are identified not with traditional farms but with irrigation schemes which grow crops such as cotton and sugarcane. According to Sorbo, Sudanese agricultural projects expose the society and its economy to considerable instability (Sorbo, 1980:2).

What has happened over the last few years in the Sudan is the creation of a mobile working class; a new class with a promising but uncertain future. This class will not assume old status roles similar to those in traditional villages and may emerge as a class with new values. Such a class, based primarily in the rural areas will become an important political force as the economic crisis grows in intensity. As the supply diminishes there is a higher demand for labor. The "new" farmer has begun to understand the value of his labor and to bargain for better work relationships and contractual terms. Greater awareness and agitation contribute to increasing conflict and instability.

The Sudan lacks a plan for comprehensive rural development.[5] Today the modern agricultural sector expands at the expense of the traditional sector, even though the productivity of the modern farmer is on the decline. The development of markets through the expansion of agriculture has resulted in a new structure of production in places such as the export-oriented Gezira. However, the problems in the Sudan are graver than they appear. The communication infrastructure is still in its infancy. The few roads which connect the production areas to the nearest markets are in poor repair. In many instances the poor transportation and communication system is the reason why traditional farmers produce enough for household consumption but cannot produce and market a surplus. Besides a lack of infrastructure, the traditional farmer does not contribute to the modern market because "customary land rights, which evolved to regulate subsistence and wealth in a traditional society, are not well adapted to the demands of the market economy" (Sorbo, 1980:2).

Large schemes decrease the amount of available land to the subsistence farmer and the traditional agricultural sector is being encroached upon by wealthy, private members of Sudanese society. Having the financial means at their disposal, they can exploit large tracts of land using modern farming methods and then store and transport grain to the major markets. Rather than work the land himself, the entrepreneur might live in an urban area and hire people to work and manage his land. The entrepeneur, unlike the traditional farmer, does not have long-term interest in the land. After farming an area for a number of years, the entrepeneur moves on to a different economic venture. When he leaves his scheme, the soil is depleted of nutrients and is prey to desertification. The traditional farmer does not continue to cultivate a piece of land until it is completely stripped of its nutrients, but lets it go fallow first. Before he cultivates the area again, he allows for long periods of bush fallow, a traditional way of replacing the store of nutrients consumed by cultivation (Adams and Howell 1979).

Rather than continue on the present path, the Sudan has to develop plans which take into account the "welfare of the people, expanded earnings and foreign exchange, and conservation of resources" (Adams and Howell 1979:513). These three priorities require both organizational and attitudinal change, and must be set against the problems of inflation. When reformulating development strategies, attempts will have to made to integrate agricultural plans with animal husbandry by liberalizing the grazing rights of the pastoralists.

At present, development plans, project implementation, and management are imposed from the top down. This does not allow for the organization or formation of grass root infrastructure. The structure of administration, as seen from the bottom, is hierarchical and complex. The responsibilities of people within the hierarchy are vaguely defined and work boundaries are unclear. In this situation, expertise in an area is not always the criterion used when making an appointment. Appointments can be, and often are, political. The results of this system are project implementation delays and confusion in regard to positional responsibilities and requirements.

Many ways to improve the agricultural sector of the Sudan have been suggested by the ILO, private planners, and economists. These range from the creation of a new ministry with new staff, to the expansion of the existing corporations. To all the people involved with development, however, it is becoming evident that there are problems. Today the tenant farmer lacks the confidence the scheme boards were supposed to generate. The corporation has become the rural farmer's stumbling block to the extent that communication has decreased and trust between two parties has been lost over the years. The present situation is basically one in which the tenant farmer and the administrators work against, rather than with, each other.

Given the present impasse there are alternatives, all equally difficult to pursue. The first is to dissolve the existing structure, commencing with the administrative system of modern irrigation agriculture. It has been stated numerous times that the administrative body is the ultimate cause of declining productivity rates. It is not merely the administration, but the lack of communication between the management and the tenant farmer that is at the root of the problem. The second is to stop expanding the area under cultivation and to concentrate on intensifying production on existing farms. Since the moderns farms are operating at declining rates of production, expanding the cultivated area does not solve but compounds the problems of productivity. Ultimately, these problems must be addressed rather than avoided or temporarily circumvented. Presently, managerial bodies are at odds with the farmers. The hierarchical nature of the system has detached the administration from its tasks. Agricultural schemes are too large and unwieldy to be handled by tenant farmers who lack direct access to technical improvements and facilities. Yet, excluding the tenant farmer from participation in the decision making process (due to a lack of technical expertise) alienates him and sets the stage for problems during implementation. The third is to recognize, once and for all, that the nomads are viable partners in development. Plans for future development projects must include livestock, because failure to deal with this problem will jeopardize any development effort.

The aim of rural development should be to improve the social and economic life of the rural poor in such a way that they remain directly involved in the production process. Today, organizational obstacles are reinforced and complemented by attitudinal obstacles. It is more prestigeous to be an administrator on a large scheme than to be a lowly field officer. The same can be said of research. It is more prestigeous to be a member of an institution than an officer on a small agricultural outstation in the rural countryside.

Understanding Social Transformations in the Sudan

Throughout this volume we criticized, implicitly or explicitly, some general theories of modernization and development, in terms of their internal inconsistencies and failure to account for specific data. We argued that many of these theories link local situations to the "west" or to the "world system" in unacceptable and unnecessary ways. Our account of local markets and legal processes in terms of cultural categories and local principles, and our study of past and present practices of development moved between general interpretations and particular sets of data in given localities. It treated politics, economics, and administration as a part of indigenous culture, and as the local and extra local forms within which development planning and implementation take place. It showed the interplay of concrete and abstract factors as these come down on the ground in villages and towns and affect the lives of people. Thus the universe of the Berta or Hamaj villager includes the Damazin merchant and administrator as much as the local Omda or lineage head. We argued that the narratives of *suqs*, courts, and offices reveal significant cultural values that impinge directly on development and on local societies in the twin towns and the countryside. Merchants and officials themselves form a society and culture with ties to the villages as well as Khartoum and their own homelands.

The Sudan, like other Third World countries, needs new solutions to old problems, new capital, new organizatonal structures, and new links between society, administration, and development. Development is no longer an economic concern, it is a human problem. However well-meaning, the suggestions we have made are mere straws in the wind. Even well-designed, small-scale projects, in keeping with such advice, fail to be put into practice. The reasons are not hard to find. Our study of regional administration, politics, law, markets, and rural social structure shows the links between levels of culture, society, and economy in the context of development. When these links are ignored, and projects proceed as if they floated *sui generis* in a vacuum, the disappointing results are inevitable.

At the present time both policies and implementation can be faulted. In the large agricultural tenancy schemes, tenants receive directives from the Board of Schemes and decisions about cropping, irrigation, and the use of fertilizers are made by the managerial body. Lack of communication between the laborers and the officials continues to trouble the work relationships and affects the projects' growth.

Historically the two forms of rural subsistence, nomadism and agriculture, coexisted in a viable, if at times troubled relationship. The current competition over grazing lands and water resources was not a feature of rural life in the past. In the 1970s and 1980s officials and administrators in power have opted to expand agricultural lands, displacing grazing lands. The balance between nomadism and farming was thrown open to competition and conflict at both the local and the national level. Sedentary villagers are now uncertain about harvesting their crops, with embittered nomads at large in the area. Larger agricultural schemes often resort to the use of police force to restore order, especially in matters of agricultural labor disputes, nomad-farmer conflicts, and other issues which affect agricultural growth and productivity.

The government's horizontal view of planning the agricultural sector affects not only the nomads but the subsistence farmers as well. As more land is allocated to large-scale schemes, the developers encroach on the nomadic grazing corridors. The nomads move into new areas for grazing, approaching the regions of rain-fed subsistence agriculture, which, in turn, have been forgotten by the developers and economic planners. Integrating livestock into agricultural cash cropping benefits the nomads, lessens the labor shortage on the schemes and minimizes nomad and sedentary clashes. But such an integration is still problematic and a successful formula has yet to be found.

The current policy of bringing more land under cultivation exposes the land to desertification, increases the problems of agricultural laborers, and encourages farmers to search for blue-collar jobs in towns. On the subsistence farms the cultivator deserts his family in search of more renumerative jobs. Tenant farmers are obligated to produce cash crops, to adhere to restricted cropping patterns, and to cover the costs of production irrespective of low world market prices. The high cost of irrigating land often results in an inability to provide for ordinary consumption needs, and tenant farmers go "scheme-hopping" in search of better paying tenancies. A turn to fundamentalist religious brotherhoods has replaced, on some schemes, the following of reformist and radical political parties. Many tenant farmers now opt to return to their old subsistence lands or to emigrate to oil producing Arab countries.

The problems have long been identified but the solutions lag behind.

Years ago, the ILO report warned that a number of central issues have to be faced in all future plans. These were: decentralizing agricultural planning; intensifying production on existing schemes; assisting small farmers; including grain production (alongside cash crops) on schemes as an incentive to tenant farmers; rethinking of mechanization and evaluation of improved agricultural practices; encouraging small and middle-level farmers with appropriate incentives. Ignoring these alternatives holds out the prospect of further desertification, encroachment of mechanized schemes, worsening condition of landless labor, continued decline of grain production, low productivity of cash crops, dependence on fluctuating (and currently low) world market prices for cotton, and the appearance of near famine conditions in parts of eastern, southern, and western Sudan. Large scale irrigated and/or mechanized schemes are still the order of the day, but these have proven to be unproductive. The import of full-fledged development projects from the West (or East) have imposed an alien framework on local agricultural communities whose cultural and social conditions have not been considered in the design and implementation of projects ostensibly set in motion for their benefit.

The context in which the development effort is conducted includes government officials, religious figures, tribal leaders, merchants, teachers, nomads, farmers, and rural traders. All these people live and work in the same locality and participate in shared cultural patterns as well as in the wider society. To design improvement for some and not others, to imagine that some aspects of society will be affected and others will remain untouched, to expect that the various elements of regional as well as national welfare and society are separable and subject to selective, modular tinkering, is to delude oneself. In considering markets, administration, law, and development schemes we have seen how complex are the interrelations, and how powerful are the sway of both old and new cultural values and meanings. Customary law attempts to deal with the distractions thrown up by the development process. But increasingly law is being rationalized by the judicial system and the consensus-compromise pattern of the older system is being replaced by punishment and retribution linked with police and state power. Our study of courts reveals, nevertheless, the continuing significance of cultural values in the context of development, and demonstrates the tensions created by rapid change.

The legal system is an uneasy blend of local customary law, Shari'a law, and a national system of justice based on British civil and criminal law. At each level, different principles operate. In cultural terms local society is closest to customary law, while development and administration rest on the uniform, national civil code. The replacement of native courts by people's courts, the supercession of the latter as well as the Shari'a Courts by Civil Law, and the subsequent elevation of Shari'a above all else may serve to achieve national political and economic objectives, but it also creates and intensifies cultural conflict in different parts of the country. Law may be an instrument of social change but it can bring about dissolution just as well as integration. Conflict and disintegration are most clearly seen in the big projects and mechanized schemes where migrant laborers from different regions and cultures are brought together outside the context of their local societies. In addition, the problems of farmer-nomad conflict seem to be beyond the powers of the courts to resolve. The system of law is seen by local societies as alien and removed from the context of everyday life. Court officials are not an integral part of local society. Judgements are made in terms of value orientations that are incomprehensible to the indigeneous people.

Economic growth has tended to reinforce and even extend existing inequalities. Women are the worst sufferers. They are forced into less profitable positions and become even more dependent on men. Men can leave the rural community in search of better jobs, but the women stay behind, ignored by planners and politicians. Although women contribute heavily to local society and economy, their activities do not come into measurable categories hence their needs are not addressed in development projects. With the emphasis on cash wages, women tend to be pushed away from their traditional sources of income. Even at that, women find it harder to provide the household food from subsistence plots in the midst of agricultural modernization.

The study of administration shows the constraints within which all planned change has to take place. It is no surprise that many development schemes and projects attempt to by-pass the local administration and establish direct lines with the central government ministries or even the Presidential Palace in Khartoum. However, these shortcuts are themselves full of pitfalls, as we saw in the case of irrigated schemes. In addition, the proliferation of such development authorities and corporations further clogs the administrative system, creating more confusion, slower decisions, competition between offices, and resentment among the local staff. From our study it should be clear that administration is itself a society, sharing the functional, structural, and symbolic aspects of the wider society. But there is a difference: the specific cultural pattern of official society places a further burden of tension and potential conflict on the *muazzafeen*. The administrative system is itself in dire need of reform in order to make it more responsive to local needs and encourage local participation. If this were not enough, our account makes clear the debilitating duplication of effort and confusion of authority between the political and administrative aspects of the government machinery. Given this state of affairs, how can planners in Khartoum, Washington, London, Belgrade, or Tokyo calculate the economic rates of return and design sound production schemes for rural Sudan? The social scientist has to consider not only local societies, Sudanese officials and politicians, but international planners, consultants, and project implementation staff who have their own links to societies and cultures within and beyond the national boundaries of the Sudan. Project planners, officials and politicians, with their well-known penchant for short term, economic considerations may pride themselves for being hard-nosed realists, yet they carry their own invisible cultural burdens that bear devastating fruit in the long run.

In earlier sections of this volume we alluded to the convergence and the divergence between theories of modernization and dependency. We emphasized the convergence. We also argued that a holistic, comparative, cultural approach may transcend the limitations of either dependency or modernization. Both theories share the values of the European enlightenment, and the implications of the 19th century emergence of the "economy" and the economic domain. The insistence of modernization theory on rationality, bureaucracy, and the political domain does not contradict but complements the economic emphasis of underdevelopment. Perhaps more than either of these theories we can still learn from Marx and Weber, the source from which these emphases emerge.

Marx recognized the dominance and uniqueness of the market economy, and his sustained study of capitalist production allowed him to set 19th century England apart from other societies. Weber, significantly later, noted the separation of economics and politics, and the dominance of the latter. Again, this allowed him to contrast European with other societies. The importance of market economy (Marx) and political power (Weber) in the context of particular historical societies should enable us to follow the spirit of these comparative approaches. We can still learn from Marx's historical analyses of class and the social organization of production, and Weber's study of the links between bureaucracy, authority, and social classes. Yet, despite Weber, contemporary modernization theories developed evolutionary and diffusionistic features, typologies of society, stages of criteria for progress, and an ideology for the "West" to encounter the rest of the world. Similarly "Marxist" theories after Marx set up stages of development, economic criteria for a typology of societies, the recreation of Western economies elsewhere, mechanistic modes of production, and ideologies for the West and the "socialist" countries to encounter the rest of the world. But even if Marx and Weber remain relevant today we have to go beyond them to understand the post-Marx and post-Weber world. Modern social theory has to account for the increasing rationality of social systems, constraints and possibilities created by markets and/or planning, the emergence of dictatorship (Nazism and Stalinism) in industrial societies, and the ideological continuities persisting in all societies.

A comparative study has to construct the differences and similarities among societies out of the culture, traditions, and history of societies. It has to recognize the contrasts between advanced industrial societies and the rest of the world, but it also has to account for the variations among and within each of these. It has to ground the relations between economy, polity, and ideology in the advanced industrial societies (small, large, capitalist, socialist, and in between) and it has to construct the hierarchy and transformation of domains in Third World societies. And finally it has to encompass all societies in its comparative, methodological, and epistemological reach. In this endeavour we cannot set up stages of development or even of revolution. We cannot look on the technologically more "advanced" as the image of the less advanced countries' future. In such a comparative study we would have to situate category, object, and subject within the structure and dialectic of social relations and processes, and we would have to regard as problematic, an area of scientific discovery, not only what is investigated but the position of the investigator as well. The latter is always situated partly inside and partly outside what we endeavour to understand.

The social scientist has a responsibility to develop a critique embracing the theories as well as the social processes these theories would elucidate. The critique should extend to the concepts of development and modernization as well as the practices that are linked to these concepts. There is little value in anthropologists becoming functionaries of intervention. Doing is no substitute for thinking and there are dangers in the speedy "application" of received social wisdom. Nor is there any point in asking for cultural or social "inputs" to match energy and technology.

We may speculate that social scientists can sustain this kind of approach in specific as well as general work. In intervention projects in specific localities the tasks of research, intervention, and critique could proceed complementarily, with the anthropologist carrying out pre-project research, contributing to the design of the plans, and continually evaluating the performance. In this, however, the researcher should not be identifed with a segment of a project, nor made to come up with palliatives and immediate applicability at every instant. Particular items of application would result from research but this alone should not become the measure of success. Beyond these, important as they are, the wider scope of comparative sociological work should not be ignored. Only through the latter can the anthropologist link local particulars to larger wholes. A total perspective will be essential if there is any attempt to build on and intensify local factors, means, and processes in continuous work toward making it possible for the people to realize their fullest capabilities. The study of local conditions and local processes should lead to an intensification of production both in relation to general development aims and the wishes of the local people. But this also calls for studies in terms of local cultural categories, and an endeavor to relate to each other the levels of a very complex system, often in tension and conflict, with the aim of transcending the stumbling blocks in the path of social transformation.

Now that some social scientists think of discarding models of modernization and others speak of post-dependency theories it may be worth pointing out that these concepts are no longer the property of academics. They lead a life of their own in societies at large, a standard fare in discussions on either side of the issues involving the New International Economic Order, the New International Information Order, and the like. Both modernization and dependency theories are incorporated, quite promiscuously, into the excrutiating jargon of international development experts and officials from both donor agencies and host countries. Theories and concepts have consequences and repercussions in the world of action, being at the same time constructed out of and creating that world. For this reason the responsibility of the scientist encompasses the relation between anthropology, the social sciences, and the whole range of societies from the United States and the Sovien Union to Chad and Bangladesh. The study of development encompasses the structure of societies as well as the officials, politicians, farmers, traders, academics, planners, and workers within societies who direct, endure, plan, profit, or suffer from development no matter in what position they are in relation to the process.

The primary task of social science is the analysis, understanding, and critique of ideas in relation to practices undertaken with an orientation toward the truth and the realization of human potential for all people. This is not a call to do the impossible, rather it is to recognize that truth is inconceivable apart from freedom and justice.[6]

Notes

[1] "National reconciliation" was an attempt by the May 1969 regime to bring into the political process the more disaffected elements of Sudanese polity.

[2] Tribal elites circulate into urban elite positions and replace the latter in Ibn Khaldun's well known theory of history.

[3] Unlike tenants on irrigated schemes, subsistence farmers have vegetable gardens tended by the household which produce enough to help alleviate the effects of *shail*. A tenant farmer is not allowed these priviledges, given the complex nature of the irrigation system and the priority placed on very specific cash crops.

[4] Market prices for groundnuts are very low and at times the cost of production is not covered sales.

[5] Axinn (1977:15) states further that "strategies for change involve change in power," so schemes of development have to consider the interdependence of economic programs and the existing power structure. Improving the situation of the rural poor is a problem which is intricately related to the presence of the rural rich. The rural rich and poor as well as the urban rich and poor participate in the same society.

[6] In Habermas's (1968) "discoursive" and "warrantable" consensus theory, truth is realized through the support of experience and the argumentation toward justified consensus.

Appendix 1:
Ingessana Muazzafeen

A small section of officials in Roseiris are members of the indigenous Ingessana.[1] The Ingessana people live in scattered clusters in the hills. The Aurs of the Ingessana, descendants of ruling families, meet in the *punuk* (the court where they consider administrative and financial problems) and are still leading and dignified figures of Ingessana society. Their authority was abolished when the Revolutionary Council liquidated the native administration in 1969. An official report to the Roseiris Regional Council pointed to "weak revenue from taxes" due to the introduction of the new system. Many educated Ingessana (including officials) wanted to promote the Ingessana region to a semi-autonomous administrative region in the provincial administration.

Merchants maintain an influential position in the hills through financial and administrative collaboration with the provincial administration which then enunciates changes for the Ingessana. This close relation generates tension between the merchants and the Ingessana. The merchants are primarily *jallaba*, men from the northern provinces of the country. The merchants also succeeded in establishing close relations with the elders of the Ingessana. Due to their long residence in the hills, and their success in establishing close ties with the Ingessana tribes, the merchants are able to influence the political, economic, and cultural life of the area. Today the close relationship is questioned because the politics of the hill tribes are undergoing change.

Ingessana officials have acquired the kind of education that leads them to view problems of social change differently from their kinsmen in the hills. They regard the old Ingessana as traditional leaders who are reluctant to initiate necessary programs to develop the area. Yet, at the same time, they are obliged to show respect to the elders. In Damazin and Roseiris, Ingessana *muazzafeen* press for recognition of their role as agents of social change in the hills. They want conditions and opportunities that would allow them to extend better services to their homeland.

These claims have increased recently since the CP promised to promote the Ingessana from a district to a regional unit of administration.

Ingessana officials criticize the provincial administration because it is not paying much attention to Ingessana needs and development problems. There is scarity of fundamental services, such as water, health, education, and communication.

Ingessana *muazzafeen* are aware of the resistance of some Ingessana cultural patterns to innovation. The six elementary schools in the hills, for example, have been handicapped by Ingessana rules restricting the admission of boys and girls. Boys are needed to graze animals while girls are kept for domestic service in the household. Ingessana officials suggest more participation in decision-making for the Ingessana people with respect to the administrative and political affairs of the region. One of their grievances is that the Ingessana Development Project, which has been approved by the Central Government in Khartoum to develop the Ingessana hills, has not yet been implemented. The project is not funded and only three tractors, whose disks are stored at the Damazin provincial headquarters, have been bought by the provincial administration. Ingessana officials comment angrily that three tractors are certainly inadequate for a project meant to develop the whole Ingessana region. Although the *muazzafeen* still respect the indigenous authority of Aurs and the *punuk*, they are commited, at the same time, to enforce the regulations of the Damazin administration. Very often conflicts occur when administrative decisions interfere with cultural and local ties.

Notes

[1] A *gabila* domiciled in the circle of hills to the southeast of Damazin, belonging to the so called pre-Nilotic linguistic groups of the area.

Appendix 2:
Methodology of the Survey

A census was conducted and two surveys were administered in the project area.[1] Formal and informal interviews held at various stages supplemented the quantifiable data. The surveys were administered simultaneously. Since the second survey was specifically drawn up for the women in the project area, female assistants were hired to gather this information.

The first survey concentrated on heads of households. Male headed households are the cultural norm, although we found evidence of female headed households. The survey involved demographic factors, migration to and from villages, professional activities and organization, kinship and family structure, household wealth, agricultural production, and income. The second, the women's survey, concentrated on women's social organization, women's activities on the farms and household chores, and women's income and expenditures.[2]

Field enumerators with some knowledge of the region were selected from Damazin and Roseiris. Six male and female enumerators were trained in field work and research. They participated in discussions of project objectives, the nature and scope of the research, the handling of questionnaires, and the conduct of the survey. The discussions covered the accuracy of data collected, individual rapport with the rural people, cultural sensitivity, and adherence to local norms and codes of conduct.

The survey established a panel family for each of the eight villages studied. The panel family is a pre-selected household for research monitoring over a period of time. In each village, we pre-selected the Sheikh, merchant, nurse, and Omda, if there was one. These families hold high positions in the village social hierarchy. In some villages we had more panel families than in others. All future research activities, the collection of agronomical data (family plots and vegetable gardens) or surveys by agricultural economists of farm and household budgets were to concentrate on these panel families.

The census survey was conducted in all project villages. The additional data were cross checked with those gathered in the two surveys. Age, sex, and tribal structure were collected, along with place of birth, residence, migration, profession, health, and annual income. After the completion of the census, we conducted time and field measurements of selected panel families. The farm lands, the distance, walked from the village to the farm, and the grain storage area and structure were measured. Using a stopwatch we measured the time spent on women's activities. This study gave a rough indication of the farming community's notion of time, distance, and size.

Notes

[1] The research effort was the result of joint work by anthropologists and an agricultural economist from ESRC and Experience Incorporated, Minneapolis. See *Blue Nile Integrated Agricultural Project* 1977.

[2] See Chapter 3 above.

References and Research Bibliography

Abbas, Ahmed Mohamed. 1980. *White Nile Arabs: Political Leadership and Economic Change.* New Jersey: Althone Press.

Abbas, Philip. 1973. "Growth of Black Political Consciousness in Northern Sudan," *Africa Today,* Summer, Vol. 20, no. 3.

Abdalla, I.H. 1971. The 1959 Nile Waters Agreement in Sudanese-Egyptian Relations," *Middle Eastern Studies.* October, Vol. 7 no. 3.

Abdel-Fadil, M. 1975. *Development, Income Distribution, and Social Change in Rural Egypt, 1952-1970: a study in the political economy of agrarian transition.* Cambridge: Cambridge University Press.

Abdel-Rahim, Muddathir. 1974. *Changing Patterns of Civilian Military Relations in the Sudan.* Uppsala, 1978, Khartoum University. Theses on the Sudan. Khartoum University Press.

Adam, Farah. 1972. "Irrigation Water Sale in the Non-Public Sector in the Northern Province, Democratic Republic of Sudan," *Agricultural Economics Bulletin for Africa.* Addis Ababa.

Adams, M.E. & J. Howell. 1979. "Developing the Traditional Sector in Sudan," in *Economic Development and Cultural Change.* April, Vol. 27, no. 3.

Afshar, Haleh (ed). 1985. *Women, Work and Ideology.* London: Tavistock Publications.

Aguda, Oluwadare. 1973. "Arabism and Pan-Arabism in Sudanese Politics," *Journal of Modern African Studies'* June, Vol. 11, no. 2.

Ahmed, Abdel Gaffar. 1976a. *Some Aspects of Pastoral Nomadism in Sudan.* Khartoum: Khartoum University Press.

Ahmed, Abdel Gaffar. 1976b. "Tribal Elite: A base for social stratification in modern Sudan," *Economic and Social Research Council.* Bulletin, Khartoum.

Ahmed, Abdel Gaffar. 1974, 1979. *Shaykhs and Followers.* Khartoum: Khartoum University Press.

Akolawin, Natale O. 1971. "Islamic and Customary Law in the Sudan," in Hassan, Yusif Fadl: *Sudan in Africa.* Khartoum: Khartoum University Press.

Albino, Oliver. 1970. *The Sudan: A Southern Viewpoint.* Oxford:Oxford University Press.

Ali, Ali A. 1973. *The Economics of the Sudan: A Selective Reading List of Books, Theses, Articles.* Dakar (U.N.), African Institute for Economic Development and Planning.

Ali, Mohammed Abdul Rahman. 1976. *Government Expenditure and Economic Development: a case study of the Sudan.* Khartoum: Khartoum University Press.

Ali, Mohammed Din bin. 1966. "Malay customary law and the family," *World Muslim League,* Singapore, no. 9.

Allum, Percy. 1979. "The Sudan: Numeiry's Ten Years of Power," *Contemporary Review.* November, 235.

Amin, Samir. 1974. *Accumulation on a World Scale.* New York: The Monthly Review Press.

Amin, Samir. 1974. *Neocolonialism in West Africa.* New York: The Monthly Review Press.

Anderson, J.N.D. 1950. "Recent Developments in Shari'a Law in the Sudan," *Sudan Notes and Records.* XXXI, 1.

Anderson, J.N.D. 1960. "The Modernization of Islamic Law in the Sudan," *Sudan Law Journal and Reports.*

Anderson, J.N.D. 1965. "The Adaptation of Muslim Law in Sub-Saharan Africa," in Kuper & Kuper (eds.) *African Law: Adaptation and Development.* Berkeley: University of California Press.

Anderson, J.N.D. 1963. "The Future of Islamic Law in British Commonwealth Territories in Africa," in Baade (ed.).

Anthony, K.R.M., B.F. Johnston, W.O. Jones and V.C. Uchendu (ed.). 1979. *Agricultural Change in Tropical Africa*. Ithaca: Cornell University Press.

Apthorpe, Raymond J. (ed.). 1970. *Rural Cooperatives and Planned Change in Africa: case materials*. Geneva: United Nations Research Institute for Social Development.

Arrighi, E. & Saul. 1973. *Essays on the Political Economy of Africa*. New York: The Monthly Review Press.

Asad, Talal. 1966. "A Note on the History of the Kababish Tribe," in *Sudan Notes and Records*. XLVII.

Asad, Talal. 1972. "Political Inequality in the Kababish Tribe" in Cunnison, I. & W. James (eds.) *Essays in Sudan Ethnography*. New York: Humanities Press.

Asad, Talal. 1964. "Seasonal Movements of the Kababish Arabs," in *Sudan Notes and Records*. XLV, 1964.

Asad, Talal. 1970. *The Kababish Arabs*. New York: Praeger.

Atiyah, P.S. 1958. "Some Problems of Family Law in the Sudan Republic," in *Sudan Notes and Records*. XXXIX.

Axinn, G. 1977. "The Development Cycle: New Strategies from an Ancient Concept," *International Development Review* Vol. 4.

Baade, Hans W. (ed.) 1963. *African Law: New Law for New Nations*. New York: Ocean Publishing Co.

Baddour, Abd el-Fattah Ibrahim el-Sayed. 1960. *Sudanese-Egyptian Relations, A Chronological and Analytical Study*. The Hague: M. Nijhoff.

Bakheit, Ja'far M.A. 1965. *British Administration and Sudanese Nationalism*. Unpublished Ph.D. Thesis. Cambridge University, England.

Bakheit, Ja'far M.A. 1971. "Native Administration in the Sudan and its Significance to Africa," in Yusuf Fadl Hassan (ed.) *Sudan in Africa*. Khartoum: Khartoum University Press.

Bandeleben, M. 1973. *The Cooperative System in the Sudan: Development, Characteristic and Importance in the Socio-economic Development Process.* Munchen: Weltforum Verlag.

Banton, M. 1965. *The Relevance of Models for Social Anthropology.* ASA Monographs, London: Tavistock Publications.

Barclay, Harold B. 1964. *Buurri al Lamaab, A Suburban Village in the Sudan.* Ithaca: Cornell University Press.

Barnett S., Fruzzetti L. & Östör A. 1976. "Hierarchy Purified," *Journal of Asian Studies,* Vol. xxxv.

Barnett, T. 1977. *The Gezira Scheme, Illusion of Development.* London: Frank Cass & Co. Ltd.

Barth, F. (ed.) 1969. *Ethnic Groups and Boundaries: The Social Organization of Cultural Differences.* Boston: Little, Brown & Co.

Barth, F. 1961. *Nomads of Persia.* London: Allen & Unwin.

Baudrillard, Jean. 1975. *The Mirror of Production.* St. Louis: Telos Press.

Bechtold, Peter K. 1976. *Politics in the Sudan: Parliamentary and Military Rule in an Emerging African Nation.* New York: Praeger.

Bedri, Ibrahim, "More Notes on the Padang Dinka," in *Sudan Notes and Records.* Vol. 29, Part I.

Bernstein, H. 1973. *Underdevelopment and Development.* Hammondsworth: Penguin Books.

Beshir, Mohamed Omar. 1977. Educational Policy and the Employment Problem in the Sudan. Monograph Series No. 3, Development Studies & Research Centre, Faculty of Economic and Social Studies, University of Khartoum.

Beshir, Mohamed Omar. 1974. *Revolution and Nationalism in the Sudan.* New York: Barnes and Noble.

Beshir, Mohamed Omar. 1975. *The Southern Sudan: From Conflict to Peace.* New York: Barnes and Noble.

Birks, J.S. & C.A. Sinclair. 1982 "Employment and Development in Six Poor Arab States: Syria, Jordan, Sudan, South Yemen, Egypt and North Yemen." *International Journal of Middle Eastern Studies.* February, Vol. 14, no. 1.

Blue Nile Integrated Agricultural Development Project. 1977. Washington: United States Agency for International Development.

Boddy, Janice. 1982. "Womb as Oasis: The Symbolic Context of Pharaonic Circumcision in Rural Northern Sudan," *American Ethnology,* November, Vol. 9, no. 4.

Boserup, E. 1970. *Women's Role in Economic Development.* New York: St. Martins Press.

Boserup, E. & C. Lijencrantz. 1975. *Integration of Women in Development, Why, When and How.* United Nations Development Programme, New York.

Brewer, William D. 1982. "The Libyan-Sudanese 'Crisis' of '81: Danger for Darfur and Dilemma for the United States," *Middle Eastern Journal,* Spring, Vol. 36, no. 2.

Briggs, John A. 1978. "The Development of Irrigated Agriculture in the Sudan," *Journal of the Geographical Asociation of Tanzania.* Dar es Salaam, June.

Burton, John W. 1983. "Same Time, Same Space: Observations on the Morality of Kinship in Pastoral Nilotic Societies," *Ethnology.* April, Vol. XXII, no. 2.

Burton, John W. 1982a. "Nilotic Women: A Diachronic Perspective." *Journal of Middle Eastern Studies,* September, Vol. 20, no. 3.

Burton, John W. 1982b. "Gifts Again: Complimentary Prestation among the Pastoral Nilotes of the Southern Sudan," *Ethnology.* January, Vol. XXI, no. 1.

Burton, John W. 1979. "Benign Neglect: British Administration and Local Response Among the Pastoral Nilotes of the Southern Sudan," *Anthropos.* May-December, Vol. 3, nos. 1 & 2.

Burton, John W. 1978a. "Ghost Marriage and the Cattle Trade among the Atout of the Southern Sudan," *Anthropos* Vol. 48, no. 4.

Burton, John W. 1978b. "Ghosts, Ancestors and Individuals among the Atuot of the Southern Sudan," *Man*. December, Vol. 13, no. 4.

Campbell, K.O. 1979. *Food for the Future: how agriculture can meet the challenge*. Lincoln: University of Nebraska Press.

Caplan, Patricia & Janet M. Bujra (eds.) 1979. *Women United, Women Divided: Comparative Studies of Ten Contemporary Cultures*. Bloomington:Indiana University Press.

Cardoso, F.H. 1972. "Dependency and Development in Latin America," *New Left Review*, 74.

Cardoso, F.H. 1973. "Associated Dependent Development," in ed. A. Stepan *Authoritarian Brazil*. New Haven: Yale University Press.

Carr, M. 1978. *Appropriate Technology for African Women*. African Training and Research Center for Women, Economic Commission for Africa, United Nations. Addis Ababa.

Chabra, Han Sharan. 1974. "Sudan - Its Agricultural Potential," in *Indo-African Trade Journal*. New Delhi, Africa Publications, October-December.

Chaney, E.M. 1980. "Women, Migration and the Decline of Smallholder Agriculture: An Exploratory Study." Paper prepared for the Office of Women in Development, US/AID under AID/OTR - 147-80-94/95.

Charnay, J.P. 1971. *Islamic Culture and Socio-economic Development*. Leiden: J. Brill.

Charter for National Action 1971. The Secretariat-General, Sudanese Socialist Union, Khartoum.

Chayanov, A.V. 1966. *The Theory of Peasant Economy*. American Economic Association, Illinois.

Clammer, J. (ed.) 1978. *The New Economic Anthropology*. New York: St. Martin's Press.

Cockroft, J.D., Frank, A.G. & Johnson, D.L. 1972. *Dependence and Underdevelopment*. New York: Doubleday.

Collins, R.O. 1983. *Shadows in the Grass, Britain in the Southern Sudan 1918-1956*. New Haven: Yale University Press.

Bibliography

Collins, Robert & Robert L. Tignor. 1967. *Egypt and the Sudan.* Tanglewood-Cliff: Prentice-Hall.

Critchfield, Richard. 1979. "The Changing Peasant: Part 1: The Magician." Hanover: *American University Field Staff*, No. 28.

Cummins, S.L. 1904. "Sub-tribes of the Bahr el Ghazal Dinkas," in *Journal of Anthropological Institute*. Vol. XXXIV.

Cunnison, I. (ed.) 1972. *Essays in Sudan Ethnography.* London: Hurst.

Cunnison, I. 1971. *The Kababish Arabs.* London: Oxford University Press.

Dalby, David. 1976. "Drought in Sudanic Africa," *The Round Table.* London, January, pp. 57-64.

Deng, F.M. 1978. *Africans of Two Worlds: The Dinka in Afro-Arab Sudan.* New Haven: Yale University Press.

Deng, F.M. 1972. *The Dinka of the Sudan.* New York: Holt, Reinhart & Winston.

Deng, F.M. 1973. *Dynamics of Identification.* Khartoum: University of Khartoum Press.

Deng, F.M. 1971. *Tradition and Modernization.* New Haven: Yale University Press.

Deutsch, K.W. 1961. "Social Mobilization and Political Development," *American Political Science Review*, 55.

Department of Statistics, Sudan. 1968. A report on the sample census sample census of agriculture for the year 1964-65, Khartoum.

Development Forum: Anthropologists and Development Situations. 1976. Mouton: The Hague.

Dixon, R. 1978. *Women's Cooperatives and Rural Development.* Baltimore: Johns Hopkins University Press.

Duffield, M. 1981. *Maiurno: Capitalism and Rural Life in the Sudan.* London: Ithaca Press.

Dumont, Louis. 1977. *From Mandeville to Marx.* Chicago: University of Chicago Press.

Dumont, Louis. 1970. *Homo Hierarchicus*. Chicago: University of Chicago Press.

Dumont, R. 1969. *Development et Socialismes*. Paris: Editions du Seuil.

Dyson-Hudson, N. 1980. "Pastorial Production Systems and Livestock Development Projects: An East African Perspective," *International Development Review*.

Dyson-Hudson, N. 1971. "Inheriting and Extending Men's Oldest Techniques of Survival..." in R.L. Breenen (ed.) *Nomads of the World*. Washington, D.C.: National Geographic Society.

Ebrahim, Mohammed H.S. 1983. "Irrigation Projects in the Sudan: The Promise and the Reality," *Journal of African Studies*, Spring, Vol. 10, no. 1.

Eisenstadt, S.N. 1966. *Modernization: Protest and Change*. Englewood Cliffs: Prentice-Hall.

Eisenstadt, S.N. 1973. *Tradition, Change, and Modernity*. New York: Wiley.

Elam, Y. 1979. "Nomadism in Ankole as a Substitute for Rebellion," in *Africa*. 49 (2).

El Bushra, El-Sayed. 1979. "Some Demographic Indicator for Khartoum Conurbation, Sudan," *Middle Eastern Studies* October, Vol. 15, no. 3.

El-Hadari, A.M., 1972. "Irrigated Agriculture in the Sudan: New Approaches to Organization and Management," in *Indian Journal of Agricultural Economics*. April/June.

El-Hadari, A.M., 1974. "Some Socio-Economic Aspects of Farming in the Nuba Mountains, Western Sudan," in *Eastern Africa Journal of Rural Development*. (Kampala) no. 1-2.

El Hassan, Ali M. (ed.) 1976. *An Introduction to Sudan Economy*. Khartoum: Khartoum University Press.

El-Mahdi, Mandour. 1965. *A Short History of the Sudan*. London: Oxford University Press.

El Samman, M.O. 1977. "The Sudan: The Social Impact of Desert Encroachment," in *Ekistics*. Athens, May.

Bibliography

El Tayab, S.A. 1978. *Agriculture and Natural Resources, Abyei District.* Khartoum: Khartoum University Press, no. 6.

El Tom, Mahdi A., 1973. "A Harmonic Analysis of the Rainfall over the Sudan," *The Journal of Tropical Geography.* December.

Emmanuel A. 1972. *Unequal Exchange.* New York: Monthly Review Press.

Epstein & Penny (eds.) 1972. *Opportunity and Response.* London: C. Hurst and Co.

Erb, G., F. Guy & V. Kallab. 1975. *Beyond Dependency: The Developing World Speaks Out.* Overseas Development Council, Washington, D.C.

Erb, G. 1975. "The Developing World's Challenge in Perspectives," in Guy Erb & V. Kallab (eds.) 1975.

Esposito, J.L. (ed.) 1980. *Islam and Development: Religion and Socio-Political Change.* Syracuse: Syracuse University Press.

Esposito, J.L. 1982. *Women in Muslim Family Law.* Syracuse: Syracuse University Press.

Evans-Pritchard, E.E. 1932. "Ethnological Observations in Dar-Fung," *Sudan Notes & Records.* Vol. 15.

Evans-Pritchard, E.E. 1927. "A Preliminary Account of the Ingessana," *Sudan Notes and Records.* Vol. 10.

Evans-Pritchard, E.E. 1972., Cunnison, I. and James, W.R. (eds.) *Essays in Sudan Ethnography.* New York: Humanities Press.

Fallers, L.A. 1974. *Social Anthropology of the Nation State.* Chicago: Aldine.

Fallers, T. 1963 "Customary Law in the New African States," in Baade (ed.).

Farvar, T.M. & Milton, J.P. (ed.) 1968. *The Careless Technology: Ecology and International Development.* Conservation Foundation.

Fernea, E.W. & Bezirgan, B.Q. 1977. *Middle Eastern Women Speak.* Austin: University of Texas Press.

Fife, D.C.W. 1927. *Savage Life in the Black Sudan.* Philadelphia: Lippincott Co.

Finkle, J.L. & R.M. Gable (eds.) 1966. *Political Development and Social Change.* New York: John Wiley.

Fluehr-Lobban, Carolyn. 1981. "Josina's Observations of Sudanese Culture," Chicago: *Human Organization.* Vol. 40, no. 3.

Food and Agriculture Organization of the United Nations. 1968. *Land and Water Resources Survey in the Jebel Mara Area: the Sudan.* Rome: United Nations Development Programs.

Forde, D. 1956. "Primitive Societies," in Shapiro (ed.) *Man, Culture and Society.* New York: Oxford University Press.

Forde, D. 1971. "Ecology and Social Structure," *Proceedings of Royal Anthropological Institute for 1970.*

Foster, Phillips. 1967. *Research on Agricultural Development in North Africa.* New York: Agricultural Development Council.

Frank, A.G. 1971. "The Development of Underdevelopment," "Economic Dependence, Class Structure, and Underdevelopment Politics," "Sociology of Development and the Underdevelopment of Sociology," in Cockroft, Frank, & Johnston (eds.).

Friedman, J. 1979. "The Crisis of Transition: A critique of strategies of crisis management," *Development and Change.* Vol. 20, no. 1.

Fruzzetti, L. 1985. "Farm and Hearth: Rural Women in a Farming Community." in H. Afshar (ed.) *Women, Work and Ideology in the Third World,* London: Tavistock.

Fruzzetti, L. 1982. *The Gift of a Virgin: Analysis of Women, Marriage, Ritual and Kinship in Bengali Society.* New Brunswick, Rutgers University Press.

Fruzzetti, L. 1979. "Socio-Economic Survey of the Blue Nile Agricultural Development Project", *Economic and Social Research Council, National Council for Research,* Research Report No. 7 Khartoum, October.

Fruzzetti, L. and Ákos Östör. 1984. *Ritual and Kinship in Bengal,* South Asia Publishers, New Delhi.

Fruzzetti, L., F. Bender, K. Eubanks, A.S.Farrah and J. Lea. 1982. "Economic and Social Factors in The Blue Nile Project Area", *Blue Nile Integrated Agriculture Development Project.* Experience Incorporated, Minneapolis, MN.

Furtado, C. 1964. *Development and Underdevelopment.* Berkeley: University of California Press.

Gaitskell, A. 1959. *Gezira: Story of Development in the Sudan.* London: Faber & Faber.

Garang, J. 1969. "On Economic and Regional Autonomy," published by Ministry for Southern Affairs, Khartoum.

Geertz, C. (ed.). 1963. *Old Societies and New States*, Glencoe, Illinois: The Free Press.

Geertz, C. 1968. *Islam Observed*, Chicago: University of Chicago Press.

Geertz, C. 1973. *Interpretation of Cultures.* New York: Basic Books.

Germaine, A. 1976-77. "Poor Rural Women: A Policy Perspective," *Journal of International Affairs.* Vol. 30, no. 2, Fall/Winter.

Giddens, A. 1971. *Capitalism and Modern Social Theory.* Cambridge: Cambridge University Press.

Giddens, A. 1973. *The Class Structure of the Advanced Societies.* New York: Harper.

Glickman, M. 1971. "The Nuer and the Dinka: A Further Note," *Man.* Vol. 7, no. 4.

Godelier, M. 1978. "The Object and Method of Economic Anthropology," in Seddon, D. (ed.) *Relations of Production.* London: Frank Cass & Co.

Goody, J. 1971. *Technology, Tradition and the State in Africa.* London: International African Institute.

Gough, K. and Hari P. Sharma. 1973. *Imperialism and Revolution in South Asia.* New York: Monthly Review Press.

Grunnet, Niels. 1962. "An Ethnographic-ecological Survey of the Relationship between the Dinka and their Cattle," in *Folk.* Vol. IV.

Gudeman, S. 1978. *The Demise of a Rural Economy.* London: Rutledge and Kegan Paul.

Gusfield, Joseph R. 1971. "Tradition and Modernity: Misplaced Polarities in the Study of Social Change," in Finkle, Jason L. and Gable, Richard W. (eds.), *Political Development and Social Change.* New York: John Wiley and Sons Inc.

Gusten, Rolf. 1966. *Problems of Economic Growth and Planning: Aspects of the Current Ten-Year Plan.* Springer-Verlag.

Gutkind, P.C.W. 1974. *Urban Anthropology.* Assen: Van Gorcum.

Haaland, G. 1969. "Economic Determinants in Ethnic Processes." in Barth F. (ed.).

Habermas, J. 1968. *Knowledge and Human Interests.* Boston: Beacon Press.

Habermas, J. 1975. *Legitimation Crisis.* Boston: Beacon Press.

Hameed, K.A. 1974. *Enterprise: Industrial Entrepreneurship in Development.* Beverly Hills: Sage Publications.

Hammer, Richard M. 1973. "Application and Consequences of Precipitation Observations in the Republic of Sudan in View of the Nomadic Life and Economy," *Geoforum.* no. 14.

Hart, K. 1982. *The Political Economy of West African Agriculture.* Cambridge: Cambridge University Press.

Hartwig, Gerald. 1981. "Smallpox in the Sudan." *International Journal of African Historical Studies,* Vol. 14, no. 1.

Hassan, Yusif Fadl. 1963. "The Penetration of Islam in the Eastern Sudan," *Sudan Notes and Records.* Vol. XLIV.

Hassan, Yusif Fadl. 1967. *The Arabs and the Sudan.* Edinburgh: University of Edinburgh Press, 1967.

Hassan, Yusif Fadl. 1971. *Sudan in Africa.* Khartoum: Khartoum University Press.

Hayes, Rose Oldfield. 1975. "Female Genital Mutilation, Fertility Control, Women's Roles, and the Patrilineage in Modern Sudan: A Functional Analysis," *American Ethnologist* Vol. 2, no. 4.

Hendry, Peter. 1979. "Options for the Sudan" in *Ceres.* Rome, July/August.

Hill, Richard L. (ed.) 1970. *On the Frontiers of Islam: two manuscripts concerning the Sudan under Turco-Egyptian rule 1822-1845.* Oxford University: Clarendon Press.

Hirschmann, A. 1971. *A Bias for Hope: Essays on Development of Latin America.* New Haven: Yale University Press.

Hirschmann, A. 1967. *Development Projects Observed.* Washington: Brookings Institute.

Hirschmann, A. 1981. *Essays in Trespassing: Economics to Politics and Beyond.* Cambridge: Cambridge University Press.

Hirschmann, A. 1977. *The Passions and the Interests: Political Arguments for Capitalism Before its Triumph.* Princeton: Princeton University Press.

Hirschmann, A. 1968. *Foreign Aid - A Critique and a Proposal.* Princeton: Princeton University Press.

Hirschmann, A. 1958. *The Strategy of Economic Development.* New Haven: Yale University Press.

Hirschmann, A. 1979. *Toward a New Strategy for Development.* New York: Pergamon Press.

Hoagland, Edward. 1979. *African Calliope: A Journey to the Sudan.* New York: Random House.

Holt, P.M., Lambtan, Ann K.S., and Bernard Lewis (eds.). 1970. *Cambridge History of Africa,* vol. IV. Cambridge: Cambridge University Press.

Holt, P.M. 1963. "Fung Origins: A Critique and New Evidence," *Journal of African History.* IV, 1.

Holt, P.M. 1956. "Sudanese Nationalism and Self-determination," *The Middle East Journal.* Vol. 10, no. 3.

Holt, P.M. 1961. *A Modern History of the Sudan, from the Fung Sultanate to the Present.* Oxford: Clarendon Press.

Holt, P.M. 1967. *Holy Families and Islam in the Sudan.* Princeton, Princeton University.

Holt, P.M. 1958. *The Mahdist State in the Sudan 1881-1898.* London: Oxford University Press.

Holy, L. 1974. *Neighbours and Kinsmen.* London: C. Hurst & Co.

Horowitz, M.M. (ed.) 1976. *Colloquium on the Effects of Drought on the Productive Strategies of Sudano-Sahelian Herdsmen and Farmers.* Binghamton, NY: Institute for Development Anthropology.

Horowitz, M.M. 1979. *The Sociology of Pastoralism and African Livestock Development.* Binghamton, NY: Institute for Development Anthropology.

Howell, J. and M. Adams. 1979. "Developing the Traditional Sector in the Sudan." *Economic Development and Cultural Change.* vol. 27, no. 3.

Howell, P. 1951. "Notes on the Ngok Dinka," *Sudan Notes & Records.* Vol. 32.

Hoyle, S. 1977. "The Khasm el Girba Agricultural Scheme: an example of an attempt to settle Nomads,"in O'Keefe and B. Wisner (eds.) *Land Use and Development.* London: International Africa Institute.

Ibrahim, Hassan Ahmed. 1980. "Imperialism and Neo-Mahdism in the Sudan: A Study of British Policy Towards Neo-Mahdism, 1924-1927," *International Journal of African Historical Studies.* Vol. 13, no. 2.

Ibrahim, Hassan Ahmed. 1979. "Mahdist Risings Against the Condominium Government in the Sudan, 1900-1927," *International Journal of African Historical Studies.* Vol. 12, no. 3.

Ibrahim, Hilmy. 1966. *The literature of Egypt and the Sudan from the earliest times to the year 1885 inclusive: a bibliography of books, articles.* London, 1886. Neudeln, Liechtenstein: Kraus Reprint.

Ibrahim, F. 1978. *Problem of Desertification in the Sudan.* Social Research Council, Khartoum.

International Labor Organization Report. 1974. *Growth, Employment and Equity: a comprehensive strategy for the Sudan.* Rome.

Irons, W.G. 1965. "Livestock Raiding among Pastoralists: an Adaptive Interpretation." *Papers of the Michigan Academy of Sciences, Arts and Letters,* 50.

Jakobson, Roman. 1966. *Collected Works.* Vol. 1, 1961 and Vol. 1V. The Hague: Mouton.

Jalee, Pierre. 1977. *How Capitalism Works.* New York: Monthly Review Press.

Jalee, Pierre. 1969. *The Third World in World Economy.* New York: Monthly Review Press.

Jalee, Pierre. 1968. *The Pillage of the Third World.* New York: Monthly Review Press.

James, W. 1975. "Sister-exchange Marriage," *Scientific American.* Vol. 233, no. 6.

James, W. 1971. "Social Assimilation and Changing Identity in the Southern Fung," in Y.F. Hassan (ed.) *Sudan in Africa.*

James, W. 1970. "Why the Uduk Won't Pay Bride-price," *Sudan Notes & Records*, Vol. 5, 1.

James, W. 1979. *'Kwanim Pa, The Making of the Uduk People.* Oxford: Clarendon Press.

Janowitz, Morris. 1964. *The Military in the Political Development of New Nations.* Chicago: University of Chicago Press.

Johnson, D.L. 1969. *The Nature of Nomadism.* Chicago: University of Chicago Press.

Johnson, Douglas. 1982. "Evans-Pritchard, The Nuer, and the Sudan Political Service," *American Anthropologist*, April, Vol. 81, no. 323.

Jong, Joeslin de. 1968. "Customary Law: A confusing ficton." *Medelelingan Van de Koninbelike Vereningin Indisch Institute*, Amsterdam, XXX, no. 1.

Kaikati, Jack G. 1980. "The Economy of Sudan: A Potential Breadbasket of the Arab World?" *International Journal of Middle Eastern Studies*, February, Vol. 11.

Kay, G. 1975. *Development and Underdevelopment: A Marxist Analysis.* New York: St. Martin's Press.

Keenan, Jeremy. 1977. "The Tuareg Veil." *Middle Eastern Studies*, January, Vol. 13, no. 1.

Kenneth, Anthony R. 1979. *Agricultural Change in Tropical Africa.* Ithaca: Cornell University Press.

Kirk-Greene, A.H.M. 1982 "The Sudan Political Service: A Profile in the Sociology of Imperialism," *International Journal of African Historical Studies*, Vol. 15, no. 1.

Konczacki, Z.A. 1978. *The Economics of Pastoralism*. London: Frank Cass.

Kuper, H. & L. Kuper. 1965. *African Law: Adaptation and Development*. Berkeley: University of California Press.

Laroui, A. 1976. *The Crisis of the Arab Intellectual*. Berkeley: University of California Press.

Lees, Francis A. 1977. *The Economic and Political Development of the Sudan*. London: Macmillan.

Leinhardt, G. 1963. "Dinka Representations of the Relations Between Sexes," in *Royal Anthropological Institute Occasional Papers*. no. 16.

Leinhardt, G. 1958. "The Western Dinka" in Middleton, J. & Tait, D. (eds.) *Tribes Without Rulers*. London: Routledge & Kegan Paul

Lele, Uma. 1975. *The Design of Rural Development: Lessons from Africa*. Baltimore: Johns Hopkins University Press.

Levi-Strauss, Claude. 1968. *The Savage Mind*. Chicago: University of Chicago Press.

Levy, Marion. 1972. *Modernization: Latecomers and Survivors*. New York: Basic Books.

Livingstone, Ian. 1977. "Economic Irrationality Among Pastoral People: Myth or Reality?"in *Development and Change*. no. 8.

Little, K. 1973. *African Women in Towns*. Cambridge: Cambridge University Press.

Little, K. 1973. *Urbanization as a Social Process*. London: Routledge & Kegan Paul.

Lloyd, P.C. 1974. *Power and Independence*. London: Routledge & Kegan Paul.

Lobban, Richard A. 1982. "Class and Kinship in Sudanese Urban Communities," *Africa*. Vol. 52.

Logan. 1867. "The Laws of the Indian Archipelago and East Asia," *JIAEA*. Singapore.

Loutje, M. 1982. *Rural Women: Unequal Partners in Development*. Geneva: ILO.

Lovejoy, Paul E. & Stephen Baier. 1975. "The Desert-Side Economy of the Central Sudan," *International Journal of African Historical Studies*, Vol. 8, no. 4.

Mackray, W.H. & Pan, C.W.C. 1910. "Rembau, Its History, Constitution and Customs," *Journal of the Singapore Branch of the Royal Asiatic Society* vol. 56.

MacMichael, Sir Harold Alfred. 1912. *The Tribes of Northern and Central Kordofan*. Cambridge: Cambridge University Press.

Mahmoud, Mahgoub El-Tigani. 1983. *The Impact of Partial Modernization on the Emigration of Sudanese Professionals and Skilled Workers*. Unpublished Ph.D. Dissertation, Department of Sociology, Brown University.

Mahmoud, Mahgoub El-Tigani. 1981. *Personalization and Hierarchy Problems in Sudanese Bureaucracy*. Unpublished M.A. Thesis, Department of Sociology, Brown University.

Mangam, J.A. 1982. "The Education of an Elite Imperial Administration: The Sudan Political Service and the British and the British Public School System," *International Journal of African Historical Studies*, Vol. 15, no. 4.

Martin, P.F. 1921. *The Sudan in Evolution: A study of the economic, financial and administrative conditions of the Anglo-Egyptian Sudan*. London: Constable and Co. Ltd.

Matthews, D.G. 1965. *A current bibliography on Sudanese affairs: a select bibliography from 1960-64*. Washington, D.C.

McClelland, D. 1961. *The Achieving Society*. New York: Monthly Press.

McClintock, David William. 1970. "The Southern Sudan Problem: Evolution of an Arab-African Confrontation," *Middle Eastern Journal*, Autumn, Vol. 24, no. 4.

McLoughlin, Peter F. 1967. *Research on Agricultural Development in East Africa*. New York: Agricultural Development Council.

Medani, A.I., 1975. "Elasticity of the Marketable Surplus of a Subsistence Crop at Various Stages of Development," in *Economic Development and Cultural Change*. Chicago, April.

Meillassoux, C. 1978. "The Economy in Agricultural Self-Sustaining Societies: A Preliminary Analysis," in Seddon, D. (ed.) *Relations of Production*. London: Frank Cass & Co.

Meillassoux, C. 1964. *L'Anthropologie economique des Gouro de Cote d'Ivoire*. Paris: Mouton.

Meillassoux, C. (ed.) 1971. *The Development of Indigenous Trade and Markets in West Africa*. London: Oxford University Press.

Mellor, J. 1976. *The New Economics of Growth*. Ithaca: Cornell University Press.

Ministry of Agriculture, Food and Natural Resources. 1969. *Bulletin of Agricultural Statistics of Sudan*. Statistics Section, no. 10.

Monod, T. (ed.) 1975. *Pastoralism in Tropical Africa*. Oxford: Oxford University Press.

Muhamed, Abu Ramat Sayyid. 1960. "The Relationship between Islamic and Customary Law in the Sudan," *Journal of African Law*,

Muncie, Peter, 1975. "Equating Health with Wealth," in *Finance and Development*. June.

Musa, Omar el-Hag. 1973. "Reconciliation, Rehabilitation and Development Efforts in Southern Sudan," *Middle Eastern Journal*, Winter, Vol. 27, no. 1.

Mustafa, Z. 1971. *The Common Law in the Sudan*. Oxford: Clarendon Press.

Myint, H.A. 1971. *Economic Theory and the Underdeveloped Regions*. Oxford: Oxford Univesity Press.

Myrdal, G. 1968. *Asian Drama: An Inquiry into the Poverty of Nations*. 3 Volumes. Middlesex: Penguin.

Nair, K. 1979. *In Defense of the Irrational Peasant*. Chicago: University of Chicago Press.

Nelson, N. 1981. *African Women in the Development Process*. London: Frank Cass.

Bibliography

Nelson, Nici. 1979. *Why Has Development Neglected Rural Women?* New York: Pergamon Press.

Netting, R. Mc. 1971. *The Ecological Approach in Cultural Study.* Addison-Welsely, Module no. 6.

Niblock, Timothy C. 1974. "A New Political System in Sudan." *American Anthropologist* Vol. 73, no. 293.

Nordenstam, Tore. 1968. *Sudanese Ethics.* Scandinavian Institute of African Studies.

Nur, M.I. El, 1960. "The Role of the Native Courts in the Administration of Justice in the Sudan," *Sudan Notes and Records.* XLI.

O'Ballance, Edgar. 1977. *The Secret War in the Sudan: 1955-1972.* London: Faber & Faber.

O'Brien, D.B. 1975. *Saints and Politicians.* Cambridge: Cambridge University Press.

O'Brien, J. 1979. *The Political Economy of Development and Underdevelopment.* Development Studies and Research Center, University of Khartoum.

O'Fahey, R.S. & J.L. Spaulding. 1974. *Kingdoms of the Sudan.* London: Methuen.

O'Fahey, Rex S. 1970. *States and State Formation in the Eastern Sudan.* Sudan Research Unit, University of Khartoum.

Oduho, Joseph. 1963. *The Problem of the Southern Sudan.* Oxford: Oxford University Press.

Okwerosa, E.A. 1976. *New Direction for Economic Development in Africa.* London: Africa Books.

Oltenacu, E.A., A. Martinez, H.A. Glimp & H.A. Fitshugh. 1976. *The Role of Sheep and Goats in Agricultural Development.* Arkansas: Winrock International Center.

Onwukuemeli, Emeka. 1974. "Agriculture, the Theory of Economic Development and the Zande Scheme," in *Journal of Modern African Studies.* December.

Östör, Ákos and Lina Fruzzetti. 1978. "Anthropology and the Question of Change". *Economic and Social Research Council, National Council for Research*, Bulletin No. 70, Khartoum.

Östör, Á., L. Fruzzetti, M. El-Tigani and A.H.M.Osman. 1981. "Law, Trade, Administration and Development in the Blue Nile Province of the Sudan", *Economic and Social Research Council*, Research Report No. 10, Khartoum, February.

Östör, Á. 1980. *The Play of the Gods: Locality, Ideology, Structure and Time in the Festivals of a Bengali Town*. Chicago, University of Chicago Press.

Östör, Á. 1984. *Culture and Power: Legend, Ritual, Bazaar and Rebellion in a Bengali Society*. New Delhi and Beverly Hills: Sage Publications.

Östör, Á. 1986. "Time and the Comparative Study of Societies." *Man in India*, Vol. 66, no. 1.

Östör, Á., Fruzzetti, L. and S. Barnett (eds). 1982. *Concepts of Person: Kinship, Caste and Marriage in India*, Cambridge: Harvard University Press.

Owusu, M. (ed.) 1975. *Colonialism and Change*. Mouton: The Hague.

Oxaal, I., T. Barnett & D. Booth (eds.) 1975. *Beyond the Sociology of Development*. London: Routledge & Kegan Paul.

Papanek, H. 1979. "The Differential Impact of Programs and Policies on Women in Development," Center for Asian Development Studies, Boston.

Parkyns, Mansfield. 1851. "The Kababish Arabs between Dongola and Kordofan," in *Journal of Royal Geographic Society*. XX.

Parmor, S. 1975. "Self Reliant Development in an ˇInterdependent' World," in Erb, Guy & Kallab, V. (eds.), 1975.

Parson, T. 1951. *The Structure of Social Action*. Glencoe: The Free Press.

Paul, Andrew. 1954. *A History of the Beja Tribes of the Sudan*. Cambridge: Cambridge University Press.

PDU: Project Development Unit: Juba. 1978. *Livestock Husbandry and Agriculture among the Dinka*. Regional Ministry of Agriculture, Southern Sudan, May.

PDU: Project Development Unit: Juba. 1978. *Result of a Farm Management Survey carried out in Rumbek Area.* Regional Ministry of Agriculture, Southern Sudan, August.

PDU: Project Development Unit: Juba. late 1978. *Social and Economic Characteristic of Livestock Traders in one Cattle Producing area in Southern Sudan.* Regional Ministry of Agriculture, Southern Sudan.

Peel, S. 1904. *The binding of the Nile and the new Sudan.* London: E. Arnold.

Peled, M. 1977. "Portrait of an Intellectual." *Middle Eastern Studies.* May, Vol. 13, no. 2.

Piaget, Jean. 1970. *Structuralism.* New York: Basic Books.

Pitt, D. 1976. *Development from Below: anthropologists and development situations.* The Hague: Mouton.

Planhol, Xavier de. 1961. "Nomades et Pasteurs I," in *Revue Geographique de L'Est.* 1 (3).

Polanyi, K., M. Arensberg, W.H. Pearson (eds.). 1957. *Trade & Markets in the Early Empires.* Glascoe: Early Press.

Porter, P.W. 1965. "Environment Potentials and Economic Opportunities: a background for Cultural Adaptation," in *American Anthropologist,* 67.

Pye, L. 1961. "Armies in the Process of Political Modernization," *Archives Européennes de Sociologie,* 2.

Radwan, S.M. 1977. *Agrarian Reform and Rural Poverty, Egypt 1952-1975.* Geneva: ILO.

Rahman, Fazlur, 1969. "The Impact of Modernity on Islam," in J. Jurji (ed.) *Religious Pluralism and World Community.* Leiden: E. J. Brill.

Republic of Sudan. Census of 1973. Khartoum.

Republic of Sudan. 1971. *Charter for National Action.* Khartoum: The Sudanese Socialist Union.

Republic of Sudan. 1951. *The Local Government Ordinance.* In Sudan Laws, the Judiciary, Khartoum.

Republic of Sudan. 1971. *The People's Local Governments Act.* Ministry of Local Governments, Khartoum.

Republic of Sudan. 1960. *The Provincial Administration Act.* The Records Office, Khartoum.

Riddel, D. 1972. "Toward a Structuralist Sociology of Development?" *Sociology.* 6 (i).

Robinson, A.E. 1929. "Abu El Kaylik, The Kingmaker of the Fung of Sennar," *American Anthropologist.* n.s. 31.

Roden, D. 1971. "Changing Patterns of Land Tenure Amongst the Wulsa of Central Sudan," in *Journal of Administration Overseas.* London, October.

Roden, D. 1976. "Regional Inequality and Rebellion in the Sudan," in *The Geographical Review.* October.

Rodinson, M. 1979. *The Arabs.* Chicago: University of Chicago Press.

Rodinson, M. 1973. *Islam and Capitalism.* New York: Pantheon Books

Rodney, Walter. 1974. *How Europe Underdeveloped Africa.* Washington: Howard University Press.

Rondinelli, Dennis A. 1981. "Administrative Decentralization and Economic Development: The Sudan's Experiment with Devolution," *Journal of Middle Eastern Studies.* December, Vol. 19, no. 4.

Rosen, L. 1978. "Law and Social Change in the New Nations," *Comparative Studies in Society and History,* Vol. 20, no. 1, Cambridge: Cambridge University Press.

Rostow, W.W. 1956. "The Take-off into Self-Sustained Growth," *The Economic Journal,* 66.

Rueschemeyer, Dietrich. 1976. "Partial Modernization," in Loubser et al. (eds.) *Explorations in General Theory in Social Science.* vol. 2, New York: The Free Press.

Sabah, M.A. Abu. 1978. *Abyei Project: Tribal Structure of the Ngok Dinka of Southern Kordofan Province.* Development Studies Center, University of Khartoum.

Sacks, Karen. 1979. "Causality and Chance on the Upper Nile." *American Ethnologist,* August, Vol. 6, no. 3.

Safwat, A. "The Theory of Muslim," *Malayan Law Journal,* XL-XLIV.

Sahlins, M. 1976. *Culture and Practical Reason.* Chicago: University of Chicago Press.

Sahlins, M. 1974. *Stone Age Economics.* Chicago: Aldine.

Salaam, M.A. 1979. *The Institutional Development of the Sudan Gezira Scheme.* Reading, England: University of Reading, Dept. of Agricultural Economics and Development, Doctoral Dissertation.

Salah El-Din, El Shazali Ibrahim. 1980. *Beyond Underdevelopment.* Bergen occasional papers in Social Anthropology no. 22, Bergen University, Bergen.

Salih, H.M., A. Ostor, & L.M. Fruzzetti. 1978. *Abyei Project: Main Report of the Socio-Economic Survey.* Development Studies and Research Center, University of Khartoum.

Salzman, P. 1980. *When Nomads Settle.* New York: Praeger.

Sanderson, G.N. 1963. "The Modern Sudan, 1820-1956: The Present Position of Historical Studies," *Journal of African History.* IV, 3.

Sanderson, Lilian Passmore. 1980. "Education in the Southern Sudan: The Impact of Government-Missionary- Southern Sudanese Relationships upon the Development of Education during the Condominium Period, 1898-1956," *American Anthropologist* April, Vol. 79, no. 315.

Santi, P. & R. Hill. 1980. *The Europeans in the Sudan 1834-1878.* Oxford: Clarendon Press.

Schneider, David M. 1972. "What is kinship all about?" in P. Reining (ed.) *Kinship Studies in the Morgan Centennial Year.* Seattle: Univesity of Washington Press.

Schneider, H.W. & Proosdij, B.A. Van, (eds). 1968. "Impact of Modern Culture on Traditional Religions," *Proceedings of XI International Congress of International Association* for *History of Religions,*

Seidman, R. 1966. "Law and Economic Development in Independent, English-Speaking, Sub-Saharan Africa," in T.W. Hutchinson (ed.) *Africa and Law.* Madison: University of Wisconsin Press.

Seligman, C.G. & B.Z. Seligman. 1918. "The Kababish, a Sudan Arab Tribe," *Harvard African Studies.* II.

Seligman, C.G. & B.Z. Seligman. 1932. *Pagan Tribes of the Nilotic Sudan.* London: Routledge & Kegan Paul.

al-Shahi, Ahmed & F.C.T. Moore (eds.). 1978. *Wisdom from the Nile: A Collection of Folk Stories from Northern and Central Sudan.* Oxford: Clarendon Press.

Shaked, Haim. 1978. *The Life of the Sudanese Mahdi.* New York: Transaction Books.

Shepherd, Andrew. 1983. "Capitalist Agriculture in the Sudan's Dura Prairies," *Development and Change.* Vol. 14, no. 2.

Shibeika, Mekki. 1959. *The Independent Sudan.* R. Speller.

Shils, E. 1975. *Center and Periphery.* Collected Papers. Vol. 2, Chicago: University of Chicago Press.

Shiner et al. 1975. "Debate on Modernization," *Comparative Studies in Society and History.* Vol. 17.

Smith, Donald Eugene (ed.). 1974. *Religion and Political Modernization.* New Haven: Yale University Press.

Smith, J. (ed.). 1980. *Women in Contemporary Muslim Societies.* Lewisburg: Bucknell University Press.

Smock, David R. 1982. "Eritrean Refugees in the Sudan." *Journal of Modern African Studies.* September, Vol. 20, no. 3.

Sorbo, G. 1972. "Off-Scheme Interests & Economic Differentiation in Sudanese Tenant Communities," World Bank paper, Washington, D.C., 1980.

Spaulding, Jay. "The Fung: A reconsideration." *Journal of African History.* XIII, 1.

Spaulding, Jay. 1974. "The Government of Sennar." *The International Journal of African History.* Vol. 1, 1.

Spaulding, Jay. 1985. *The Heroic Age in Sinnar.* African Studies Center. Michigan State University, East Lansing.

Spaulding, Jay. 1982. "Slavery, Land Tenure and Social Class in the Northern Turkish Sudan," *International Journal of Historical African Studies:* Vol. 15, no. 1.

Spooner, Brian. 1973. *The Cultural Ecology of Pastoral Nomads.* Reading, Mass: Addison-Wesley Publishing Co.. (Module no. 45).

Staudt, K. 1978. "Agricultural Productivity Gaps: A Case Study in Male Preference in Government Policy Implementation," *Development and Change* 9, No. 3.

Staudt, K. 1979. "Tracing Sex Differentiation in Donor Agricultural Programs," Paper read for the American Political Science Association Annual Meeting, Washington, DC, August 30-September 3, 1979.

Staudt, K.A. 1975-76. "Women farmers and Inequities in Agricultural Services." *Rural Africana.* no. 29, Winter.

Stenning, D.J. 1958 "Household Viability Among the Pastoral Fulani," in J. Goody (ed.) *The Developmental Cycle in Domestic Groups.* Cambridge: Cambridge University Press.

Streeter, P. 1977. "The distinctive Features of a Basic Needs Approach to Development," *International Development Review.* Vol. 19, no. 3.

Strobel, M. 1979. *Muslim Women in Mombasa 1890-1975.* New Haven: Yale University Press.

Stubbs, J.M. & C.G.T. Morison. 1944. "The Western Dinka, their land and their agriculture," in *Sudan Notes and Records.*

"Sudan Economic Survey", *African Development.* London, January 1976.

"Sudan Economic Survey", in *African Development.* London, January 1973.

"Sudan Economic Survey", *African Development.* London, January 1975.

Sudan Intelligance Reports, Cairo. Africa 3715, 3F.

Sudan, Department of Statistics. 1968-69. Census of agriculture: a brief report on the sample census of agriculture for the year 1964-65. Khartoum.

Sudan, Department of Statistics. 1969. A report on the sample survey carried out in 1967-68 in the tract to be covered by the first phase of the Rahad Irrigation Project. Khartoum.

Sudan, Egyptian, Janglei Investigation Team. 1954. The equatorial Nile project and its effects in the Anglo-Egyptian Sudan. Khartoum

Sudan, The Ministry of Information and Culture. 1972. *Revolution's achievements in three years -- 1969/1972.* Khartoum, Government Printing Press.

The Sudan. 1947. *A record of Progress 1898-1967.* Khartoum, Sudan Government.

Sudan. 1920. *The Sub-Manner's handbook; Lectures on the criminal and civil codes; and notes on accounts, agriculture, forestry, and sanitation,* Khartoum. Printed by McCorquodale.

"Sudan: Special Issue". 1974. *Arab Economist, Monthly Survey of Arab Economies.* Supplement, November.

Suliman, Ali A. 1971. "The Effect of Labour Turnover and Absenteeism on the Cost of Production in the Sudan Textile Industry," in *Eastern Africa Economic Review.* Nairobi, December.

Suliman, Ali Ahmed. 1973. "Deficit Finance and Economic Development in the Sudan," *Journal of African Studies,* December, Vol. 11.

Suliman, Mohamed. 1971. *Alyassar El-Sudani fi Ashrat A'wam 1954-1963.* (The Left in the Sudan for Ten Years 1954-1963) Medani.

Sylvester, Anthony. 1977. *Sudan Under Nimeiri.* London: Bodley Head.

Taha, S.A.R. 1977. *Society, Food and Nutrition in the Gezira.* Khartoum: Khartoum University Press.

Ten Years of Economic and Social Development, 1961/62-1970/71. 1965. Khartoum, Sudan Survey Department.

Terray, E. 1972. *Marxism and Primitive Societies.* New York: Monthly Review Press.

Tinker, I. 1976. "The adverse impact of Development on women", in I. Tinker & M. Bramsen (eds.) *Women and World Development.* Overseas Development Council, Washington, D.C.

Tinker, I. 1979. *New Technologies for Food Chain Activities: The Imperative Equity for Women.* Paper prepared for the Office of Women in Development (PPC/WID) AID.

Tothill, J.D. 1954. *Agriculture in the Sudan: being a handbook of agriculture as practised in the Anglo-Egyptian Sudan.* London: Oxford University Press.

Traore, S. 1975. "An African Experiment in Grass Roots Development," in Erb & Kallab (eds.) *Beyond Dependency.*

Trimingham, J.S. 1949. *Islam in the Sudan.* London: Oxford University Press.

Tubiana, Marie-Jose & Joseph Tubiana. 1977. *The Zaghawa from an Ecological Perspective: Foodgathering, the Pastoral System, Tradition and Development of the Zaghawa of the Sudan and the Chad.* ARotterdam: A.A. Balkena.

Turner, Bryan. 1974. *Weber and Islam.* London: Routledge and Kegan Paul.

Turner, Victor. 1967. *The Forest of Symbols.* Ithaca: Cornell University Press.

Utas, Bo. 1983. *Women in Islamic Societies.* Scandinavian Institute of Asian Studies. Atlantic Highland: Humanities Press.

Verholst, Thierny. 1968. *Safeguarding African Customary Law.* No. 7, African Studies Center. Berkeley: University of California Press.

Voll, John. 1985. "Effects of Islamic Structures on Modern Islamic Expansion in the Eastern Sudan," *The International Journal of African Studies.* Vol. 11.

Voll, John. 1972. "Mahdis, Walis, and New Men in the Sudan." In N. Keddie (ed.) *Saints and Sufis.* Berkeley: University of California Press.

Voll, John. 1971. "The British, the 'Ulama' and Popular Islam in the Early Anglo-Egyptian Sudan," *International Journal of Middle Eastern Studies*, July, Vol. 2, no. 3.

Voll, John. 1979. "The Sudanese Mahdi: Frontier Fundamentalist." *International Journal of Middle Eastern Studies*, Vol. 10.

Voll, John. 1982. *Islam, Continuity and Change in the Modern World.* Boulder, Colorado: Westview Press.

Voll, Sarah. 1980. *A Plough in The Field Arable. Western Agribusiness in the Third World Agriculture.* Hanover: University Press of New England.

Wai, Dunstan. 1980. "Pax Brittanica and the Southern Sudan: The View from the Theater," *African Affairs*, July, Vol. 79, no. 316.

Wai, Dunstan. 1979. "The Sudan: Domestic Politics and Foreign Relations under Nimiery," *African Affairs*, July, Vol. 78, no. 312.

Wai, Dunstan. 1981. *The African Arab Conflict in the Sudan*. New York: Africana.

Wallerstein, Immanuel. 1976. *The Modern World System*. Chicago: Aldine.

Warburg, Gabriel. 1973. "From Ansar to Umma: Sectarian Politics in the Sudan, 1914-1945," *Asian and African Studies* Vol. 9, no. 2.

Warburg, Gabriel. 1971. "Religious Policy in the Northern Sudan: Ulama and Sufism 1899-1918," *Asian and African Studies* Vol. 7.

Warburg, Gabriel. 1978. "Slavery and Labour in the Anglo-Egyptian Sudan," *Asian and African Studies* Vol. 12, no. 2.

Warburg, Gabriel. 1978. *Islam, Traditionalism, and Communism in a Traditional Society: The Case of the Sudan*. London: Frank Cass.

Wells, A. 1972. "Toward an empirically grounded theory of development." *British Journal of Sociology*. Vol. 23.

Whetham, E.H. (ed.). 1968. *Co-operation, land reform and Land settlement: report on a survey in Kenya, Uganda, Sudan and Ghana, Nigeria and Iran*. London: Plunkett Foundation for Co-operative Studies.

Weiner, Myron. 1968. *Party Building in a New Nation*. Chicago: The University of Chicago Press.

Wilber, C.K. (ed.). 1973. *The Political Economy of Development and Underdevelopment*. New York: Random House.

Winstead, R.O. 1921. "Indian and Malay Beliefs." *Journal of Singapore Branch of the Royal Asiatic Society* 87.

Woodward, Peter. 1981. "Nationalism and Opposition in the Sudan." *African Affairs*, July, Vol. 80, no. 320.

Woodward, Peter. 1979. *Condominium and Sudanese Nationalism*. New York: Barnes Noble Books.

World Bank. 1978. *Sudan Livestock Marketing I & II*. Eastern Africa Region.

Periodical Title Abbreviations

A	Africa
AA	African Affairs
AAS	Asian and African Studies
AE	American Ethnologist
AF	Anthropological Forum
AJ	Africana Journal
AM	American Anthropologist
AQ	Anthropological Quarterly
ASR	African Studies Review
CA	Current Anthropology
DC	Development and Change
IJAHS	International Journal of African Historical Studies
IJMES	International Journal of Middle East Studies
JAR	Journal of Anthropological Research
JAS	Journal of African Studies
JCFS	Journal of Comparative Family STudies
JFH	Journal of Family History
JMAS	Journal of Modern African Studies
JNES	Journal of Near Eastern Studies
MANK	Mankind
MEJ	Middle East Journal
MER	Middle East Review
MERIP	Middle East Research and Information Projects
MES	Middle Eastern Studies
UA	Urban Anthropology

Index

Aba, 117
Abala (plots), 135, 137, 139
Abyei project, 151
Adat (custom), 89
Agadi State Farm, 53
Administration, 102-3, 173-5, 188
Administration, history, 104-6
Administration, organization, 107-11
Administration, markets, 119-21
Ahal, 117
Al-Kibashab, 13
Amm/amma, 117
Angareb (string bead), 48
Anthropological theory, 3, 171 185, 190
Applied anthropology, 9, 190
Arab, 116
Arrida, 85
Awlad, (family), 178
Balakh, 85, 86
Beledi, 42, 43
Belt of fire, 13, 88
Benefit, 46-47
Berta, 11, 31, 90, 91, 116, 127, 185
Big merchants, 120
Bilaad (vegetable and farm land), 90, 93

Bildaat, 137, 139
Blue Nile Integrated Agricultural Development Project, 127, 130
Blue Nile Province, 13
Bokassis, 37
Bornu, 38
Capitalism in societies, 24, 25
Civil Courts, 88
Civilizing mission, 176
Civil Law, 80, 187
Colonial administration, 83
Cultural categories, 3, 9, 67, 171, 185, 190
Customary laws, 80, 187
Dahari, 32, 131, 137, 142
Damazin markets, 47
Damazin merchant, 185
Damazin town, 29
Dawla, 94
Dependency theories, 3, 18, 20, 24-26, 171-72, 188
Designing of new projects, 15, 128, 188, 190
Development ideology, 16, 18-20, 175, 190
Development of markets, 183
Development of underdevelopment, 20
Development plans, 144-46, 148-49, 171, 184
Dia, 89

227

Din (Islam), 49
Dinka, 31, 90
Dokan, 33, 40, 127, 141, 150
Dura, (sorghum), 139, 159, 163
Duwerta, 139
Dyn, 159
Economic Growth, 16
Effendi, 13, 31, 102
Eisenstadt, 28
Eritrean refugees, 31
Es Suki, 10, 163-65
Expansion of mechanized farms, 122
Faki, 74, 90
Farmers on subsistence, 159
Farrashas, 36
Feddans, 147, 155, 160, 161, 180
Fellata, 28, 29, 90, 92, 93, 131, 151, 175
Free markets, 49
Fulani, 13, 31, 38, 90
Funj Sultanate, 10
Gabila, (tribe), 11, 12, 13, 38, 39, 41, 51, 55, 80, 83, 90, 108, 116, 127, 140, 178, 195
Gattai traiders, 33, 40, 41, 43, 44, 45, 46, 47, 48
Gezira scheme, 125, 153, 154, 156, 157, 163, 167, 173
Gimaii, 86
Gisim, 83
Grazing lands, 142
Green Revolution, 18
Habermas, 191, 192
Haj, 10
Hamaj, 11, 90, 127, 173, 185
Hara, 117
Harig (setting fire to fields), 88
Hash, 139
Hausa, 29, 31, 90, 131
Hawashas, 161
Ideology of development, 177
Ihtiram, 49
Ijma, 81

Imperialism, 24, 26
Implementation, 15
Indaiyas, 90, 92
Indirect rule, 81
Ingessana, 11, 12, 31, 46, 193-95
Inhilal (social disintegration), 76
Integrated rural development, 21
Irfa, 142
Irrigated schemes, 157
J'amaia, 145, 147
Ja'alyn, 116
Jallaba (merchants), 30, 42
Jebelawin, 127
Jebels, 36, 51
Jedda, 150
Jumla merchants, 33, 39, 40, 41, 43, 44, 45, 46, 47, 48
Jumla-gattai, 48
Juruf (river), 31, 32, 88, 90
Juruf, 135, 137, 139
Kadalu, 116
Kadeb, 139, 142
Kantar, 150
Kenana, 90, 116, 122
Khal/khala, 117
Khalwa (Koranic) schools, 29, 135, 163, 177
Khashm El Girba, 53
Khordawat, 39, 40, 41, 44, 45
Kisra, 67, 68
Koran, 28
Kushuks, 36, 39, 44
Lablab, 146
Law case studies, 89-97
Law in development, 79-82, 97-99, 187
Law courts, 83-87
Madaniia, 86
Mahdi, 131
Mahdiya, 173
Mahr, 91
Majalisa, 94
Makhsan, 33
Maktab, 39
Managil Extension, 10

Index

Marisa (local beer), 51, 91
Market economy, 139
Market of the sun, 36
Marx, 20-21, 189
Marxist rhetoric, 19, 20, 24, 189
Mashiakh, 83, 94
Mashrubat, 48, 52, 94
Mata'an, 48
Matmura, 150
Mechanization, 48, 144, 155
Mechanized agriculture, 2, 13, 31, 142, 157, 174
Mechanized Farms Corporation (MFC), 52-54, 84-86
Mechanized infrastructure, 157
Mediating agents, 43
Mek, 12, 80
Mek's rule, 173
Metropolis, 24
Modern agriculture, 180
Modern society, 22, 23
Modernization theory, 2, 18, 20-23, 189
Modernization of agriculture, 13-15, 18, 48, 127, 153-54, 180-84
Modernization, 167, 182, 188-90
Montega, 41
Muazzafeen, 13, 102, 103, 107-10, 113, 116-17, 120-24, 178, 188, 193-194
Mudriya, 38, 46, 50, 174-75, 178
Mur, 139, 142
Nabaha, 13
Nafir (communal labor), 126, 139, 140, 142, 145, 149, 155, 158, 169
Nasaba, 117
Native administration, 83
Native Courts, 12, 84
Nazir, 10
Neo-imperialism, 24
Neo-Mahdism, 103
Neocolonialism, 24

Nesah, 13
Nuba, 53, 90
Nuer, 90
Off-scheme, 143
Officials (see Muazzafeen)
Omda system, 12, 14
Omda, 126, 185, 195
Omodias, 83, 84
People's Council, 107
People's Courts, 83, 84, 85, 86, 88, 90, 95
Peoples' market, 36
Peripheral capitalism, 24
Politics in administration, 112-115, 175, 177-180, 188
Pre-Nilotic, 11, 12
Qadis (Judges), 11
Qyias, 81
Rahad, 10, 53
Rakouba, 126
Registered land, 137
Resident Magistrate's Courts, 13, 85, 86, 87, 88, 92
Roseiris dam, 29, 131
Roseiris Native Court, 83
Roseiris Rural Council, 110
Rufa'a al Hoi, 31, 90, 95, 116, 122
Rural development, 183, 185
Sagia, 2
Saiif, 139
Samada, 160
Samasra, 42, 49
Scheme managers, 155
Scheme-hopping, 186
Shadouf, 2
Shail repayment, 159
Shail, 31, 61, 141, 142, 150, 159, 192
Shakhi, 85
Sharaka, 166
Shari'a law, 80, 81, 104, 117, 187
Shari, 75

Sheikhs, 14, 74
Shilluk, 90
Shipi-jumla, 46
Simsim (sesame), 40, 42, 50
SSU, 54, 112-116, 174-175
Structure, 9, 24
Subsistence economy, 180, 183
Subsistence farming, 61
Sufi orders, 11
Suluh (peace), 14, 89
Sunna, 81
Suq al shaabi, 36
Suq al shams, 36
Suq hierarchy, 177
Suq hurr, 42, 177
Suq shops, 48
Suq (markets), 10, 12, 33, 37, 38, 41, 42, 44, 45, 46, 47, 49, 51, 55, 120, 147, 171, 176, 177, 178, 185
Suweba, 150
Symbolic meanings, 3
Taadi, 88, 98
Taban, 176
Tahnia, 40, 47
Tahrir al mara, 76, 85
Tajir, 33
Takamul agricultural scheme, 30, 174
Talef (trespass), 88, 96, 98
Tariga (religious brotherhood), 11, 12, 13, 76, 80, 117, 177-80
Tenant farmer, 181, 186
Tenmiya, 175, 177
Theories of modernization, 21-23, 185
Third World countries, 15, 17, 19, 21, 24, 28, 65, 185
Tigar, 120
Tob, 43
Tradition, 22, 23, 26, 172

Traveling merchants, 42
Tribes, *(gabilas)* 80, 172, 174
Uduk, 11
Um Bororo, 13
Umbahate, 139
Umma Party, 103
Umma, 117, 177
Unauthorized schemes, 38
Underdevelopment theorists, 24, 26
Underdevelopment, 20, 24, 189
Unregistered lands, 137
Value, 3, 9, 28
Village development, 125-26
Wakil, 33, 43
Walis, 80
Wallerstein, E., 24, 26
Wandering merchants, 43, 44, 45
Wasiq, 42, 43
Watawit, 11
Weber, Max, 20-21, 189
Women in development, 57-59, 75-77
Women's activities, 66-69
World system, 185